AS/A-LEVEL
Economics

John Hearn

Exam Revision Notes

Philip Allan Updates
Market Place
Deddington
Oxfordshire
OX15 0SE

tel: 01869 338652
fax: 01869 337590
e-mail: sales@philipallan.co.uk
www.philipallan.co.uk

ISBN 0 86003 430 5

Printed by Raithby, Lawrence & Co Ltd, Leicester

Contents

Unit 3 The financial structure of the economy

Unit 4 The economy as a whole

Unit 5 The international structure of the world economy

The revision process

Using revision notes

Before you look at these revision notes, you will have read the recommended textbooks, written your own notes and, where relevant, constructed essays, answered multiple-choice and data-response questions and generally felt knowledgeable about each part of the course as you studied it. The examinations are now getting closer and it is time to put together all your notes and start a revision programme.

Most A-level courses in economics require you to cover the whole syllabus. Certain papers give you no choice of questions; you have to answer them all. This volume of revision notes covers the entire course. The notes are not exhaustive – they are **prompts to your memory**, foundations which can support the rest of your knowledge and catalysts to your thought processes.

It is likely that you will have important tests throughout your course and it is possible to use the revision notes in preparing for these tests as well as for the final examinations, but only after you have completed all the groundwork.

All economics examinations require you to show two broad skills. First, you must thoroughly understand economics to the level where you can answer multiple-choice questions, and not feel, as many unprepared students do, that they are multiple-guess questions. Second, you must be able to **express your knowledge** of economics clearly and concisely to an examiner in the form of short answers and essays.

Revision notes are an important step towards achieving your best in the examination. The final step, however, is how you apply this knowledge in response to data, case studies and essay questions. You must look upon these revision notes as the first part of the final stage in your preparations. These notes will not tell you how to write essays or respond to data questions but, without the appropriate knowledge, you will not be able to complete the final steps successfully.

Many examination questions require you to **apply economic theory** to a real world situation. Writing about the real world situation without showing a clear understanding of the economic theory will gain very few marks. For example, if you are asked about privatising the National Health Service, it is no good releasing all those pent-up emotions and producing a political diatribe. You are an economist and you must look at supply, demand, market places, optimal and efficient resource allocation. You must ask questions about whether the product of the NHS is a private good. Does it have significant externalities which class it as a merit good? Are parts of the service public goods, for example the prevention of contagious disease? If this is so, then economics implies that taxation is the only efficient way to provide public goods. If you provide the service free, how do you deal with the problem of consumers using the product up to the point where marginal utility is zero?

This is what these revision notes will do for you. They will give you the economist's perspective. There are brief notes on all the basic theory. Important terms are defined and important diagrams are set in context. Certain parts of the new specifications in AS/A-level economics have been emphasised in a little more detail compared with the traditional subject areas that are already covered well by the current textbooks.

The revision plan

At least 1 month before the examination you need to devise a **revision plan**, and then you need to **stick to it**. Divide up the course into manageable portions and aim to complete the revision process a week before the examination. This gives you some leeway in case you are unwell or an unexpected event leaves you unable to complete a day or two of revision.

Remember that some of your examinations will be in the morning and your brain will need to be functioning early in the day. Get used to rising early and going to sleep before midnight. It takes several weeks for the body to settle into a routine and you do not want to be at your best at 9.00 p.m. and at your worst at 9.00 a.m.

As an economist you know the trade-off between **investment** and **consumption**. Look upon completing your revision plan as investment in your future. Consumer activities like clubs, discos, cinemas, etc. will raise your standard of living during the last month before your exams, but forego this consumption, invest in your future and you are likely to raise your standard of living for the rest of your life.

Ergonomics and economics

Ergonomics studies the efficiency of people in their working environment and it has been found that efficiency can be significantly raised by **working in the right way**. If you have not already done so, get organised! **Minimise disturbance to maximise returns**. The revision process requires a little reading and a lot of writing – you do not communicate with the examiner orally or through telepathy but by how well you can write.

Locate a table and chair (not too comfortable) facing a wall – not a window – and eliminate all possible distractions. Some students argue in favour of music while they revise. If you are listening to the music, you are not revising. If the music is drowning out other extraneous noises, then it could be an advantage to play music without lyrics by an artist you do not like.

As you revise, separate what you already know from what you have forgotten. By skimming through this book you can identify areas which require you to return to the main text. **Time is at a premium** and you need not waste it by rereading what you already know. Get permission to place a lot of lists around the house – one of the best places is behind the toilet door.

The day of the examination

Remember to wear comfortable clothes and take some extra clothing just in case it is colder than expected. Nice warm feet are a real bonus during the examination. It is better to look like a 'dork' and feel comfortable than to act like one.

As well as the obligatory sweets and bottled water, do not forget pens, pencils, rubbers, rulers, a watch and two calculators or one with fresh batteries.

You will already know the structure of the examination paper, how many questions you need to answer and roughly how much time to allocate to each question. Once in the examination room, check all these details are correct and **manage your time efficiently**.

The most common criticism of students by examiners is that they do not answer the set question. **Read the question carefully** and separate relevant from irrelevant detail. It is frustrating that you know so much and only a small fraction of your knowledge can be used in the examination, but do not fall into the trap of writing all you know – **only write what is relevant**.

The single most important rule of examinations should be obvious: **never leave the examination room before the end of your allotted time**. You only get one chance to communicate to the examiner that you deserve a grade A. Do not waste the opportunity. Remember that deep down inside everyone there is a creative person waiting to get out. If you feel you have absolutely nothing more to say, then let your creative juices flow. Look for ways of amplifying the points you have made, add examples from your own experiences and, where discussion is an option, do not be afraid to question the answers as well as answer the questions.

If you inadvertently press the panic button, then close your eyes and count to 30. Your mind will clear, the override will kick in and new ideas will come flooding in. No matter how hard or easy the examination seems, do not give up. Remember that your *relative* performance, rather than your *absolute* performance, is important. If everyone finds the examination difficult, there is a good chance that pass rates and grade boundaries will be lowered. If the paper is easy, standards will be higher.

Exam revision notes structure

It is traditional to divide economics into microeconomics and macroeconomics. Microeconomics looks at the small economic unit, the individual, the household, the firm. The chosen unit is put under the economist's microscope and analysed in detail, while the rest of the economic system is held constant (*ceteris paribus*) on the assumption that the relative neglect will not lead to serious error. Often these studies are referred to as partial equilibrium analysis. Macroeconomics looks at large economic units such as the national economy and international groups like the European Union. This is often referred to as general equilibrium analysis.

When students come across this division, they should remember that in reality studies in economics range between two finite extremes: the small unit (individual) to the large unit (world) and there is no clear point of division.

All macroeconomic analysis can be broken down into its microeconomic components and vice versa. For this reason, these revision notes do not stress the division into micro and macro, but look at five main areas of study. These are entitled:

Unit 1	An introduction to economics
Unit 2	The industrial structure of the economy
Unit 3	The financial structure of the economy
Unit 4	The economy as a whole
Unit 5	The international structure of the world economy

Although we will look at a more widely recognised definition of economics in this book, I suggest you think of economics as 'the allocation of scarce resources to the production and consumption of goods and services'. After the introductory unit, we look at the way goods and services are produced, followed by money and the institutions through which it flows. Combining these two gives a view of the aggregate balances between supply and demand in the economy as a whole. Finally, we look at how one economy relates to another through international trade.

The structure described above makes economics easier to understand and therefore easier to recall. The topics approach is often adequate when examinations give you a choice of questions, but when you are required to answer all questions on a paper, you need a coherent structure rather than disjointed bits and pieces.

You may have played the game in which a tray of objects is placed in front of you for a few seconds and then is taken away. The object is to recall as many objects as you can. Because the objects are randomly chosen with no obvious relationship, it is difficult to remember them, though you will have committed a few to short-term memory. If you are given a picture of a house to look at for a similar length of time and then asked to describe it, you will remember more because a house has an easily recognisable structure. Even more interesting is the effect on your longer-term memory. If, after several days, you are asked to recall the tray of objects, you will probably have forgotten all of them. However, if you are asked to describe the house in the picture, you will remember much more. If you can see economics as a structure that fits together, it will be much easier to revise and recall the relevant information in an examination.

Throughout these revision notes, headings are weighted. Each of the five units is subdivided as follows:

Main headings	**A**	**B**	**C**
Subdivided	**1**	**2**	**3**
Subdivided again	**1.1**	**1.2**	**1.3**
Subdivided yet again	**1.1a**	**1.1b**	**1.1c**

Given this structure, it should be easy to identify how things fit together. Each page is split so that the main body of text is separated from a 'comments' column which is used to highlight important and interesting points. In the main text, important terms are emboldened to attract your attention. For those students studying the A-level in a modular form, the A-level board specification and their own notes will direct them to the relevant parts of this revision book.

The division between AS and A2

For identification purposes, the narrow panel that separates the main body of text on the right from the comments column on the left includes a symbol that denotes relevance to AS or A2.

The Qualifications and Curriculum Authority (QCA) imposes constraints on the examining boards which mean that in most areas of the specification they are 'singing from the same song sheet'. There are a few minor differences, however, which are set out below. The three main examining boards are AQA, Edexcel and OCR, and the criterion for determining whether a heading is categorised by AS or A2 is when at least two of the three boards are in agreement. This means that the few exceptions that follow are specific to only one of the boards.

Specifically AQA

From Unit 2, 'The industrial structure of the economy', AQA includes supply and demand analysis as it is applied to factor markets and an explanation of consumer surplus and producer surplus in A2.

From Unit 5, 'The international structure of the world economy', it is only necessary to understand the main components of the current account of the balance of payments and the meaning of a current balance deficit or surplus. Also, it is only necessary to be able to make a brief descriptive reference to what happens to import and export prices when the exchange rate of a currency changes.

Specifically Edexcel

From Unit 2, 'The industrial structure of the economy', the division of labour and specialisation of function are included at AS.

From Unit 5, 'The international structure of the world economy', a more profound understanding of the gains from trade is required, including the difference between absolute and comparative advantage.

Specifically OCR

From Unit 1, 'An introduction to economics', cost–benefit analysis is required at AS.

From Unit 2, 'The industrial structure of the economy', students must be able to apply supply and demand analysis to the money market at AS.

From Unit 5, 'The international structure of the world economy', it is necessary to include an analysis of free trade and protected trade as well as a more detailed approach to the accounting structure of the balance of payments.

Note: in Unit 2 part C, 'The theory of demand', I find it difficult to see how a student can understand demand theory without making reference to utility, budget lines and indifference curves. For this reason, point 1, 'The concepts used in demand analysis' and point 2, 'Consumer theory' remain in the text, but are not labelled AS or A2 as they are not specifically required by the examining boards.

Acknowledgements

I must recognise a debt of gratitude to the following people: the economists whose textbooks I have used in the past – Lipsey, Stanlake, Begg et al; those inspirational economists Smith, Keynes, Friedman and Hayek who made me think; my colleagues, particularly Martin Tucker and Stuart Luker; my students, who have kept me on my intellectual toes; my sons, Ben and Chris, who were also my students; and above all my wife, Geraldine, who types, edits and reorganises all my work.

John Hearn

This is the briefest of the five units, but it is very important. It sets the scene and justifies the subject you are studying. The definitions provide a source for multiple-choice questions. The economic problem, how resources are allocated in different political systems, and opportunity cost are often subjects for essays or components of essay questions.

A The nature and scope of economics

1 Definitions

There are many definitions of economics linked to scarcity and the allocation of resources. Arguably the most quoted definition is that from Lionel Robbins who wrote that economics is:

'...the science which studies human behaviour as a relationship between ends and scarce means which have alternative use.'

If you want to impress your examiner, learn this quote. It comes from 'An Essay on the Nature and Signifi-cance of Economic Science' (Lord Robbins).

In this context, economic goods include services. Economics studies these allocative mechanisms in detail.

2 The economic problem

Economic problems like inflation and unemployment are symptoms of (and therefore should not be confused with) **the economic problem**. The economic problem is **scarcity**, i.e. not enough resources to satisfy everyone's demand. All **economic goods** are scarce, some more and some less so, but all require an **allocative mechanism**. The only goods that do not require an allocative mecha-nism are **free goods**. An example of a free good is air, although it is interesting to note that in a polluted city like Los Angeles fresh air is likely to become an economic good.

Given a limited ability to obtain resources, both **consumers** and **producers** must choose between alternative products. Scarcity leads to **choice** and in theory it is assumed that, in a free market, economic units make **rational decisions**.

Look at Eastern Europe.

In a centrally controlled economy the aim is to maximise the **total welfare** of society. In reality, the sheer size of an undertaking which tries to match the sum of individual demands and direct resources to them has led to the **decline** of this allocative mechanism.

3 Political systems and the economics of resource allocation

3.1 INTRODUCTION

All economies require allocative mechanisms. At the theoretical extremes, economies are divided into:

- free market or capitalist
- centrally-controlled or command

In reality all countries are a mixture of central direction and market places. More freedom in markets and the economy will be described as capitalist; more control in markets and the economy will be described as command. In command economies a lot of trade takes place on illegal or black markets.

3.2 FREE MARKET CAPITALISM

Minimal government is concerned with creating a framework of rules that protects:
- freedom of contract
- private property rights

In the past, slavery meant people were owned.

Producers are free to buy, hire and own non-human factors of production but only to hire and fire labour. They compete in product and productive factor markets.

Producer sovereignty is a market imperfection caused by monopolies.

Consumer sovereignty determines what is produced, who produces it and how it is produced. The market place is where the **invisible hand** of competition will harness the self-interest of the individual so that society benefits from the pursuit of **profit**. The invisible hand is a powerful concept in economics, first introduced by Adam Smith in his book, *Wealth of Nations*, published in 1776.

3.3 THE COMMAND ECONOMY

Government tries to solve the economic problem by total planning. There are no rights to own property. Incomes are received for work, not as the result of ownership. Production and productive factors need to be under the direction of a central authority. Quotas are established for productive units. Consumption by workers can be directed through vouchers used as a part share of planned output. Alternatively incomes can be awarded through central planning and consumers can choose how to spend their incomes. The marketplace must be part of a system aimed at bringing about an equitable distribution of resources. Therefore, prices may be fixed and shortages and surpluses used as signals to expand or contract output.

In the heyday of the command economy, some economists estimated that between 30% and 50% of all trade was through black markets.

Many command economies are currently going through a transitional phase as they free up their markets to competition. This has caused a number of problems as their industries are not competitive. Many of their resources need to be shifted from state bureaucracy and producer goods like armaments to the provision of consumer goods.

3.4 THE MIXED ECONOMY

3.4a The disadvantages of free market capitalism

Externalities are a very important concept throughout economics. These will be introduced in more detail under heading 5.

- Instability in the form of **booms** and **depressions**.
- Product sovereignty caused by powerful single firm industries.
- **Inequalities:** millionaires and beggars.
- **Externalities:** uncontracted costs or benefits which are not paid for when goods are produced or consumed.

Would you work harder if you were to get an individual grade at A-level or an average grade for the group?

In Moscow in the 1970s it was reported that Muscovites spent several hours every day in queues.

Without some degree of government intervention, there would be anarchy, where resources would be allocated by the laws of the jungle.

A common mistake by students is to include education and health as public goods because they are paid for out of the public purse.

Arguably, some forms of clothing are not pure private goods as they are worn to have an effect on other people.

3.4b The disadvantages of a command economy
- Lack of incentive in pursuing collectivist ideals.
- **A paradox of equality.** On the surface it is easy to create an equality of ownership by removing private property – it is not so easy to ensure an even distribution of the resources that make up a person's standard of living.
- Resource misallocation as consumer demand is not satisfied by producer supply.
- Shortages, and rationing through a queuing system.

4 The rationale behind economic intervention

4.1 INTRODUCTION
Philosophers of political economy argue a case for the mixed economy based upon the observation of weaknesses at both extremes. The argument for intervention by government is associated with the identification of various types of economic good ranging from:
- the **pure public good** to
- the **pure private good**

4.2 TYPES OF ECONOMIC GOOD

4.2a Pure public good
A pure public good is necessarily collectively consumed. It is **non-rival** and **non-excludable**. If one person has it, the whole group can have it. If any producer provides it for one consumer, it is provided for all other members of the group. The often-quoted examples are street lighting, water purification, prevention of contagious disease, law and order and internal and external defence. The fact that individuals will not buy the product is an economic justification for taxation and collective demand but does not necessarily mean that the product should be produced by the state.

4.2b Quasi-public good
A quasi-public good is something that is likely to have started as a public good, usually because property rights have not been recognised or, if recognised, have not been implemented. This means that it has the potential to become a private good. For example, a beach could be fenced off and made excludable.

4.2c Pure private good
If a pure private good is consumed by one person, it cannot be consumed by anyone else; and if provided for one person, it cannot be provided for anyone else. Therefore it is completely **rival** and **excludable**. Examples include food and clothing.

4.2d Club goods
These are public goods inside an organised group which are private with respect to people outside the group. The cinema and the discotheque are rival and excludable to those outside but non-rival and non-excludable to those inside.

4.2e Merit goods

These are private goods, but they are **under-consumed** as a result of market imperfections. Arguably, in order to benefit society, the government needs to become involved in the supply and/or demand for these products. The most commonly-quoted examples are the National Health Service and state education.

This point is arguable because many countries do not recognise the need to intervene.

4.2f Demerit goods

These are also private goods, but they are **over-consumed** as a result of market imperfections. Arguably, government can benefit society by restricting the consumption of these products. Examples include smoking, drinking alcohol and gambling. It is interesting to ask the question: how would government manage without the revenue from these three products if people really did give them up?

5 _Externalities_

Be warned: it is a common error to think of social costs and externalities as the same thing.

- Private costs or private benefits + external costs or benefits = social (total) costs or social (total) benefits.

Externalities can occur as the result of either **production or consumption**. For example, if a firm discharges waste into a local river and kills the fish, this is an external cost. If it discharges a waste product that feeds the fish and improves local fishing, this is an external benefit. Externalities are often referred to as **spillover** effects on third parties. There is never a contract to pay for external costs or benefits. If there is, then they are no longer external but become private costs or benefits.

The extent to which there are externalities is used to justify government intervention. This will be looked at in more detail later in these revision notes.

6 _Optimality and efficiency_

Vilfredo Pareto, 1848–1923.

6.1 PARETO OPTIMALITY

Most students know that a best case exists when the economy's resources are allocated in such a way that no reallocation can make anyone better off without making someone else worse off. However, they do not know how it is achieved. There are three maximising conditions.

- An optimal distribution of products between consumers requires that:

$$\frac{MUXA}{MUYA} = \frac{MUXB}{MUYB}$$

where MU = marginal utility
X and Y = products
A and B = consumers

Optimal comes from the Latin 'optimus' which means 'best'.

- Optimal allocation of productive factors occurs where:

$$\frac{MPLX}{MPCX} = \frac{MPLY}{MPCY}$$

where MP = marginal product
X and Y = products
C and L = productive factors

- Optimal output is where:

$$\frac{MUX}{MCX} = \frac{MUY}{MCY}$$

where MU = marginal utility
X and Y = products
MC = marginal cost

More detail under 'The theories of the firm', Unit 2F.

6.2 ECONOMIC EFFICIENCY

There are three types of efficiency commonly referred to:

- **allocative efficiency:** firms produce where price equals marginal cost
- **productive efficiency:** firms produce at the lowest average cost
- **dynamic efficiency:** firms reduce costs over time

7 | An introduction to welfare economics

7.1 TOTAL COSTS AND TOTAL BENEFITS

Arguably all or almost all products give rise to externalities and these complicate the theories of optimality and efficiency. The divergence between the private costs and social (total) costs of production and the private benefits and social (total) benefits from consumption are referred to as **market imperfections**.

In order to make decisions, it is useful to complete a **cost–benefit analysis**, where total costs and benefits are measured. It is the task of cost–benefit analysis to estimate all costs and benefits in money terms. Private costs and benefits are relatively easy to measure. Unfortunately, external costs and benefits are very difficult to measure. If total costs are less than total benefits, a certain type of resource allocation will benefit society, even though private costs may have been greater than private benefits. In this case resource allocation would have produced losses in a private market.

This is a good critical point to bring out in essays.

Some economists have suggested that almost any cost–benefit analysis can produce a positive or negative answer. It all depends upon what is included in (or excluded from) the analysis, and the money values given to intangibles like human life and the preservation of the countryside.

7.2 POSITIVE AND NORMATIVE STATEMENTS

The degree of government intervention is a fundamental argument which has shifted throughout this century. Traditionally, Tories are associated with free markets and Labour with intervention. However, the reality is that some Tory governments have supported intervention

Welfare economics highlights the importance of identifying the difference between the terms positive and normative. A positive statement usually includes **'was'**, **'is'** or **'will be'** whereas a normative statement usually includes **'ought'**, **'should'** or **'must be'**.

A positive statement is an actual or probable event that is described by an economist, whereas a normative statement is a subjective value judgement that is more likely to be made by a politician.

7.3 DIFFERENT POINTS OF VIEW

- Welfare economists envisage an important role for government in correcting market failure.

while some Labour governments have encouraged free markets.

- Free market economists cast doubt on the ability of government to acquire the knowledge necessary to improve upon the market. They would like to limit the government role to easing entry into the market place through the clarification of **private property rights**.

The opportunity cost of resource allocation

One of the most important concepts in economics is **opportunity cost**. It is fitting to complete this first unit by identifying its relevance to the analysis so far and introducing its importance to the study of economics in general.

- Opportunity cost is a real measure in terms of the foregone alternative at the level of either production or consumption.

All the time that products and productive factors are scarce in economic terms, then transactions can be measured by opportunity cost. There is one good which is not scarce and therefore does not have an opportunity cost: **the free good**.

All economic goods have an opportunity cost of production. When they are provided free to the consumer, they do not have an opportunity cost of consumption.

Type of product	Opportunity cost of production	Opportunity cost of consumption
Free good	No	No
Public good	Yes	No
Merit good	Yes	No
Club good	Yes	Yes
Private good	Yes	Yes

Opportunity cost is often illustrated using a **production possibility boundary** (Figure 1.1).

This is the first diagram in these notes. It is therefore timely to remind you that all diagrams must be drawn correctly with full labelling. Written work can be considerably enhanced by clear illustrations which are both correct and relevant.

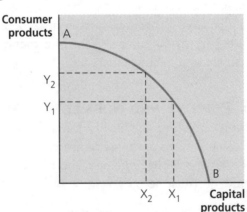

Figure 1.1 Production possibility boundary

The line AB represents the maximum quantity or combination of consumer and capital goods that can be produced given current resources. If Y_1X_1 represents current output, then the opportunity cost of moving from Y_1 to Y_2 is a contraction from X_1 to X_2.

For those of you who enjoy thinking about economics, try this quotation: 'It is an economic axiom as old as the hills that goods and services can only be paid for with goods and services' (A. J. Nock).

Breaking with tradition, we will not start by looking at supply, demand and pricing. Let us go right back to the beginning with what is available to produce, namely the productive factors. Economics looks at certain laws and concepts to do with the size and scale of productive units. After this, we will study the theories underlying pricing. A very important part of economic theory is analysing the theories of the firm. The rules of pricing can then be applied to the productive factors and the unit will be completed by considering a more complex analysis of pricing and resource allocation.

The unit is subdivided into the following major headings:

A The factors of production
B The size and scale of production
C The theory of demand
D The theory of supply
E The elementary theory of price
F The theories of the firm
G Some further analysis of price determination and resource allocation
H The pricing of productive factors

A-level specifications usually identify four factors of production – land, labour, capital and enterprise – although some economics texts identify only land, labour and capital, preferring to consider enterprise as a component of the productive factor, labour.

Question: When does a spear become a consumer good? Answer: When it is used as a javelin.

A The factors of production

1 Definitions

AS

- **Land** includes all natural resources, the original raw materials of production. It is important to remember that in economics the sea is land, but do not try walking on it.
- **Labour** involves all human economic effort, whether it be mental, physical, skilled or unskilled, applied to the production of goods and services.
- **Capital** is a produced means of production. The essential characteristic of capital is its quality of being able to produce more, having been produced itself. The early forms of capital were spears to kill animals, ploughs to cultivate land and nets to catch fish.
- **Enterprise** describes the factor of production which takes the risks and uncertainties of bringing together the other factors of production in the hope of a profitable return from the sale of their product.

2 Labour

2.1 LABOUR AND POPULATION SIZE

A2

2.1a The dependency ratio

The dependency ratio changes over time and is different between countries. It is strictly the ratio of:

$$\frac{\text{Unable to work}}{\text{Able to work}}$$

Its significance is in a relatively crude observation that those who are working to produce goods and services are supporting not only themselves but also those who are not working. As the UK economy matures, so more people seem to be supported by a shrinking workforce. Whether or not this is a problem makes for an interesting debate.

A2

2.1b Are there limits to the size of a population?

The Reverend Thomas **Malthus** wrote in 1798 that the productivity of finite resources is likely to grow arithmetically (1, 2, 3, 4) while the population is likely to grow geometrically (1, 2, 4, 8). The result will be poverty, plagues, wars and starvation. These will bring back the population size to a level that the land can support.

Today this view is often overlooked in more developed countries, but considered much more seriously in those countries still suffering from these problems.

A2

2.1c The optimum size of a population

In theory it is quite clear:

● The optimum size of a population is that which gives rise to the highest average output for an economy.

In reality it is not quite so clear. For example, it cannot be **proved** that India is overpopulated and Australia is underpopulated. They probably are, but there is no way of telling. This is an interesting point because many political debates take place on the assumption that overpopulation is proved. What is more worrying is that knowledge of the theory may encourage leaders of a country to pursue sterilisation policies or limit families to only one child. Suppose a UK government decided that unemployment was a measure of overpopulation and suggested that all people with blue eyes and blonde hair should be repatriated to Scandinavia.

Do economists have a moral responsibility to point out that although countries have an optimum population size, it is not possible to identify this size in reality?

Another important point to note is that optimum population size continually changes as technology changes. This means that a new invention or discovery may change a country almost overnight from being overpopulated to under-populated.

2.2 THE MOBILITY OF LABOUR

AS

2.2a The economic importance of mobile labour

It is a common error to refer to the UK as a developed economy. The UK is a developing country, as are all countries – it is just that some countries are further down the endless road than others.

In order to maintain economic development and improve efficiency, all product-ive factors must be sufficiently mobile to accommodate all the economic changes that take place.

Mobility not only refers to movement from place to place, i.e. **geographical or lateral mobility**, but also movement from one job to another, i.e. **occupational or vertical mobility**.

Ask yourself if you would be prepared to go anywhere and do anything and then ask your parent(s) the same question.

AS

2.2b Frictions and lateral mobility

Labour is not perfectly mobile in response to changing economic circumstances. Because the word 'labour' is a collective noun, it does not require each individual

worker to be responsive to economic change. Only a proportion of the workforce needs to be mobile as economic conditions change.

A rough rule of thumb is that the faster the rate of economic growth, the more mobile the workforce needs to be to facilitate the necessary economic change.

2.2c Frictions and vertical mobility

If one unit of labour was a perfect substitute for another, then many frictions associated with occupational mobility would not exist.

Older members of the workforce find it more difficult to adjust to changes and to acquire new skills.

In addition, the abilities of labour are unevenly distributed. Only a limited number of people have the ability to become premier league footballers, first-rate mathematicians, linguists or steeplejacks.

2.2d Removing mobility frictions: a political dilemma

If the choice was between starvation and mobility, the workforce would be more mobile than it is today. Herein lies the dilemma: a civilised society will want to protect its members from the genuine hardship that can come with unemployment. However, in doing this it can reinforce the frictions which slow the engine that raises living standards.

A case can also be made for the protection of certain occupations by artificial barriers:
- Do you need a degree to be a competent chartered accountant?
- Did you need to be the son of a miner to become a good miner?
- Do you need an Equity card to be a fine actor?

The question an economist must ask is whether these barriers bring about a more efficient allocation of resources or whether they do exactly the opposite and preserve unnecessarily high incomes.

2.3 THE DIVISION OF LABOUR INTO SPECIALISED FUNCTIONS

2.3a Advantages

These are well documented in textbooks and include:
- improved dexterity
- efficient use of skills
- production line methods
- greater use of machinery

However, examinations usually want you to understand how division of labour allows output to expand through the **theory of comparative advantage**. In order to understand this theory it is necessary to be clear about the difference between absolute advantage and comparative advantage.
- Absolute advantage is where a productive unit, like a person, a firm or a country, can produce more output than another productive unit given the same resources.
- Comparative advantage can exist where one productive unit has absolute

---

Margin notes:

The word 'friction' is used as it denotes the forces that stop labour moving.

In the 1960s the equivalent of five GCSE passes including mathematics and English was the entrance requirement for chartered accountancy.

The importance of the theory of comparative advantage will be reinforced when we look at international trade.

disadvantage in producing all products, but has a **lower opportunity cost** of producing one or some of the products.

The theory is best understood by following through a simple example. Suppose that over a specific period of time two people could produce the quantities of loaves of bread and pints of beer shown in Table 2.1.

This will also illustrate the theoretical basis of all trade.

	Loaves of bread	Pints of beer
Geraldine	24,000	16,000
John	12,000	9,000
Total	36,000	25,000

Table 2.1

In this example, Geraldine has **absolute** advantage in the production of both bread and beer. At first sight it would seem that specialisation would not increase total output. However, before reaching a conclusion it is necessary to apply the concept of opportunity cost. What we need to know is how much bread has to be given up to produce more beer and vice versa. Table 2.2 shows the opportunity cost of producing one loaf of bread and one pint of beer.

The ratios are always the reciprocal of each other.

	One loaf of bread	One pint of beer
Geraldine	$^2/_3$ pint of beer	$^3/_2$ loaves of bread
John	$^3/_4$ pint of beer	$^4/_3$ loaves of bread

Table 2.2

In terms of opportunity cost, John gives up fewer loaves of bread to produce a pint of beer while Geraldine gives up fewer pints of beer to produce one loaf of bread. **Comparative advantage occurs when one productive factor has a lower opportunity cost for producing one product.**

Although Geraldine has absolute advantage in producing bread and beer, John has comparative advantage in producing beer. If they both concentrate on the product for which they have comparative advantage, we get the results in Table 2.3.

	Loaves of bread	Pints of beer
Geraldine	48,000	0
John	0	18,000

Table 2.3

Geraldine produces 12,000 more loaves than the previous total while John produces 7,000 fewer pints. The gain of 12,000 loaves is at an opportunity cost of 8,000 pints, but only 7,000 are lost. A loss of 7,000 pints would be at an opportunity cost of 10,500 loaves, but overall 12,000 loaves are gained. It is therefore advantageous for each to specialise.

However, so far we have not increased the total of one product without reducing the other total.

Suppose Geraldine produced only 9,000 more loaves at a cost of 6,000 pints while John produced 6,000 more pints at a cost of 8,000 fewer loaves (Table 2.4).

A

Table 2.4

	Loaves of bread	Pints of beer
Geraldine	33,000	10,000
John	4,000	15,000
Total	37,000	25,000

It is always possible to produce more of both products. As a bit of fun, see if you can do it.

We have proved that **when opportunity costs are different it is always possible to produce more of one product without producing less of the other product**.

A final very important point is illustrated by changing the original situation very slightly (Table 2.5).

Table 2.5

	Loaves of bread	Pints of beer
Geraldine	24,000	16,000
John	12,000	8,000

A simple rule for calculating opportunity cost: if you are dealing with output, place the number on the right **over** the number on the left to get the ratio, e.g. 16,000/24,000 = $^2/_3$. If you are dealing with costs, then the number on the right goes **beneath** the number on the left.

In this situation there is no comparative advantage. You can check this by working out the opportunity costs. Do this and you will see they are the same. Play around with the numbers and you will find that it is now no longer possible to increase the output of both products. Changing one number very slightly has created a situation where there can be no advantage in specialising function. **If opportunity costs are the same, there cannot be any gains from trade.**

A2

2.3b Disadvantages

Again, these are well documented and include:
- monotony and boredom
- a loss of craftsmanship and variety of expression
- interdependence within one firm and between firms which creates a greater risk of unemployment

The tenuous thread which binds the modern economy's productive processes is both its strength and potentially its greatest weakness.

3 *Enterprise*

AS

3.1 THE FUNCTIONS OF THE ENTREPRENEUR

The entrepreneur is the risk-taker who has no guaranteed rate of return. Whereas labour can insure itself against a cessation of income through ill health or redundancy, the entrepreneur takes an uninsurable risk.

It is usual for the entrepreneur to sign contracts to pay for the use of productive factors, but there is no contract with the consumer that can guarantee profits.

A2

3.2 THE DECISION OF OPTIMUM FACTOR COMBINATION

The successful entrepreneur will find the most efficient mix of productive factors. This decision is illustrated using Figure 2.1.

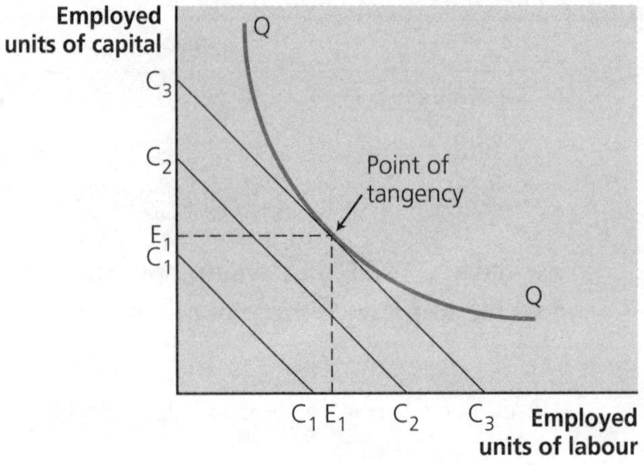

Figure 2.1

The line QQ is an isoquant. **Isoquants join together different combinations of productive factors (in this case labour and capital) which can be used to produce the same quantity of a product.** The lines C_1C_1, C_2C_2 and C_3C_3 are isocost lines. **An isocost line joins together different combinations of productive factors that can be employed for the same total cost.** The point of tangency between C_3C_3 and QQ is the least cost combination of productive factors to produce a specific quantity.

The point of tangency has an algebraic formulation as it is the point where:

$$\frac{\text{Marginal physical product of labour}}{\text{Price of labour}} = \frac{\text{Marginal physical product of capital}}{\text{Price of capital}}$$

> Although this is the most efficient combination, it does not tell us anything about revenues and profits. It only identifies costs.

4 | *Land*

4.1 INTRODUCTION

Land can be available for repeated use, e.g. agricultural land, or it can be used up in the production process, e.g. fossil fuels.

It is not possible to replenish many natural resources which took millions of years to form, so those **non-renewable resources** are only available for a particular use over a limited period of time. This has led to a debate between conservationists and others.

4.2 CONSERVATION OR NOT: THE DEBATE

4.2a Conservationists

Problem: Non-renewable resources will be used up over a relatively small number of years and some renewable resources will be exhausted (for example, by overfishing and destruction of hardwood forests) if the firms and nations of the world compete for their use.

Solution: Far-sighted national and international agencies must manage the controlled use of these resources.

4.2b The others

Problem: The opposing argument questions the reality of cooperation at a national and international level and even suggests that resources will be used up, without replacements coming on stream, as the market mechanism is ignored.

Solution: Let the market mechanism work – shortages will lead to higher prices and profits, which will in turn encourage the search for substitutes and synthetic alternatives. Private property rights should be clearly established and resources will then be carefully farmed. As long as land remains common to all, it will be misused and exhausted.

This leads to a difficult philosophical point, namely who should **own** the free gifts of nature if common ownership is inefficient.

4.2c Conclusion

Many economists have predicted the total exhaustion of certain raw materials. For example, the fossil fuel oil will not last long into the next millennium. In contrast, other economists have said that if the price mechanism is allowed to work, then in 500 years time there will still be huge quantities of oil unused throughout the world.

Who is right? It is your future.

5 Capital

5.1 INTRODUCTION

Capital can only be formed if current consumption is foregone. This means that if you want to be better off in the future, it will be necessary to lower your standard of living in the present. This has been referred to as one step back in order to take two steps forward.

All capital is wealth, but not all wealth is capital.

5.2 SOME IMPORTANT DISTINCTIONS

Capital and wealth: Wealth is what you own, capital is that part of your wealth which is used to derive a flow of income. Your car is wealth – it becomes capital if you use it as a taxi.

Gross and net capital investment: Capital is consumed or used up in the production process. This **depreciation** occurs through wear and tear or deterioration and can also be the result of **obsolescence** when more efficient alternatives are developed.

Gross investment is the total amount of new capital produced. **Net investment** is the total produced over and above that required to cover depreciation. For a productive unit to become more productive, net investment must be greater than zero.

5.3 THE IMPORTANCE OF CAPITAL

In all countries of the world where living standards are high, large amounts of capital per head of the population have been produced and are being used. However, **although capital investment is a necessary condition for a high standard of living, it is not sufficient on its own to guarantee economic growth.** This is particularly obvious where a country has invested large amounts in non-productive capital such as armaments.

B The size and scale of production

1 Introduction

1.1 TYPES OF PRODUCTIVE UNIT

It is very important not to confuse the terms 'industry' and 'firm'.

The process of producing goods and services is usually classified by industries. **An industry is a collection of firms producing the same or similar products**, e.g. the car industry. The term is sometimes used to identify all the economic activity in a certain geographical area, e.g. British industry.

A firm is a legal entity distinguished from other firms by ownership. It could be as small as one person or it could be owned by thousands of shareholders, employ hundreds and thousands of people throughout the world and produce products in many different industries.

The size of the firm relative to the size of the industry is important in understanding the relationship between producer and consumer.

- many firms – competitive industry – consumer sovereignty
- one firm – monopoly – producer sovereignty

1.2 OUTPUT AND TIME PERIODS

Production time periods relate to the amount of time required to change output.

It is useful to identify four periods, although short run and long run are most often used in theoretical models.

- The **very short run** (momentary period) is that period of time during which it is not possible to change output.
- The **short run** allows the producer to change most of the productive factors, but at least one factor is fixed and cannot be changed.
- The **long run** allows the producer to expand or contract output by adjusting the use of all the productive factors.

In each of the above, technology has been held constant.

- In the **very long run** it is possible that technological developments can change the quality of the products or the efficiency of the productive factors.

2 In the short run

2.1 INCREASING MARGINAL RETURNS AND THE LAW OF VARIABLE PROPORTIONS

This law is sometimes known as the law of diminishing marginal returns. It is important to remember that returns refers to output, not revenue or profits.

In the short run **variable** factors can be added to **fixed** factors, and it is likely through specialisation of function and division of labour that the addition to total output (marginal output) will at first rise. It is, however, not definite. What is certain, and is therefore given the status of law, is that when additional units of a variable factor are added to a fixed factor, then at some level of input of the variable factor, the addition to output will begin to diminish.

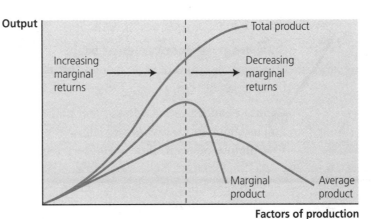

Figure 2.2

MP will always cut AP at its highest point when numbers rise and then fall.

The marginal product curve in Figure 2.2 clearly illustrates the point where the law of variable proportions kicks in.

2.2 HOW DO COSTS BEHAVE IN THE SHORT RUN?

It is important to remember that the **law of variable proportions** is about **output in the short run**. However, it is obvious that it has implications for the costs of production. To illustrate this we must define two costs:

- **Fixed costs** are those costs of production which remain the same at all levels of output including zero.
- **Variable costs** are incurred as soon as the first unit is produced and subsequently vary with output.

Because fixed costs remain the same at all levels of output, they must always fall on average as output expands. If we assume that the additional costs of employing factors is constant, then falling average costs plus increasing marginal returns must bring costs down. However, as output expands the fall in average fixed costs becomes weaker and diminishing marginal returns set in. Hence the normal shape for cost curves is as shown in Figure 2.3.

Figure 2.3

When numbers fall and then rise, MC will cut AC at its lowest point.

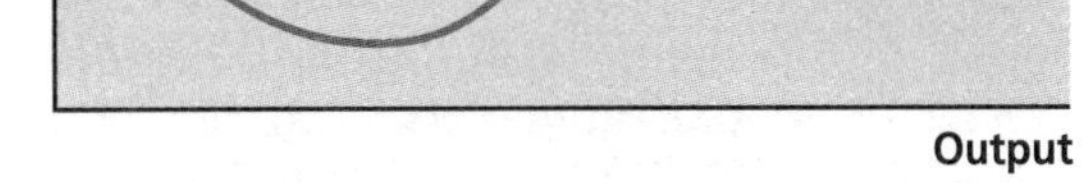

3 *In the long run*

3.1 A COMMON CONFUSION

Returns to scale should not be confused with the increasing marginal returns that occur when factor proportions vary in the short run. They occur when factor inputs are changed in the same proportion. Increasing returns to scale give rise to **economies of scale**.

Questions on economies and diseconomies of scale are quite popular at A-level.

3.2 ECONOMIES OF SCALE

3.2a Internal economies of scale

Internal economies of scale result from actions taken inside the firm that reduce unit or average costs.

Capital economies include the fact that machines can be used 24 hours a day and usually refer to two principles:

- **Principle of multiples:** Suppose three machines produced components for the final product. Machine A produced 40, B produced 70 and C produced 80 per time period. The least common multiple of these three numbers is 560. Therefore, to achieve maximum efficiency 14 As must be linked with 8 Bs and 7 Cs.
- **Principle of increased dimensions:** Double the size of a container and the volume is increased eight times – a considerable saving in transport and storage costs.

Buying economies: Bulk buying of materials can reduce the prices below those quoted to small firms.

Selling economies: The marketing and advertising budget can be spread over many more units.

Financial economies: Large firms can raise loans at more favourable rates than small firms.

Managerial economies: If two firms merge, one management team takes over and the other becomes redundant.

3.2b External economies of scale

External economies of scale result from actions taken outside the firm that almost inadvertently reduce their unit costs.

Training: A firm's training budget is reduced if a local college starts offering relevant courses.

Infrastructure: A large firm in an area may lead to improvements in the transportation and communication networks.

Support services: Trade magazines, research units and component suppliers may be drawn towards a large firm.

3.2c Internal diseconomies of scale

Internal diseconomies of scale result from actions in the firm that raise unit costs of production.

There is an interesting debate about whether these exist only as the result of the human problem. As firms grow larger it becomes more difficult to manage, control and coordinate the workforce. This is supported by the fact that internal diseconomies do not occur in all similar firms at the same level of output. For example, Japanese workers seem much more controllable in large numbers than their UK counterparts.

3.2d External diseconomies of scale

External diseconomies of scale result from actions outside the firm that raise unit costs of production.

Productive factors are scarce. As firms and industries grow larger, so increased competition for their use can create external diseconomies, for example:

- higher wages
- higher price for raw materials
- congestion on the roads
- cost of renting space

3.3 HOW DO COSTS BEHAVE IN THE LONG RUN?

Changing the scale of activity in the long run is likely to produce economies and diseconomies of scale, as illustrated in Figure 2.4.

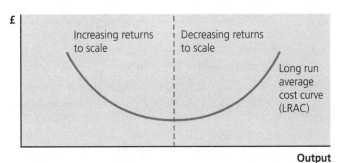

Figure 2.4

The long-run average cost curve is tangent to each of the short-run average cost curves, as shown in Figure 2.5.

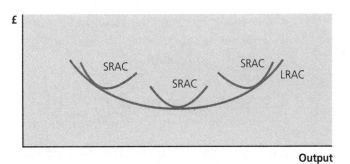

Figure 2.5

Points of tangency have the same slope. Therefore as LRAC falls, so it touches SRAC where it is also falling. Only at the lowest point on LRAC will SRAC be at its lowest.

4 *In the very long run*

The main difference between the long run and the very long run is that the average costs of production can change **without** a change in output. In this case inventions, innovations, changes in technology, etc. will shift the cost curves vertically downwards, as illustrated in Figure 2.6.

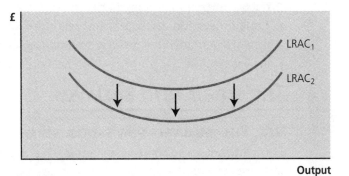

Figure 2.6

5 The optimum size of a firm

A2

The **optimum size** of a firm is when it is producing at the **lowest point** on the average cost curve, i.e. Q_1 in Figure 2.7.

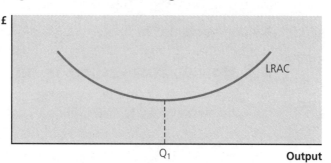

Figure 2.7

These points will be explained in more detail under 'The theories of the firm', Unit 2F.

Optimum size should not be confused with optimum resource allocation which occurs when firms produce where **price = marginal cost** or with the most profitable output which is where **marginal cost = marginal revenue**.

6 The growth of firms

A2

6.1 WHY FIRMS GROW

- To take advantage of increasing marginal returns and returns to scale. Both of these will increase profitability.
- Increasing the economic security of the firm by diversifying the product range.
- In pursuit of status, power, market dominance and the removal of actual and potential competitors.

Most economic model building of firms assumes profit maximisation as the main motivation.

A2

6.2 HOW FIRMS GROW

Firms grow **internally** by ploughing back profits.

They grow **externally** by vertical integration, horizontal integration or by conglomeration.

- The production process is a link between suppliers of raw materials, product providers, wholesalers, retailers and even after-sales service. If a firm takes over or merges with another firm that is at a different stage in the production process, this is described as **vertical integration**. This integration can be backwards when a product provider joins with its suppliers or forwards when it joins with the retailer.

How many shops in your local high street are owned by a manufacturer or product provider?

- **Horizontal integration** is where similar firms at the same level in the production process join together.
- **Conglomeration** is where firms which are producing fundamentally different products join together, usually to produce security through diversity.

7 The small firm survives

It is common for examiners to ask why small firms survive in view of all the advantages of being large.

A2

7.1 THE DEMAND FOR SMALL FIRMS

As incomes rise, so there is a demand for more **variety**. This is a movement away from the mass-produced, standardised product.

Quality and lasting value may be more forthcoming from a small firm.

The **limited size** of certain markets may mean it is unprofitable for a large firm with indivisible units of capital to produce at a level of output which will bring down unit costs without over-supplying the market.

Personal service may be lost in large firms but be required by customers of, for example, doctors, dentists, lawyers, accountants.

A2

7.2 THE SUPPLY OF SMALL FIRMS

The point at which a firm reaches its optimum size will be an important factor determining its profit-maximising level of output. The degree to which firms can take advantage of economies of scale varies and this will produce different optimum sizes. Some firms may not reach optimum size until their daily production run is several hundred thousand. In contrast, firms in other industries may reach their optimum size after 50 units have been produced. Industries comprising these firms will only be profitable if they are made up of many small firms.

There seems to be no shortage of entrepreneurs willing to set up business in a small way. Small firms are more flexible. Producers do not feel so divorced from their customers and the workforce may have a greater sense of responsibility and may produce work of a higher quality.

7.3 CONCLUDING POINTS

A2

7.3a Point 1

A-level questions quite often ask why some industries have both small and large firms, for example the UK car industry includes Ford and Morgan. In order to answer this question, segment the overall market and you will find the part supplied by Morgan will have all the characteristics of a small market.

A2

7.3b Point 2

Up until now it has often been stated that small firms have been and will eventually be forced out of business by large firms. However, we may see the very opposite in the new millennium. Higher incomes may lead to greater demand for variety and personal service. In addition, many large firms are breaking up into smaller units as they outsource peripheral parts of the business and concentrate on their core activity.

C The theory of demand

See note on p. 5.

1 *The concepts used in demand analysis*

1.1 UTILITY

1.1a Introduction

Utility is defined as a measure of the satisfaction which is derived from the consumption of a good or service. The units of measurement are known as 'utils'.

Consumer theory is based upon the assumption that individuals will arrange their pattern of expenditure to maximise utility.

In reality most individuals will admit to purchasing something which gave them little or no satisfaction. This is usually explained by imperfect knowledge or pressure from advertising.

1.1b The law of diminishing utility

Over a specific period of time and assuming the consumption of other products is fixed, the utility derived from consuming successive units of the same product will add less to a rising total and may even reduce total utility past a certain level of consumption.

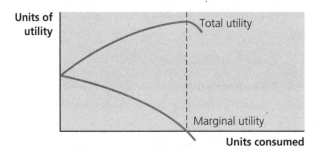

Figure 2.8

Figure 2.8 shows that marginal utility is falling as total utility rises by ever decreasing amounts.

A common mistake is to write that marginal utility rises before it starts to fall.

1.1c Can utility be measured?

It may seem strange to be asking this question after diagrams have been drawn. However, in reality it is not possible to measure utility in any meaningful way that allows comparisons between one consumer and another. It is, though, much easier to rank products for each individual consumer. Their expenditure reflects the expected utility that will be derived from each unit of money spent.

Alfred Marshall (1842–1924) solved the problem.

1.1d The paradox of value

Some early economists were confused by the fact that people were prepared to pay high prices for non-essential goods like diamonds when they spent little or nothing on essential goods like water.

Ask yourself this question: You are dying of thirst in the desert and one glass of water can save your

The confusion was generated by looking at the high marginal utility from the last diamond and the low marginal utility from the last drop of water. The answer was found by looking at relative scarcity and the total utility derived from each product. The total utility from water was much greater than the total utility from diamonds, as shown in Figure 2.9.

life. Someone offers you either water or the world's biggest diamond. Which will you take?

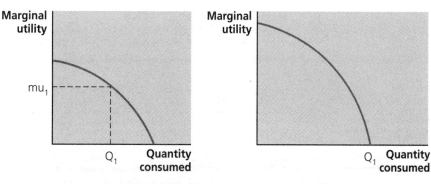

Figure 2.9a Marginal utility schedule for diamonds

Figure 2.9b Marginal utility schedule for water

1.2 INDIFFERENCE CURVES

1.2a The indifference curve

The law of diminishing marginal utility states that increased consumption of one product will add successively less to total utility. If we assume that a person consumes only two products, X and Y, and that a preference for a certain combination of X and Y has been revealed, then in order to maintain the same total utility from combinations which have less and less X, the consumer must add ever increasing amounts of Y to achieve the same total utility. Therefore the indifference curve has a concave shape, as illustrated in Figure 2.10.

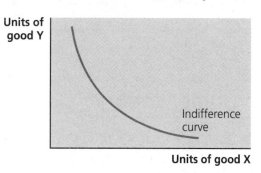

Figure 2.10

The word 'indifference' is often explained as the consumer being indifferent to various combinations.

The indifference curve joins together all the points where different combinations of two products give rise to the same total utility.

1.2b The indifference map

The indifference curve joins together all combinations of products with the same total utility. To the right of any curve there will therefore be curves which join together points of higher total utility and to the left, curves of lower total utility (Figure 2.11).

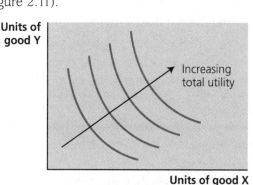

Figure 2.11

When you draw an indifference map, remember that curves cannot cross. If they did, it would mean a consumer could get higher utility from consuming less of both products.

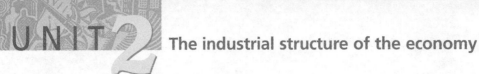
1.3 THE BUDGET LINE

The budget line joins together different combinations of X and Y that can be purchased given a fixed sum of money (Figure 2.12).

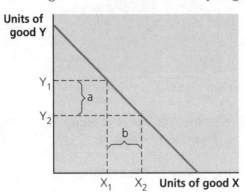

Figure 2.12

The slope of the budget line identifies the opportunity cost of more X or more Y.

Opportunity cost of X $= \dfrac{a}{b}$

Opportunity cost of Y $= \dfrac{b}{a}$

Parallel shifts in the budget line occur if income changes or if each price changes by the same percentage.

The **slope** of the budget line changes when relative prices change, i.e. one price changes by a different percentage from the other.

2   *Consumer theory*

2.1 THE INDIVIDUAL DEMAND CURVE

The demand curve for an individual establishes the functional relationship between the price of a product and the quantity demanded.

This can be illustrated in its simplest form if we assume a person has only £50 to spend on one product and total utility increases with each successive purchase. Table 2.6 shows how many will be purchased at various prices.

This is a very simple example but we will use the same numbers to build up a more complex model. If you get lost, then keep going back to pick up the argument.

Price	Quantity demanded
£50	1
£25	2
£10	5
£5	10

Table 2.6

I will leave you to graph this function, remembering that the convention is price on the vertical axis and quantity on the horizontal axis.

Now let us make it a little more difficult by assuming the consumer has a choice of two products X and Y, the same expenditure constraint, i.e. £50, and a price for both products of £5. In order to answer this, let us use some made-up numbers for marginal utility (Table 2.7).

Units consumed	Marginal utility of X	Marginal utility of Y
1st	20	15
2nd	18	12
3rd	16	10
4th	14	8
5th	12	6
6th	11	5
7th	10	2
8th	4	1
9th	3	0
10th	1	0

Table 2.7

The answer is that the consumer will purchase 7X and 3Y and will maximise utility at 138 utils. No other pattern of expenditure can achieve this total.

To work this out, you can proceed in an iterative way, i.e. the first purchase of X gives 20, the second purchase gives 18 and so on until all the money is gone. Alternatively, you can search for the expenditure pattern which spends all the money and equals the marginal utility of the last pound spent on X and Y, i.e.:

$$\frac{\text{Marginal utility of X (MUX)}}{\text{Price of X (PX)}} = \frac{\text{Marginal utility of Y (MUY)}}{\text{Price of Y (PY)}} = \frac{10}{5}$$

The analysis is made more complex if we assume a change in relative prices. Suppose the price of X rises to £10 and the same expenditure constraint remains. To approach this in an iterative way, notice that doubling the price of X halves the utility from each pound spent.

Using $\dfrac{\text{MUX}}{\text{PX}} = \dfrac{\text{MUY}}{\text{PY}} = \dfrac{16}{10} = \dfrac{8}{5}$

the answer is 3X and 4Y with utility maximised at 99 utils.

2.2 USING INDIFFERENCE CURVES AND BUDGET LINES

Using the figures from above:

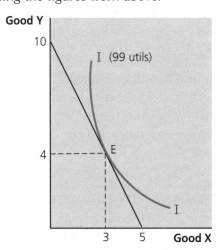

Figure 2.13

In examinations, calculations are always doctored so that the answer can be worked out precisely.

Some specifications no longer require you to understand indifference curves. This means that you cannot directly be asked questions on them. However, in essay answers they can be useful to explain certain points and, as you will see, they are not difficult to understand.

The budget line would join 10Y and 5X. The consumer-maximising choice is 4Y and 3X and the indifference curve which is tangent to the budget line at E has a value of 99 utils.

Now let us assume that the consumer income constraint rises to £100. The budget line will shift out parallel to itself. The **new equilibrium** must lie in the shaded area of Figure 2.14 because a point of higher utility must include at least the same amount of X and more Y or the same amount of Y and more X. The exact point can be found by looking at the previous marginal utility schedules for X and Y. The answer is 6Y and 7X and a new indifference curve which joins together all combinations achieving 157 utils.

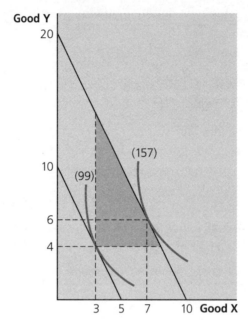

Figure 2.14

The point where the consumer maximises total utility is both where there is an equality between the utility derived from the last pound spent on each item and where the indifference curve is tangent to the budget line.

3 *Market demand*

AS

3.1 THE NORMAL PRODUCT DEMAND CURVE

The total demand for an individual product is referred to as the market demand. It is the horizontal sum of each individual demand curve and its normal shape is downward sloping from left to right.

> 'Horizontal sum' means you are adding up on the horizontal axis while the vertical axis remains constant.

The uneven distribution of income in a country like the UK will mean that as the price falls, so more consumers will be able to enter the market. Each consumer will also gain more utility per pound spent as the price falls and will therefore increase consumption as purchases are rearranged to maximise utility.

AS

3.2 SHIFTS AND MOVEMENTS IN A DEMAND CURVE

If the first thing that changes in the relationship between price and quantity demanded is **price**, then this will be represented by a **movement** along the demand curve. If it is **quantity demanded**, then this will be represented by a **shift** in the demand curve.

A movement along a demand curve occurs as the result of a change in price whereas more or less of the product demanded at the same price constitutes a shift.

Consider one final variation to make sure you have got this right: **more or less demanded at different prices is a movement; more or less demanded at the same price is a shift.**

Shifts in the demand curve can be the result of:
- rising real income
- economic growth
- change in consumer tastes
- new products entering the market
- new ways of buying and selling, e.g. the Internet
- the cost of loans
- advertising
- change in the price of other competing or complementary products
- change in the structure or size of the population

3.3 NORMAL GOODS AND INFERIOR GOODS

Normal goods have two characteristics:
- The quantity demanded is negatively related to price, i.e. a fall in price raises demand.
- The quantity demanded is positively related to income, i.e. a rise in income raises demand.

Inferior goods have only one characteristic:
- The quantity demanded is negatively related to income, i.e. a rise in income causes a fall in demand.

It is common to identify two types of inferior good, one of which has a normal demand curve while the other has a perverse demand curve. The distinguishing feature is the relative strength of the income effect of the price change.

It is important to understand that a change in price has two effects:
- It changes **real income** by raising or lowering spending power.
- It causes a **substitution** of one product for others as the utility per pound spent changes.

Although these two effects take place simultaneously, their separation clearly identifies the two types of inferior good.

4 *Price elasticity of demand*

4.1 INTRODUCTION

The elasticity coefficient measures the responsiveness of a change in demand to a change in price. Theoretically this relationship is precise and relatively easy to calculate while in reality the inclusion of many more variables than just price and quantity demanded make it impossible to identify with the precision implied by theory.

Point elasticity: Every point along a demand curve has an elasticity value that can be calculated using a ruler. All you have to do is measure the projected distance from the point to the quantity axis and divide it by the projected distance to the price axis (Figure 2.15).

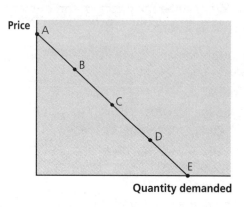

Figure 2.15

$$\text{Point A} \quad = \quad \frac{AE}{A} \quad = \quad \text{infinity}$$

$$\text{Point B} \quad = \quad \frac{BE}{BA} \quad = \quad \text{elastic}$$

$$\text{Point C} \quad = \quad \frac{CE}{CA} \quad = \quad \text{unitary}$$

$$\text{Point D} \quad = \quad \frac{DE}{DA} \quad = \quad \text{inelastic}$$

$$\text{Point E} \quad = \quad \frac{E}{EA} \quad = \quad \text{zero}$$

Doing this reminds you that every straight line has a different elasticity at every point. If the line is not straight, use tangents to make the calculations.

4.2 THE ALGEBRA

The universal equation that you must familiarise yourself with is:

$$\text{Price elasticity coefficient of demand (c)} \quad = \quad - \quad \frac{\text{Percentage change in quantity demanded}}{\text{Percentage change in price}}$$

An alternative calculation using averages is:

$$c \quad = \quad - \quad \frac{\text{Average price} \times \text{Change in quantity demanded}}{\text{Change in price} \times \text{Average quantity}}$$

Both calculations produce slightly different answers as one is a percentage change from one point to another whereas the other is the average of a number of points. Do not worry about this – either answer will be accepted.

4.3 THE GRAPHS

As well as the straight line in Figure 2.15, there are three **uniform** shapes.

Sidebar notes:

For those of you who find elasticity difficult, there is good news and bad news: point elasticity is simple to understand and very helpful but does not attract examination questions.

It is a common mistake to assume that a straight line has uniform elasticity.

All calculations produce a positive answer and strictly there must be a minus sign in front of the percentage changes.

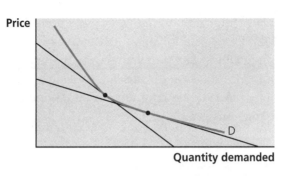

Figure 2.16
The unitary curve

The shape in Figure 2.16 is a rectangular hyperbola. Although it is a curve, each point is equidistant from each axis along the tangent and therefore it has a value of 1.

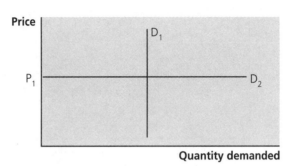

Figure 2.17
The perfectly elastic/inelastic curves

D_1 is perfectly inelastic (0): as price changes there is no change in demand.
D_2 is perfectly elastic (infinite): as the price rises above P_1, demand is zero. At and below P_1, the demand is infinite.

4.4 EXPENDITURE AND THE PRICE ELASTICITY OF DEMAND

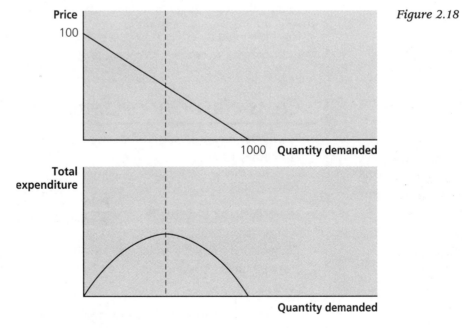

Figure 2.18

Most students will say that demand rises when price goes down. Ask them what happens to expenditure on the product as demand rises and they will usually start by saying that expenditure rises. Place two numbers on the axes and they will realise that selling nothing at £100 or giving away 1,000 at a zero price produces no revenue.

Figure 2.18 shows that as price falls there is a range over which:
- demand rises and expenditure rises
- demand rises and expenditure stays the same
- demand rises and expenditure falls

Many firms around the world have gone bankrupt because they do not understand this relationship. Ask a person in business how they will improve profitability. 'Sell more' is usually the answer. How will you sell more? 'Lower the price' may be the answer. As we can see, there is a price range over which this is exactly the **right answer** and a price range over which this is exactly the **wrong answer**.

Another interesting point is illustrated by the unitary demand curve: whatever the price, the expenditure on the product remains unchanged. In Figure 2.19, multiply the price by the quantity sold.

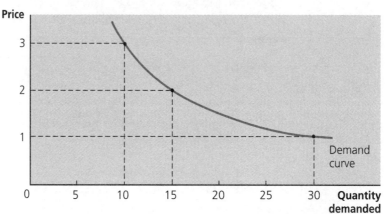

Figure 2.19

4.5 BE THANKFUL FOR SMOKERS, DRINKERS AND GAMBLERS

We have already pointed out that, in reality, you cannot calculate precisely an elasticity. However, anyone who changes a price does so with some expectation about the effect it will have on demand. Firms do this all the time, as does government when changing the indirect tax on a product.

No-one should be advised to become a smoker, drinker or gambler, so look back in your main notes to remind yourself why we must all be grateful to them.

5 *Cross elasticity of demand*

This is the responsiveness of demand for one product to a change in the price of another product.

The formula is:

Cross elasticity of demand $= \dfrac{\text{Percentage change in demand for X}}{\text{Percentage change in the price of Y}}$

Competitive products which are **substitutes** for each other will have a **positive** cross elasticity: a rise in the price of one product will raise demand for the other product.

Products in **complementary** or **derived demand** will have a **negative** cross elasticity: a rise in the price of one product will reduce the demand for the other product.

Independent products will have a zero or infinite cross elasticity of demand, i.e. a change in one product will not affect the other product.

Here the + or – signs used to record a rise or fall are important as they are the first sign of the possible type of relationship between two products. A positive or negative cross elasticity is a **necessary**, though on its own not a **sufficient**, condition to prove the relationship. Products could have changed together but be totally independent.

6 *Income elasticity of demand*

Income elasticity of demand is the degree of response of demand to a change in income.

The formula is:

$$\text{Income of elasticity of demand} = \frac{\text{Percentage change in quantity demanded}}{\text{Percentage change in income}}$$

Consumption of a **normal** good will rise as income rises.

Normal goods which are **necessities** will at some point have elasticities which tend towards zero, i.e. at some point as your income rises you will want to stop eating more food. Normal goods which are **luxuries** will produce income elasticities with higher numerical values.

Inferior goods will have income elasticities of demand which are negative because a rise in income will lead to a fall in demand.

In all three elasticity calculations the quantity demanded is on the top. If you remember this, you are less likely to make a mistake.

D The theory of supply

1 The individual firm's cost and supply curves

AS

1.1 DEFINITIONS

We have already identified how total costs can be divided into fixed costs and variable costs (**B2.2** on p. 19). Other important definitions which need to be clear before we proceed are:

- Average total cost $= \dfrac{\text{Total cost}}{\text{Total output}}$

- Average fixed cost $= \dfrac{\text{Total fixed cost}}{\text{Total output}}$

- Average variable cost $= \dfrac{\text{Total variable cost}}{\text{Total output}}$

- Marginal cost $=$ Additional cost of producing one more unit

A2

1.2 THE FIRM'S SUPPLY CURVE

The following simplifying assumptions apply:
- firms aim to maximise profits
- in Figure 2.20, firms can sell unlimited amounts of their product at a fixed price
- the cost curves are a normal shape

We will question this in section H: 'The pricing of productive factors'.

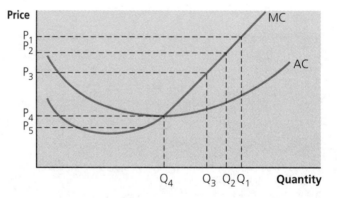

Figure 2.20

The profit-maximising rule for a firm is that output will continue to expand until **marginal cost = marginal revenue**.

Marginal revenue is the additional revenue from selling one more unit. In Figure 2.20, the fixed price means that price and marginal revenue are equal. Therefore at P_1 the firm will produce at Q_1. As the price falls, output contracts to P_4Q_4. Any price below P_4 will not produce any output in the long run. The reason for this is obvious as the firm cannot cover its costs and therefore make a profit.

Output can occur in the short run given certain rules that are explained in section F: 'The theories of the firm'.

In this very simple example we have proved that the supply curve for a firm is the functional relationship between price and quantity supplied. This function is represented by the **marginal cost curve** where it rises above the **average cost curve**.

2 The industry supply curve

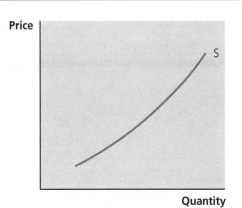

Price

S

Quantity

*Figure 2.21
Industry supply curve*

Under normal circumstances the industry supply curve is upward sloping from left to right. As the industry is a collection of firms, its supply curve is the **horizontal** sum of all the individual firms' supply curves.

3 Shifts and movements in supply curves

If the first thing that changes in the relationship between price and quantity supplied is price, this will be represented by a **movement** along a supply curve. Alternatively, if the first thing that changes is quantity supplied, then this will be represented by a **shift** in the supply curve.

This may be easier to remember in the following form: more or less supplied at **different** prices is a movement; more or less supplied at the **same** price is a shift.

Shifts may occur as the result of:
- weather variability – often related to the agricultural industry
- technical progress
- changes in the price of productive factors
- changes in the price of other factors
- changes in indirect taxation
- changes in subsidies

4 Goods in joint supply

It is a common mistake to assume that demand for these products is also linked.

Goods in joint supply create some interesting special cases as the production of one product inadvertently produces another product. Such goods include:
- wood and sawdust
- lead and zinc
- mutton and wool
- beef and hides
- pork and pigskin

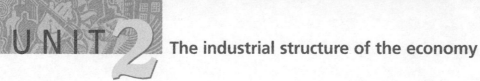

A change in the demand for one of the products shifts the supply curve for the other product.

5 *The elasticity of supply*

5.1 INTRODUCTION

Because a certain period of time must elapse before a producer can change the supply of a product, the elasticity also varies over time (Figure 2.22).

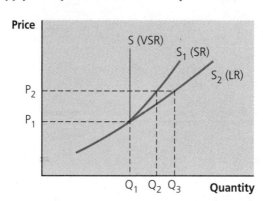

Figure 2.22

See B1.2 on p. 18 for definitions.

In the **very short run**, supply is perfectly inelastic as output cannot change. In the **short run**, output can adjust, but not fully, so the supply function is likely to be more inelastic than in the **long run** when a full adjustment can be made.

5.2 THE ALGEBRA

As with demand, from a given supply schedule it is possible to calculate a coefficient as a measure of supply elasticity. Again, this determines the relationship between a change in market price and a change in the quantity supplied.

The same formulae can be used but adjusted for supply rather than demand. The most common is:

The slope is positive. It is therefore not necessary to have a minus in front of the equation to produce a positive answer.

$$c = \frac{\text{Percentage change in quantity supplied}}{\text{Percentage change in price}}$$

5.3 THE GRAPHS

There are three uniform shapes. Two are obvious, namely perfectly elastic and perfectly inelastic, as illustrated in Figure 2.23.

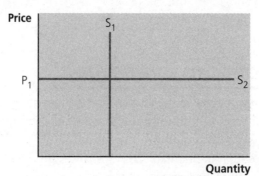

Figure 2.23

Although this is a theoretical extreme, it is also realistic. There

S_1 is **perfectly inelastic** and a rise in price will have no effect on the quantity supplied ($c = 0$).

are some products where output cannot change whatever price is offered. An artistic example can be found in the anagram ANILMASO (4,4).

At price P_1 and above, an infinite quantity will be supplied if the supply curve is **perfectly elastic**, as in S_2. Below P_1 nothing will be supplied (c = infinity).

The third uniform shape is **unitary** supply, which is any straight line that passes through the origin of the graph (Figure 2.24).

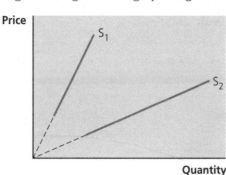

Figure 2.24

Mathematicians can prove this using similar triangles.

Surprisingly, both S_1 and S_2 have the same percentage change on each axis.

Straight lines which would pass through the vertical axis have **elastic** values (greater than one) while straight lines which would pass through the horizontal axis have **inelastic** values (between 0 and 1) (Figure 2.25).

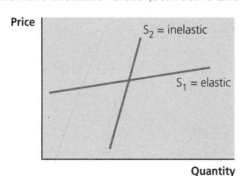

Figure 2.25

5.4 FACTORS WHICH INFLUENCE SUPPLY ELASTICITY

5.4a Supply elasticity is influenced in the short run by:
- the amount of excess capacity in a firm
- the level of stocks held
- the law of variable proportions
- access to unemployed resources

5.4b Supply elasticity is influenced in the long run by:
- the technology involved in production
- internal and external economies and diseconomies of scale
- access to productive factors

6 An introduction to theories of the firm

The detail required in A2 is included in part F of this unit.

At AS, an elementary description of the main market structures that supply an economy is required. All the firms in each market structure are assumed to be faced with competing buyers while they are motivated to maximise profits. The defining characteristics of each theory are set out below.

Perfect competition
- Many firms with no barriers to entry into or exit from the industry.
- Identical products.
- Normal profits in the long run.

Monopolistic competition
- Many firms with no barriers to entry into or exit from the industry.
- Differentiated products.
- Normal profits in the long run.

Oligopoly
- A few large firms with barriers to entry and exit.
- Differentiated products.
- The potential to make excessive profits in the long run.

Monopoly
- A single firm industry with barriers to entry.
- The potential to make excessive profits in the long run as the result of being able to set a price.

E The elementary theory of price

1 Equilibrium price and output

AS

Although we have looked independently at supply and demand, in reality they cannot be separated. It is their interaction, without any conscious control, which determines price and output.

The supply and demand curves have been specially drawn so that they can produce surpluses and shortages using only three quantities. To construct this correctly, draw a square and pass D and S through the corners.

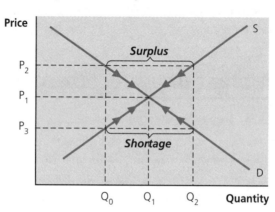

Figure 2.26

An easy way to understand price is to place a normal supply and demand curve on the same diagram (Figure 2.26).

P_1Q_1 is the equilibrium point where **quantity supplied = quantity demanded**.

This equilibrium or point of balance will remain unchanged if nothing else changes. At any other price, forces will be set in motion to move the market back into equilibrium.

This type of analysis is referred to as static and it is often criticised because the world is dynamic and ever-changing. However, bearing this in mind, it is a simple way to start the analysis.

If price is **too high** at P_2, producers will have an incentive to produce more and Q_2 will be produced while only Q_0 is demanded by customers. This surplus will force producers to lower price until the market is cleared.

If price is **too low** at P_3, consumers demand a quantity Q_2, but producers only find it profitable to produce Q_0. This shortage allows producers to raise their price and profits until the market is cleared.

2 Changes in supply and demand functions

AS

In the theories of demand and supply we have explained the difference between a shift and a movement and we have identified the factors which have brought about a shift.

Now that we are looking at the interaction of supply and demand, we need to recognise an important additional point: **a shift in either curve will bring about a movement along the other curve**. For example, if demand shifts to the right

In examinations, be careful to use the step-by-step approach. Identify the shift first and then the movement. If two things change, then there are likely to be two shifts and two movements.

or left, then in order to establish a new equilibrium there will be a movement along the supply curve (Figure 2.27).

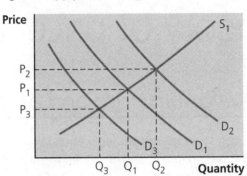

Figure 2.27

The same thing will happen when supply shifts, namely a movement along the demand curve.

3   *Market imperfections*

3.1 INTRODUCTION

In reality, markets do not always work as described above. A lot of time is given in economics to studying these imperfections and decisions have to be made as to whether corrective action can improve upon the imperfection. We will look at three situations where the price mechanism does not clear the market.

3.2 PRICE LOW: POTENTIAL DEVELOPMENT OF A 'BLACK MARKET'

A black market is often, but not always, an illegal market. It could be a secondary market which clears the market imperfection.

A good example of this type of market imperfection is when a promoter books a stadium for a rock concert. Rock bands are reputedly temperamental and if the stadium is not full, then the band may refuse to play. The probability of setting a ticket price in advance that will just fill the stadium is very low. There are therefore many examples of prices being set too low, as illustrated in Figure 2.28.

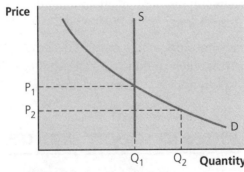

Figure 2.28

P_1 = price that would have cleared the market
Q_1 = fixed number of tickets
P_2 = ticket price
Q_2 = demand for tickets

It may be that the shortage of tickets between Q_1 and Q_2 may leave some customers unsatisfied. Alternatively, if people can get hold of tickets they do not

The FA Cup Final is a similar example, where prices are kept low to reward the true fan. How many other such instances can you think of?

want to use, then a black market will exist where **touting** for higher prices will occur. This may or may not be illegal.

3.3 PRICE HIGH: DEVELOPMENT OF A SURPLUS

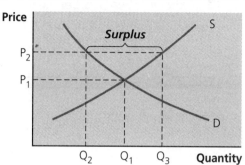

Figure 2.29

For a price to be set too high, it will usually involve a third party. The most obvious example is when government gets involved in the agricultural industry. In order to stabilise farm income, prices are sometimes fixed too high. Surpluses develop, as illustrated in Figure 2.29. This can lead to problems, as we will see when we look at the Common Agricultural Policy in Unit 5.

3.4 MAXIMUM AND MINIMUM PRICING

It is important to note the difference between the effect on the market of a price which is fixed too high or too low, as opposed to a maximum or minimum price.

A maximum or minimum price only distorts the market on one side of the equilibrium.

It is common to make the mistake of responding to a question by saying that maximum or minimum distorts either side of the equilibrium.

If a **maximum price** is set **below** equilibrium, it will distort the market and cause a **shortage**. If it is **above** market equilibrium, then it will have **no effect** on the market.

If a **minimum price** is set **above** equilibrium, it will distort the market and cause a **surplus**. If it is **below** market equilibrium, then it will have **no effect** on the market.

3.5 VARIABLE SUPPLY AND THE USE OF BUFFER STOCKS

Because demand and supply are relatively inelastic for many commodities, small changes in the supply function can produce significant price volatility. One policy is to stabilise prices with the use of buffer stocks, as illustrated in Figure 2.30 below.

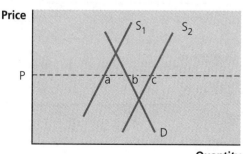

Figure 2.30

S₁ and S₂ represent the limits to output variability. In order to stabilise the price at P, when output is high, at point c, the difference between b and c will have to be purchased and placed in stock. When output is low, at point a, then the difference between a and b can be released from stock. In theory this will stabilise prices, but in practice there are potential problems:

- The range of variability may not be known.
- Administration costs might be high.
- Storage costs might be high.
- There may be a tendency for the price to be set too high and overproduction to prevail.
- Many producers, who may be in different countries, are required not to abuse the system.

4 The cobweb theory: a dynamic theory of price

A2

A theory which is useful in developing price theory, from the simple static interpretation so far undertaken to a more realistic analysis in an ever-changing world, is the cobweb theory. Usually applied to agriculture, it uses the static model but introduces a time lag between **decision** and **execution** and an output total that may vary from what was anticipated (e.g. Figure 2.31).

> It is important to draw a supply curve which is more inelastic than the demand curve; otherwise the cobweb becomes unstable and moves away from the equilibrium.

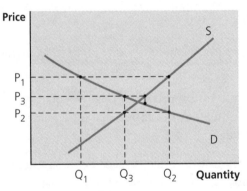

Figure 2.31 Stable cobweb

Suppose a bad harvest produces Q_1. The price will rise to P_1 and P_1 will induce a higher level of output at Q_2. Assuming no more shocks, you can follow the bold points on the curves until you disappear up the equilibrium.

5 Supply and demand curves and related products

AS

It is possible to ask a question, where products are linked, which looks at the effect on one product of a change in the demand or supply conditions of the related product.

Example 1: What will happen to the price of lead if the demand for zinc increases?

To answer this question:
- Make an assumption about the starting equilibrium position for both products.

- Identify the relationship between the products (in this case they are in joint supply).
- Proceed logically through the effects on each product as illustrated below.

The demand curve for zinc will shift to the right as more is demanded at each and every price (Figure 2.32).

One of the problems with this type of question is that you need to know that lead and zinc both come from the same ore.

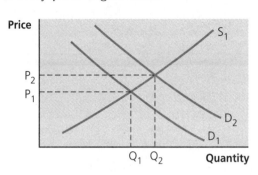

Figure 2.32 Zinc

P_1Q_1 = original equilibrium
P_2Q_2 = new equilibrium at a higher price and significantly a higher output

The supply curve will shift to the right as more is supplied at each and every price (Figure 2.33).

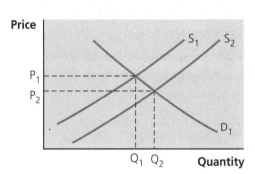

Figure 2.33 Lead

P_1Q_1 = original equilibrium
P_2Q_2 = new equilibrium at a higher output and a lower price

Answer: Price of lead falls.

Example 2: What will happen to the price of gas if a war destroys a number of oilfields?

This means less oil will be supplied at each and every price and the supply curve shifts to the left (Figure 2.34).

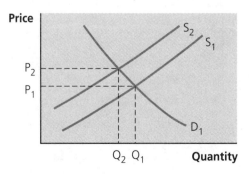

Figure 2.34 Oil

P_1Q_1 = original equilibrium
P_2Q_2 = new equilibrium at a lower output and a higher price

Oil and gas are substitutes for each other in the provision of heat and power. The relatively higher price for oil will increase the demand for gas at each and every price (Figure 2.35).

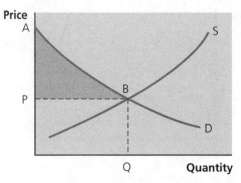

Figure 2.35 Gas

P_1Q_1 = original equilibrium
P_2Q_2 = new equilibrium at a higher output and a higher price

Answer: Price of gas rises.

6 *The consumer surplus*

6.1 DEFINITION

Alfred Marshall first identified this in his book, *Principles of Economics* (1890).

The consumer surplus is the difference between the maximum amount of money a consumer is willing to pay for a product, rather than go without, and the amount actually paid.

6.2 THE INDIVIDUAL

Suppose an individual would be prepared to pay £10 to buy the first unit of a product, £9 to buy a second unit, £8 to buy a third and £7 to buy a fourth. If the price is £7, the consumer would buy four units costing 4×7 = £28. However, the consumer would have been prepared to pay 10 + 9 + 8 + 7 = £34. Therefore the consumer surplus is 34 − 28 = 6.

6.3 THE MARKET

If the market place produces Figure 2.36, then the shaded area will represent the consumer surplus, i.e. money that consumers would be willing to pay but do not have to as the market price is established at P.

PAB = consumer surplus

7 The producer surplus

7.1 DEFINITION

The producer surplus is the revenue received by the producer above that which would have brought a particular quantity of the product onto the market for sale.

7.2 THE MARKET

In a market analysis it is the difference between the minimum payment that a producer would accept for offering a certain quantity for sale and the market price of the product. In Figure 2.37 it is the shaded area above the supply curve and below the price line.

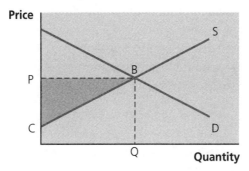

Figure 2.37

PBC = producer surplus

F The theories of the firm

1 *The theory of perfect competition*

AS

1.1 THE ASSUMPTIONS OF PERFECT COMPETITION

In order to build a simple model the following assumptions are well documented in textbooks:

- Industries comprise many relatively small firms.
- There are many competing consumers, i.e. there are no opportunities to form a **monopsony**.
- Products are homogeneous.
- There is perfect knowledge on the part of both producers and consumers.
- Firms have free entry into and exit from the industry.
- In the long run there is perfect productive factor mobility.
- There are no transport costs.

In real life these conditions may never apply or never apply simultaneously. It must be emphasised that the assumptions of perfect competition produce an extreme case which is primarily an analytical device to reach a certain level of basic understanding.

An often-quoted example that comes close is the foreign exchange market which does have a homogeneous product, i.e. currency.

1.2 IMPORTANT RULES

Although they are introduced here, these three rules apply to all the theories of the firm considered in this section.

A2

1.2a Rule One: profit maximising

It is a necessary condition for profit maximisation that output is where **marginal cost = marginal revenue**. However, it is not sufficient on its own as profits are both minimised, Q_1, and maximised at this equality, Q_2. To complete the rule, MC must be **rising** (Figure 2.38).

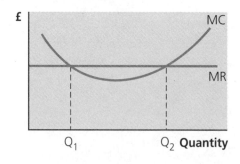

Figure 2.38

A2

1.2b Rule Two: production in the short run

A firm will produce in the short run as long as it can cover its **variable** costs. Therefore, **total revenue is equal to or greater than total variable cost**.

A2

1.2c Rule Three: production in the long run

In the long run a firm must produce where it can at least cover its total costs of production. Therefore, **total revenue is equal to or greater than total costs**.

The minimum required could vary from one entrepreneur to another and is therefore not a fixed amount.

AS

1.3 NORMAL PROFITS AND ABNORMAL PROFITS

Normal profits are the minimum reward required by the entrepreneur to remain in that line of business. In economics, normal profits are considered to be a cost of enterprise and are therefore included in the costs of the firm.

Abnormal profits can include **supernormal or excessive profits** and **subnormal profits**, which are less than normal profit, i.e. less profit than that required to keep the entrepreneur in business in the long run.

1.4 THE DEMAND CURVE FOR THE PERFECTLY COMPETITIVE FIRM

A2

The range of output over which a firm can make a profit is such a small proportion of total output that no one firm can change output sufficiently to influence price. Each firm is then faced with a **perfectly elastic demand curve** (Figure 2.39).

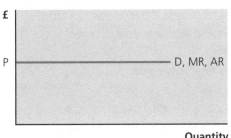

Figure 2.39

This means that the firm can sell all its products at the given market price. Therefore, the price is equal to the **marginal revenue (MR)**, which is the additional revenue from selling one more unit, and the **average revenue (AR)**, which is the price.

1.5 THE SUPPLY CURVE FOR THE PERFECTLY COMPETITIVE FIRM

A2

A firm in perfect competition only has a **short-run supply curve**. This is because in the long run there is only one point where the firm makes normal profit. The short-run supply curve is the marginal cost above average variable cost, as illustrated in Figure 2.40.

> The average variable cost curve (AVC) gets closer to the average total cost curve (ATC) as output expands. This is because the average fixed cost falls continuously as output expands.

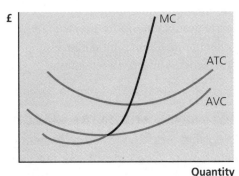

Figure 2.40

1.6 PROFIT-MAXIMISING OUTPUT OF THE COMPETITIVE FIRM

1.6a In the short run

A2

In the short run a firm can make abnormal profits or it can minimise losses. Neither of these situations can be sustained in the long run as firms have freedom to enter or leave the industry (Figure 2.41).

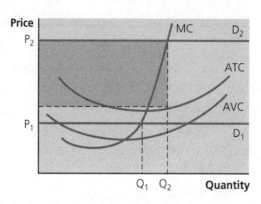

Figure 2.41

MC will cut both ATC and AVC at their lowest points.

P_1Q_1 is a loss-minimising equilibrium where firms will leave the industry. P_2Q_2 is an abnormal profit-maximising equilibrium which will attract firms into the industry. The shaded area is the area of excessive profit. For all theories of the firm, the area of excessive profit is always enclosed between the **average revenue and average cost curves**.

A2

1.6b In the long run

When firms enter or leave the industry, then those firms already present take an increasing or decreasing share of the total market and the demand curve moves towards the long-run equilibrium where only normal profits can be made (Figure 2.42).

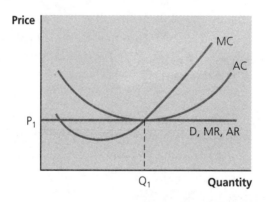

Figure 2.42

In the long run:
- All firms produce at optimum size, i.e. at the lowest point of the AC curve.
- Only normal profit can be achieved.
- Marginal cost = marginal revenue = average cost = average revenue = price.

The important equality for the entrepreneur is MC = MR, i.e. profit maximising.

A2

1.7 MARGINAL AND INTRA-MARGINAL FIRMS

There is a slight weakness in the argument so far in as much as all the firms in a perfectly competitive industry are identical. Should this not mean that when the industry is making a loss, all firms will, at the same time, make the decision to leave the industry?

Remember, normal profit is not a fixed amount: it is the minimum required by an entrepreneur to remain in business and this may vary from one entrepreneur to another.

For the theory to work, firms must leave the industry one after the other. To cope with this problem we can assume that the cost of enterprise varies and that only one or a few firms are in long-run equilibrium – **the marginal firms** – while other firms are making slightly more than normal profit – **the intra-marginal firms**.

A2

1.8 PERFECT COMPETITION AND OPTIMAL RESOURCE ALLOCATION

Optimum resource allocation or allocative efficiency occurs when firms produce at a point where price (P) = marginal cost (MC). This means that the price the community is willing to pay for the last product is equal to the additional cost of using factor resources to produce this last product.

In perfect competition in the short and long run, P = MC.

A potential problem exists if there are external costs which are not accounted for. In this situation, price will only equal marginal private cost, not marginal social cost, and therefore **resource misallocation** will exist.

1.9 THE PERFECTLY COMPETITIVE INDUSTRY

A2

1.9a The demand curve

It is often difficult to grasp how the sum of a number of horizontal demand curves for the firms can add up to produce a normal downward-sloping demand curve for the industry.

The answer is that the range over which a firm is likely to change output over the short run is considerably less than the amount required to change the market price (Figure 2.43).

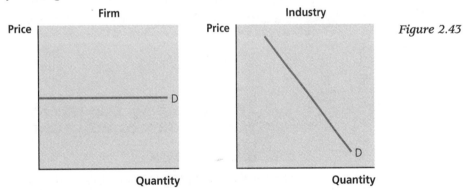

Figure 2.43

A2

1.9b The supply curves

In the short run the firm's supply curve is the marginal cost curve above average variable cost. Therefore, in the short run the industry supply curve is an upward slope from left to right (Figure 2.44).

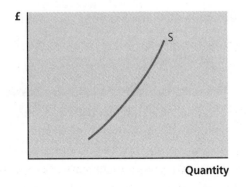

Figure 2.44
Short-run industry supply curve

If we remove the constant cost assumption and have rising costs, the long-run supply curve rises from left to right or falls from left to right with falling industry costs.

In the long run, if we assume constant costs, the perfectly competitive industry supply curve is horizontal (Figure 2.45).

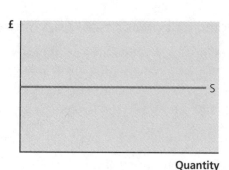

Figure 2.45
Long-run industry
supply curve

2 The theory of monopoly

2.1 CHARACTERISTICS

We are now at the other extreme from perfect competition. In theory we are concerned with a single firm industry, but in reality the UK government, through legislation, recognises that any firm which has more than a 25% share of the market is liable for investigation as a monopoly.

In theory the monopolist has complete command over the supply of a product and is referred to as a **price-maker**. However, a monopolist cannot dictate demand but is able to discover the nature of the demand and manipulate supply to make **excessive profits**. These profits can be sustained in the long run as **barriers to entry** into the industry prevent competing firms from entering the market.

A monopolist can **fix** either **price** or **output**, but **not both**.

2.2 THE CREATION OF BARRIERS AND THE FORMATION OF MONOPOLIES

2.2a Natural barriers

Geographical distribution can produce a concentration of resources that creates a true **natural monopoly**.

Technical barriers caused by economies of scale produce monopolies which are described as natural in the sense that there are no **contrived** actions. A question which asks what market structure will develop when a firm continually benefits from increasing returns to scale is looking for the answer: a monopoly.

Local monopolies are investigated by the relevant government department and can be caused by the **transport advantages** at a particular location or the **ignorance** of potential competitors.

2.2b Deliberate barriers to exclude competition

Government has been involved in the creation of monopolies which were arguably created in the **national interest**.
● The monarchy granted firms monopoly status.
● Modern government protects a firm's invention for 16 years under the **Patent Act**.
● **Public utilities** were granted monopoly status to protect the public from exploitation.

Some textbooks refer to perfect competition and imperfect competition, including monopoly as an extreme form of imperfect competition. Other textbooks include all theories of the firm which fall between perfect competition and monopoly as imperfect competition. Either interpretation would be accepted in examinations.

Why have so many public utilities been privatised?

- Legislation to protect farm incomes has created monopolies at the level of marketing and distribution.
- **Tariffs** on imports are a source of monopoly power.
- **Quotas** provide a source of monopoly power to those firms holding a share of the quota.

In the private sector the search for increased profits encourages firms to try and become monopolies through a process of **contrived scarcity** or **anti-competitive practices**. This may involve a number of actions to exclude competition:

- tied outlets for retailers
- subsidiary companies set up to make losses and force competitors out of the market
- persuasive advertising designed to lessen the degree of product substitutability
- mergers and takeovers

Although designed to achieve monopoly status, firms will probably have to settle for monopolistically competitive status.

A2   ## 2.3 CONSTRUCTION OF THE MONOPOLY MODEL

2.3a Preliminary considerations

The shape of the cost curves is the **same** as other theories of the firm. However, the revenue curves are **different**.

The firm is the industry and therefore the demand curve is a normal downward-sloping curve from left to right. The **demand curve** shows how many units will be demanded at each and every price and is therefore the **average revenue curve**.

Since the price must be lowered to sell more products, the addition to total revenue, i.e. **the marginal revenue**, is less than the average revenue. This is probably easier to see using a diagram explained previously (Figure 2.22) and some new numbers (Figure 2.46).

Can you remember the elasticity of every point on the demand/average revenue curve?

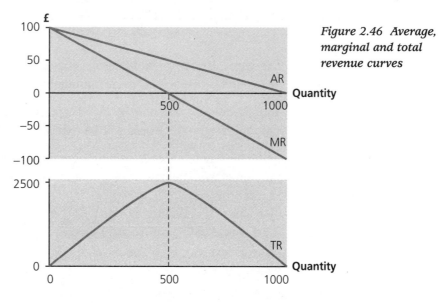

Figure 2.46 Average, marginal and total revenue curves

The simplest way to draw this diagram is to put AR and MR either side of the intersection between MC and AC. This is not a rule, as either MR or AR could intersect MC = AC, but this produces a unique rather than general case.

A2

2.3b The equilibrium of a monopolist

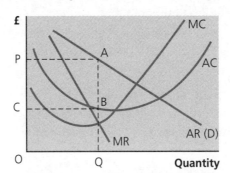

Figure 2.47

From the model in Figure 2.47, note the following points:

- The profit-maximising output is OQ where MC = MR.
- The price OP is determined by the demand curve.
- Each unit is sold for OP and costs OC to produce. Hence the rectangle, PABC, enclosed by AR and AC, is the excessive profits.
- In a monopoly there is no linear relationship between market price and quantity supplied, so there is no supply curve.
- Barriers to entry mean that the model is a long-run equilibrium.
- A distinction between short run and long run relates only to changes in the cost structure of the monopolist.

A2

2.3c Monopoly and non-optimal resource allocation

The rule for an optimum allocation of resources is P = MC.

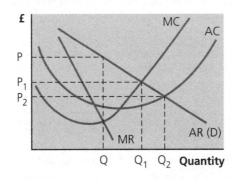

Figure 2.48

In Figure 2.48 the profit-maximising equilibrium is PQ. At this output, **P > MC** and therefore resources are **misallocated**.

The equilibrium where P = MC, P_1Q_1, is **not profit maximising**, although in this diagram profits would still be **excessive**.

Trace the line from Q_2 vertically upwards and see that resources are once again misallocated.

In the heyday of nationalisation where natural monopolies were state controlled, the rule of average cost pricing to remove capitalist profits produced an equilibrium at P_2Q_2 where P < MC.

A2

2.3d Measuring monopoly power

As we move from the theory of a single firm industry to the reality of a firm which controls more than 25% of a specified market, then it becomes clear that there must be degrees of monopoly power. Two methods are commonly used to measure monopoly power.

First, **concentration ratios** measure the proportion of sales going to the four largest firms.

The theories of the firm

Second, it may be easier to use public records to identify firms that make **large profits** and assume that these profits reflect a degree of monopoly power.

2.4 MONOPOLY: A POINT OF INTEREST

A monopolist will **never** produce where the demand curve is **inelastic** (Figure 2.49).

> A common mistake made by students is to refer to monopolists having inelastic demand curves.

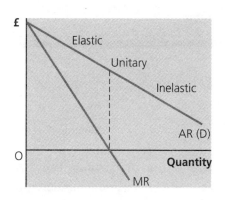

Figure 2.49

The profit-maximising rule is MC = MR. The only place that an equilibrium can be established between MC and MR is where MR is positive. As seen in Figure 2.49, this is where the demand curve is elastic.

2.5 THE MONOPOLIST AND PRICE DISCRIMINATION

2.5a Two types of discrimination

There are two types of discrimination:

- discrimination between **units sold** to the same buyer, e.g. electricity
- discrimination between **buyers**, e.g. different prices for OAPs

2.5b What turns a single price monopolist into a discriminating price monopolist?

A monopolist cannot price discriminate unless segmentation can clearly **separate** parts of the market and units cannot be **resold** between these parts.

It is easier to separate the market for services than it is to separate the market for goods. Market separation is made possible by:

- time
- transport costs
- national barriers
- quotas and tariffs
- age/sex of the consumer

2.5c Why price discrimination pays, and the perfectly discriminating monopolist

A single price profit-maximising monopolist can make excessive profits but cannot absorb the **consumer surplus**.

Price discrimination pays because it adds some or all of the consumer surplus to the profits.

Only a perfectly discriminating monopolist can absorb all the consumer surplus.

In all other theories of the firm the demand curve is the AR curve, although in perfect competition AR = MR = D.

In this case, the producer will be able to charge the full price a consumer is willing to pay for each unit. Figure 2.50 is interesting because the demand curve is the marginal revenue curve. Profits are still maximised where MC = MR, but the price varies from P_1 to P_N and ABCD is the area of excessive profits.

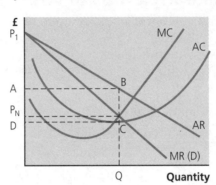

Figure 2.50

A2   2.5d   Can discriminatory pricing benefit an economy?

The word 'discrimination' is often associated with bad rather than good, so it is interesting to note that price discrimination can benefit an economy.

First, the output of a perfectly discriminating monopoly will be **higher** than a single price monopolist and the **same** as a perfectly competitive industry.

Second, suppose there is a doctor in the poor part of a country where no single price for treatment will cover costs. The AR and AC curves would not touch, as illustrated in Figure 2.51.

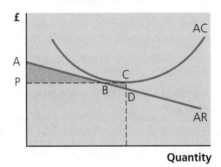

Figure 2.51

However, given price discrimination, as long as the triangle PAB is larger than the triangle BCD, the doctor will remain in business.

3   *The theories of imperfect competition*

3.1 INTRODUCTION

Given two extreme theories of the firm, namely perfect competition and monopoly, it is reasonable to accept that any industry structure which lies between the two extremes can be included under the collective heading of **imperfect competition**.

Some textbooks take all theories of the firm other than perfect competition as cases of imperfect competition; you can then include monopoly in answer to a question about imperfect competition.

In reality some industries comprise many firms, others only a few. However the difference between 'few' and 'many' is defined, it is possible to make a convenient theoretical division between **monopolistic competition** or competition among the many and **oligopoly** or competition among the few.

AS

Students are often confused by the use of the terms 'monopoly' and 'competition' in this theory. Remember: competition results from many firms and monopoly is the name or brand image.

3.2 MONOPOLISTIC COMPETITION: COMPETITION AMONG THE MANY

3.2a Characteristics
- A lot of firms in the industry.
- Free entry into and exit from the industry.
- Products are similar, but differentiated usually by a brand image.
- Product differentiation means that each firm faces a downward-sloping (left to right) demand curve.
- The demand curve is more elastic the **less** differentiated the product and less elastic the **more** differentiated the product.

A2

3.2b The equilibrium of the firm in the short run
This diagram is easy to remember in that you can use the monopoly diagram as your starting position, highlighting the area of excessive profits PABC (Figure 2.52).

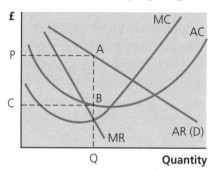

Figure 2.52

In the case of monopoly, barriers to entry maintain this equilibrium, but because there is **free entry** into this industry the excessive profits attract more firms and this shifts each firm's share of demand to the left.

A2

3.2c The equilibrium of the firm in the long run
In the long run each firm will only make **normal profits** (Figure 2.53).

When you draw this diagram it is difficult to get MR to cut MC directly below the point of tangency between AC and AR. To avoid this problem, draw curves in the following order: AC, MC, AR, marking on P and Q, and finally draw in MR.

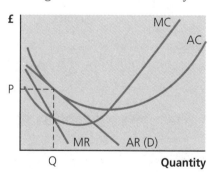

Figure 2.53

Like perfect competition, AR is now tangent to AC but at a point where AC is falling.

In the short run firms can survive making subnormal profits as long as variable costs are covered. However, in the long run firms will leave the industry until only normal profits are made at PQ by those firms left in the industry.

In the short and long run, monopolistic competition produces an equilibrium where there is a **non-optimal allocation** of resources, i.e. where **P > MC**.

Moreover, each firm is **productively inefficient**, i.e. it is not producing at the lowest point on the AC curve. As it produces at a point to the left of where it

would be productively efficient, a firm is described as producing with **excess capacity**. Only perfectly competitive firms are productively efficient and produce at **capacity output** in the long run, i.e. the lowest point on the AC curve.

3.3 OLIGOPOLY: COMPETITION AMONG THE FEW

AS

3.3a Characteristics

- **Few firms** in the industry where 'few' usually means a number which could manage collusive actions.
- **Capacity output**, which is the lowest point on the AC curve, will occur when a significant proportion of the total market is satisfied. A simple analysis might suggest that if this point is reached when 25% of the market is satisfied, there will be four firms in the industry. At 50% there would be a two firm industry, or **duopoly**, and so on.
- Other barriers to entry might include **large set up costs, large advertising budget** and **proliferation of brands** controlled by one firm.
- A **kinked demand curve** for the firm is likely to exist even though the demand curve for the industry is normal (Figure 2.54). The kink is at the prevailing market price. Raise price and the firm will lose a lot of customers to competitors. Lower price and other firms will lower prices rather than risk losing a lot of customers. All the firm will gain is a share of the overall increase in market demand.

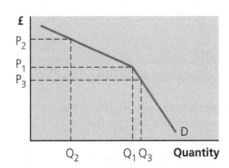

Figure 2.54

- **Administered prices** are an assumption of most theories of oligopoly behaviour. Prices are controlled by the producer rather than determined by the consumer.

A2

3.3b What determines oligopoly price?

The kinked demand curve suggests that firms have incentives to **collude** in the way that they establish prices and then try to increase market share through **non-price competition**.

If oligopolists agree to restrict output and raise price, they can make more profits, whereas if they compete, they will be forced towards a normal profit-making situation.

Game theory is often used to explain this dilemma facing oligopolists.

A covert collusion to fix prices is against the law and the cartels in banking and petroleum to fix prices during the 1960s would now be outlawed.

		Firm X Comply	Firm X Cheat
Firm Y	Comply	**A**	**B**
	Cheat	**C**	**D**

A If both firms comply with a policy to restrict output and raise price, they will make excessive profits.

B If Firm Y complies with the agreement but Firm X cheats and expands output, Firm X can make even higher profits than in A but Firm Y will make a loss.

C If Firm X complies and Firm Y cheats, Y makes profits and X makes a loss.

D If both firms cheat on each other, normal profits will prevail.

The conclusion of this game is that in order to avoid making a loss, both firms will **cheat** and the outcome will be normal profits – the same as if they **competed** with each other.

3.3c Oligopoly and the theory of contestable markets

This is interesting because it implies that even in the smallest oligopoly situation, i.e. a duopoly, the firms will be forced into a competitive equilibrium.

Contestable markets evaluate the costs of **entering** markets and distinguish between **recoverable** and **sunk** costs. A **perfectly contestable** market will have no sunk costs, while the lower the sunk costs the more contestable the market.

The theory was developed by three American professors: Baumol, Panzer and Willig.

The theory implies that even in industries that contain only a few firms, as long as **actual entry** can take place or **potential entry** is anticipated, then firms will produce at levels which achieve normal profits.

Contestable market theory and **game theory** both suggest that any form of competition will produce competitive rather than excessive profits.

4 Monopoly vs competition

4.1 THE DEBATE

Whether monopoly is bad and perfect competition good is not an economic issue. Whether monopolies are less efficient or more efficient, whether prices are higher or lower under monopoly, are economic issues which have been used to support arguments for and against monopoly and perfect competition.

In reality this debate does not concern itself with the extremes, but rather with the structures that tend towards either monopoly or competition.

4.2 IN FAVOUR OF COMPETITION

- Perfect competition produces allocative efficiency **(P = MC)**, productive efficiency **(MC = AC)** and a Pareto-optimum allocation of resources.
- Competition produces greater variety of products.
- Consumer sovereignty involves greater freedom of choice.
- Monopoly produces allocative inefficiency **(P > MC)**, productive inefficiency and is not Pareto efficient.
- In the long run, profits are normal under perfect competition, but can be excessive under monopoly.
- Producer sovereignty exists under monopoly.
- An industry comprising perfectly competitive firms produces a higher output at a lower price P_1Q_1 whereas monopoly produces a lower output at a higher price P_2Q_2 (Figure 2.55).

It is useful to learn this diagram as a simple illustration of why perfect competition is favoured.

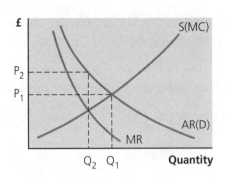

Figure 2.55

4.3 IN FAVOUR OF MONOPOLY

A2 **4.3a Removing the given cost assumption**

The last argument used in favour of competition assumes that a perfectly competitive industry transformed into a monopoly will inherit the given costs.

The diagram requires the costs to be reduced sufficiently to shift the intersection of MR and MC to the right of Q_1. At this point the firm would still be making excessive profits.

In reality the motivation to become a bigger firm in the industry is **economies of scale**. This means it is unreasonable to assume given costs and it is possible for a monopoly to have **lower prices and higher output** than the corresponding perfectly competitive industry. In Figure 2.56, P_1Q_1 represents the competitive equilibrium while P_2Q_2 could be the monopoly equilibrium.

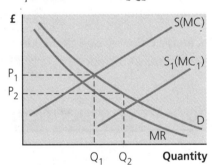

Figure 2.56

A2 **4.3b Dynamic efficiency**

A third type of efficiency can be introduced into this argument. It is how costs behave **over time**. Firms making large profits are more likely to complete research and development programmes and be more innovative than competitive firms. Their costs will therefore fall much more rapidly over time. Even though these firms remain productively and allocatively inefficient at **one point in time**, they are more dynamically efficient over time.

A2 **4.3c Is consumer choice increased under monopoly?**

When the British Broadcasting Corporation (BBC) monopolised the airwaves it was argued that it offered a variety of programmes catering for mainstream and minority interests.

More competition over the airwaves produced many more radio stations, but all of them offered a similar diet of popular music interspersed with news items.

A2 **4.3d Policy-makers take note**

UK policies, particularly those associated with **monopolies and mergers**, are usually framed on the assumption that a monopoly damages the economy. Although this may be the case, it should not be assumed, as the arguments above bring into question the foundation of the case against monopoly.

G Some further analysis of price determination and resource allocation

1 Introduction

You should now understand how resources are allocated by prices, which are in turn determined in a marketplace through the interaction of **supply** and **demand**.

This is a very simple analysis and throughout your studies you will have been made aware of factors which have changed or replaced the **price mechanism**.

These factors can be grouped together as those which have:
- influenced supply
- influenced demand
- replaced the market mechanism
- substituted for it in the absence of a marketplace

2 Supply factors which affect the price mechanism

2.1 DO FIRMS AIM TO MAXIMISE PROFITS?

2.1a A realistic rule?

It is becoming quite popular to set examination questions which question this assumption.

The assumption that firms maximise profits has been very important in the analysis of how firms operate. The profit-maximising rule that firms will produce an output and sell at a price which equates **marginal revenue** with **marginal cost** has been questioned by a number of economists.

2.1b The sales maximisation hypothesis

It is argued, particularly in large firms, that the separation of ownership of the company from its management has led to sales maximisation within a profit constraint.

This may explain why many firms force their managers to be shareholders and rely on dividends as a significant proportion of their salary.

Managers can justify raising their salaries as firms grow larger, and if the potential for increasing profits is unknown to the majority of shareholders, as may be the case in a **public joint stock company**, then they may be satisfied with a level of profits below maximum.

Figure 2.57 shows that profit maximisation occurs at Pr_1Q_1, but the firm may be able to double its size and still make sufficient profits to satisfy shareholders.

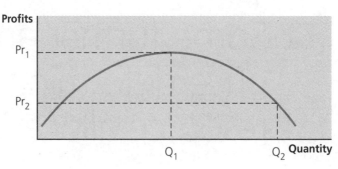

Figure 2.57

Some textbooks go a little further and separate sales revenue maximisation from sales maximisation using a normal profit constraint. The difference between the two is that sales revenue is maximised where marginal revenue is zero, whereas sales maximisation is consistent with normal profit where average cost equals average revenue.

2.1c Satisficing theory

Professor Herbert Simon suggested in satisficing theory that there is **no unique equilibrium**, but rather that firms may have many different goals including those already stated. Their other targets may include:
- a level of profits which hides potential profits from competitors
- lower profits which avoid short-term embarrassment to a well-known company
- lower profits for environmental reasons
- lower profits for ethical reasons and to identify the company as an ethical investment
- lower prices and profits to reward customer loyalty

A firm may worry about being exposed by 'Greenpeace' or 'Animal Rights' and therefore direct some potential profits into environmentally friendly projects.

2.1d Non-maximisation through ignorance

The fact that firms and their customers do not have perfect knowledge and the economic environment is always changing has led some economists to point out that profit maximisation is probably only ever achieved **by luck**. They argue that firms tend to approximate rather than actually achieve.

2.1e Cost-plus pricing

In the 1930s Charles Hitch and Robert Hall made a number of detailed case studies of pricing policy by firms in the Oxford area. They introduced the hypothesis of **full-cost pricing**. Further empirical studies supported their ideas and gave rise to what is now known as **cost-plus pricing**.

This pricing policy does not equate MC with MR. Instead, it sets price equal to average cost at capacity output plus a conventional mark-up. In this theory prices will tend to be fairly stable and adjust only to changes in costs.

Arguably cost-plus is a short-run response to changes in costs. Demand probably has the final say on pricing in the long run.

3 Demand factors which affect the price mechanism

3.1 SUPPLY CREATES DEMAND

Professor J. K. Galbraith suggested that, in certain parts of the market, it is not consumer demand which creates market signals, but large corporations which create and manipulate demand to iron out unexpected changes.

In order to guard against the impact of reductions in demand, companies spend large sums on advertising which allows them to sell what they produce rather than what consumers want to buy.

3.2 TRADE UNIONS INFLUENCE DEMAND

The weakening of trade union power has reduced their influence. However, in the past, successful lobbying of Parliament has led to the imposition of tariffs and quotas on imports to protect and redirect demand on the products of industries such as agriculture, coal mining, shipbuilding and textiles.

4 Government intervention in the supply of goods and services

4.1 NATIONALISED INDUSTRIES

Although there are fewer and fewer nationalised industries, their products have been supplied under near-monopoly conditions and their prices have often been influenced by political rather than economic circumstances.

4.2 THE EFFECT OF TAXATION AND EXPENDITURE

Expenditure taxes like VAT and excise duties change prices. These changes can be very significant as in the case of **demerit goods** like alcohol and cigarettes as well as fossil fuels, particularly petroleum.

By collectivising demand, the government changes the pattern of demand from what it would be in a free market. This is obvious in the case of **public goods** which are collectively demanded as they are unlikely to be provided in a free market. If **merit goods** are provided free to the consumer, markets will be distorted.

4.3 GOVERNMENT CONTROL OVER THE SUPPLY OF GOODS FREE TO THE CONSUMER

4.3a The case for providing products free to the consumer
- **Public goods:** There is a very strong case for supplying these **collective consumption goods** free to the consumer. Law and order and defence will be demanded collectively, but not individually because they are **non-excludable**. There is almost universal agreement among economists that taxes should be raised to finance the demand for public goods.
- **Merit goods:** The case for merit goods is not as strong. This is because **health** and **education** are **private** goods which would be traded in a marketplace. The argument which supports intervention is that these products will be underconsumed when **externalities** are taken into account.

Arguably, health and education provide external benefits to society as well as private benefits to individuals. Expenditure on these products can be considered as **investment in human capital**.

4.3b The case against providing products free to the consumer
The case against supplying the consumer with goods free is one of non-optimal allocation of scarce resources. If consumers maximise utility, they will consume

There are not many countries which provide merit goods like health and education free to the consumer.

Would all parents be prepared to pay the necessary amounts on educating their children up to the level required to benefit society?

Not to be confused with the free good, e.g. air and sun.

the 'free' good up to the point where marginal utility is zero. At this point the marginal cost of producing the last unit is likely to be relatively high and certainly higher than zero. This will bring about inefficiency because scarce resources will have been used in order to produce products that will give rise to very low additional utility.

If we assume **no externalities**, then a price charged for these merit goods will reduce consumption and release resources to produce products which have a higher marginal utility. Therefore, the **total utility** received by households will be lower if merit goods are provided free and higher if offered at a price.

However, if we assume externalities which are benefits, then the issue becomes one of providing the products either **free** or at a **subsidised** price.

The argument hinges upon the elasticity of demand for the product. If the elasticity is higher between the subsidised price and zero, then more resources will be wasted (see Figure 2.58a where MC_1 is much higher at Q_2 than in Figure 2.58b, where the elasticity is lower and fewer resources will be wasted).

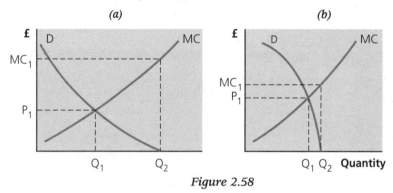

Figure 2.58

The case for providing certain goods free is based upon the **imperfections** of the market place and the implicit assumption that governments can produce a more efficient allocation of resources. This assumption has been questioned by a number of economists who argue that the **inefficiencies of government** far outweigh the inefficiencies of the marketplace.

A final point is that government intervention costs money whereas the marketplace does its job with no charge.

A question which is now being asked more forcefully is whether governments have the knowledge to improve upon the marketplace.

5 *Specialist markets*

5.1 INTRODUCTION

Across the examining boards there is an expectation that students will familiarise themselves with actual markets and be able to apply the basic economic theory of markets and market failure. The brief notes below are pointers towards specified markets that will be useful indicators on how to relate theory to reality.

5.2 THE HOUSING MARKET

This market may be dealt with as one market or segmented into:
- owner occupier
- private rented
- housing associations
- local authority

You will be expected to analyse this market in terms of how supply and demand:

- determine a price
- explain regional price differences
- explain relative prices in the segments identified above
- explain price changes over time
- produce different results with different price elasticities of supply and demand

It is also necessary to consider how the housing market is related to:

- market failure
- government failure
- government policies with particular reference to interest rates
- income elasticity of demand
- environmental problems

5.3 THE SPORT AND LEISURE MARKET

This market covers:

- holidays
- travel
- the film industry
- television
- theatre
- the music industry
- other forms of entertainment

You will be expected to analyse this market and its segments in terms of:

- how supply and demand determine the price of entering sport and leisure events
- a description of how different market structures can be applied, i.e. a degree of monopoly power for unique events such as the FA Cup Final
- applying income, cross and price elasticity of demand
- how changes in the exchange rate may affect holidays, travel and other exports and imports in this sector

5.4 THE TRANSPORT MARKET

The various transport modes include:

- road
- rail
- air
- water

and can be analysed from the perspective of:

- passenger
- freight

under the direction of:

- public enterprise
- private enterprise
- public/private partnership

The main issues include:

- market structure, e.g. natural monopoly
- deregulation
- contestability
- privatisation
- market efficiency and market failure
- an integrated transport policy
- transport investment decisions
- application of cost–benefit analysis
- public goods, quasi-public goods and private goods
- external benefits and external costs
- sustainable transport policies
- traffic congestion and road pricing
- environmental problems

H The pricing of productive factors

1 Introducing the factors

A2

The economist is not directly concerned with the question of whether the national income is shared out equally or fairly among its recipients, but rather with the forces which determine the size of the shares received by the factors.

All incomes except **transfer payments**, such as state pensions and unemployment pay, are the earnings of the factors of production.

At its simplest level the rewards to productive factors can be considered as prices:
- the price of labour is a **wage**
- the price of capital is **interest**
- the price of enterprise is **profits**
- the price of land is **rent**

Like other prices, these can be determined in a free market by the interaction of **supply** and **demand**. In markets other than free markets these may be distorted or replaced by other mechanisms.

> Transfer payments are income paid out for which no good or service is provided. They should not be confused with transfer earnings.

2 The price of labour

A2

2.1 THE FORM OF PAYMENT AND THE FACTORS WHICH INFLUENCE ITS SIZE

A salary is a wage paid to workers of a certain status, usually over intervals longer than a week. It is not generally related to a specific number of hours worked.

Payment of a wage is normally made under a legal contract for the services provided by labour.

It is important to make a distinction between **real** and **nominal** wages. Nominal wages are the units of currency paid to labour. Real wages are the products that can be purchased with any given wage.

> Remind yourself of how nominal wages can go up while real wages fall.

The common sense explanation of the observed large differences in wages between occupations is that labour is **not homogeneous**. There are many differences in skills and abilities and the demand for different workers. These give rise to many labour markets, each with its own supply and demand conditions.

Over very long periods of time it is likely that there will be some erosion of wage differentials, but they will never be eliminated because of:
- permanent differences in skills and abilities
- geographical immobility
- **pecuniary** and **non-pecuniary** rewards
- qualification barriers

> Wage differentials may exist in money terms but not exist when one takes account of non-pecuniary benefits such as job satisfaction.

- unequal opportunity
- imbalances of power between groups of people
- government policies
- dynamic changes and the need for market signals

2.2 THE DEMAND FOR LABOUR

2.2a Basic propositions

A2

Labour is not demanded for itself but for what it can produce: **derived demand**.

The **elasticity** of demand for labour is determined by the elasticity of demand for the product.

The smaller the proportion of total costs accounted for by labour the more **inelastic** is the demand curve.

The more capital can be substituted for labour the more **elastic** is the demand curve.

2.2b Marginal revenue productivity

A2

Quite often texts refer to the marginal revenue productivity theory of wages. In fact, it is not a theory of wages but a theory of the demand for labour.

In Unit 2 (B2.1) the marginal and average physical products were given a normal shape. Although physical product is important, it is not the ultimate determinant of labour demand. A firm can be productively efficient, but if it cannot sell its product it cannot make a profit.

What is important is the revenue derived from the sale of the product.

Given the following simplified assumptions:
- profit-maximising entrepreneurs
- one variable factor
- perfectly elastic demand for the product, therefore MPP × Price = MRP
- perfectly elastic supply of the productive factor

then the demand curve for labour is MRP below ARP, as illustrated in Figure 2.59.

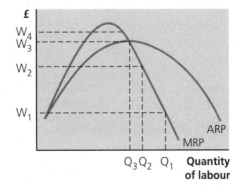

Figure 2.59

At W_1 the entrepreneur will maximise returns by employing Q_1 units of labour. As the wage rate rises up to W_3, less labour will be demanded to maintain maximum profits. At any wage rate above W_3, as illustrated by W_4, it will not be profitable to employ any units of labour and therefore **the demand curve for labour is MRP below ARP**.

2.2c Shifts in the demand curve for labour

Shifts in the demand curve for labour result from more or less labour being demanded at the same wage rate. This can occur for two main reasons:

- a change in the **physical productivity of labour**
- a change in the **demand for the product**

2.3 THE SUPPLY OF LABOUR

2.3a The individual supply of effort

It is usual to identify the relationship between wages and hours worked by the individual, as illustrated in Figure 2.60.

Students often confuse the supply of effort, which is how many hours a person will want to work at a given wage rate, with the supply of labour to a given occupation, which is the number of people willing to work at a given wage.

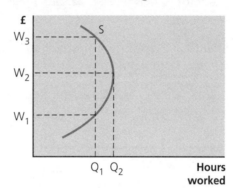

Figure 2.60

Up to W_2, a higher wage will encourage the person to work more hours and have less leisure. After this point a rise in wages will reduce the hours worked as leisure time is of greater value.

An alternative analysis uses indifference curves (Figure 2.61).

I_1 and I_2 can look as though they will cross as they represent two different situations.

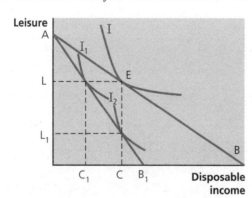

Figure 2.61

A = all leisure

B = all work

E = the chosen balance between leisure (L) and work (C) identified by an indifference curve which is tangent to the line AB

Suppose income tax rises. The highest level of disposable income falls from B to B_1.

If the person wishes to maintain income, she will position herself on AB_1 at L_1C. If she wishes to maintain leisure, she will settle at LC_1.

The debate about whether an average person would choose to sustain leisure or consumption is unresolved.

A2

2.3b The supply of labour to a given occupation

The supply curve for labour in a given labour market is a normal upward-sloping curve from left to right. The higher the wage rate, the more labour is prepared to offer itself for work (Figure 2.62).

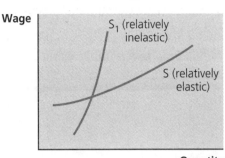

Figure 2.62

The slope of the supply curve will vary from one labour market to another. In general, the **less skills** required will produce a **relatively elastic** supply curve, while the **more skills** required will produce a **relatively inelastic** supply curve.

2.3c Shifts in the supply curve

More or less labour supplied to a particular labour market at the same wage rate will result from changes in:
- the geographical mobility of labour
- the occupational mobility of labour
- relative wage rates between labour markets

Over a longer period of time, shifts in the supply curve may result from changes in:
- population size
- the structure of population
- educational attainments
- expectations

2.4 THE THEORY OF WAGE DETERMINATION IN DIFFERENT MARKET CONDITIONS

2.4a In a free market

In a labour market where supply and demand are competitive, the **equilibrium wage** rate is determined by the intersection of the demand and supply curves (Figure 2.63).

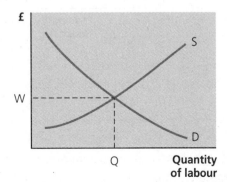

Figure 2.63

A2

2.4b In a market where labour is demanded monopsonistically

If there is a single buyer of labour (monopsony) and competitive selling of labour, then the supply curve becomes separated from the marginal cost curve. This is because as the buyer of labour wishes to attract more labour into the market the wage rate must be raised for all units of labour in order to attract the new labour.

In Figure 2.64, the profit-maximising position is where MC = MRP at WQ. This equilibrium is below the competitive equilibrium at W_1Q_1.

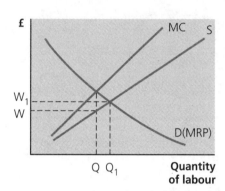

Figure 2.64

A2

2.4c In a market where labour is supplied monopolistically

This is less likely to occur today but, in the past, **trade unions** could gain total control over the supply of labour to a given occupation through a **closed shop** agreement.

In this situation the trade union action could lead to a number of outcomes.

- First, the union could raise wages and force the employer to maintain the level of employment by threat of industrial action. Industrial action is a cost to the employer and the company may set aside potential profits to avoid this cost. Therefore the union has forced the wage above the free market equilibrium without any loss of jobs, as illustrated in Figure 2.65.

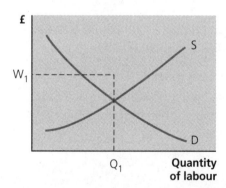

Figure 2.65

- Second, the trade union could raise the wage rate at the expense of lost jobs. In Figure 2.66 union action replaces the supply curve (S) with a curve that is perfectly elastic from the agreed wage rate until it intersects the original supply curve. If the union-controlled wage is W_1, then less labour will be demanded by employers, as illustrated by Q_0, while more people will be attracted to work in this market, with Q_1 seeking employment. The result will be a surplus of workers unable to find a job.

In order to become an actor it was necessary to be given an Equity Card from the actors' union. There were only a limited number and without one you could not get employment.

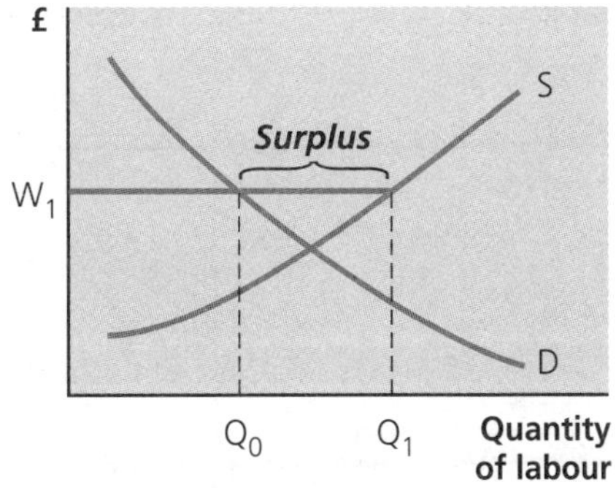

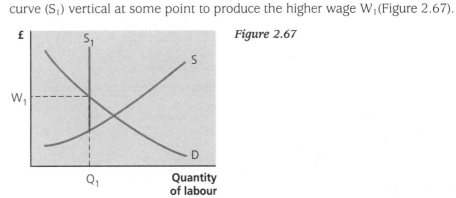

Figure 2.66

- Third, the trade union could restrict the supply of labour by such things as qualification barriers or limited apprenticeships. This would make the supply curve (S_1) vertical at some point to produce the higher wage W_1 (Figure 2.67).

The supply curve could change slope or shift to the left as the result of union action.

Figure 2.67

2.4d In a market where labour is demanded monopsonistically and supplied monopolistically

In the market where labour is demanded monopsonistically, the equilibrium is WQ (Figure 2.68). If a union enters the market, then it has the opportunity to **raise wages and employment** up to W_1Q_1. Past that point, wages can be raised to W_2 and the original level of employment Q can be sustained.

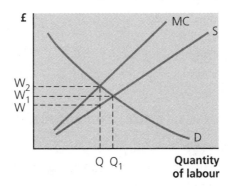

Figure 2.68

This is a popular examination question.

2.5 THE THEORY OF WAGES AND WAGE DIFFERENTIALS

Quite often wage differentials are explained using either demand or supply analysis and this can lead to the following misunderstanding: **a high level of demand or an inelastic supply of labour will produce a high wage rate**. This is incorrect in many cases because it is the interaction of supply and demand which determines the wage rate.

This point is clearer if we compare a classically trained violinist with a rock star (Figure 2.69).

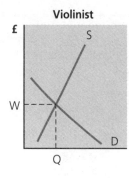
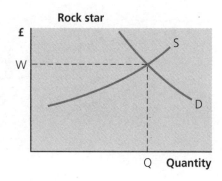

Figure 2.69

This is an important
lesson to remember:
good education and a
lot of training do not,
on their own, ensure a
high wage.

The skills required to produce a violinist are likely to give rise to an inelastic supply curve, whereas those required to become a rock star are less and the supply curve is more elastic. However, the demand for the rock star is likely to be higher than the demand for the violinist, resulting in higher wages for the rock star.

It is likely that the demand for refuse collectors exceeds the demand for surgeons, but the limited supply of surgeons produces the higher wage rate (Figure 2.70).

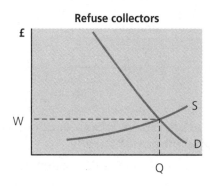
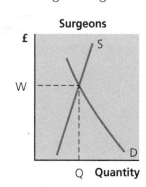

Figure 2.70

Given the interactive analysis above, it is possible to include all the usual points:

- low labour productivity
- qualification barriers
- dangerous jobs
- unique skills
- discrimination by age, sex, race, etc.

There are many social
and political reasons
used to support a
minimum wage.

A2

2.6 A TOPICAL ISSUE: THE NATIONAL MINIMUM WAGE

2.6a In favour

Supporters of a national minimum wage have suggested that it will:

- Raise productivity of labour by making it feel more highly valued.
- Have a shock effect on a company which forces it to reorganise production more efficiently.
- Raise welfare by redistributing income more evenly.

Some economists are
concerned that this is
interfering with the
allocative process of
the price mechanism
and there are more effi-
cient ways of dealing
with poverty, i.e. a
reverse income tax.

A2

2.6b Against

Detractors from a national minimum wage highlight the following:

- In order to be effective it will be set at a level above the wage being earned in some labour markets and will cause unemployment Q_1–Q_2 and an involuntary surplus of labour Q_2–Q_3 (Figure 2.71).

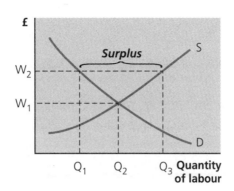

Figure 2.71

W_1 = competitive wage W_2 = national minimum wage

- There will be pressure to restore wage differentials by those already earning the national minimum wage or just above.
- A black market for labour will develop as there will be people willing to work below the minimum.
- Inflation will erode its real value.

3 The price of capital

3.1 INTRODUCTION

By strict definition in economics the price of funds for investment in capital is the **rate of interest**. For example, if an entrepreneur borrows money to build a factory, the price of capital is the rate of interest. If the investment is funded within the firm, the **opportunity cost** of funds is the rate of interest foregone.

As the rate of interest is a price, then under market conditions it will be determined by the forces of demand and supply.

3.2 THE DEMAND FOR INVESTMENT FUNDS

The demand for investment funds is a major component of the demand for loans.

As with labour, capital is a **derived demand** and changes in either the demand for the product or the revenue productivity of capital will shift the demand for capital.

The demand curve for capital is normally downward sloping from left to right. It is the same as the marginal revenue productivity curve of labour and it is referred to as the **marginal efficiency of investment (capital) curve** (Figure 2.72).

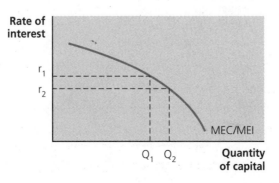

Figure 2.72

The entrepreneur will employ capital up to the point where the rate of interest is equal to the marginal efficiency. If the rate of interest falls from r_1 to r_2, it will be profitable to employ more capital (Q_2 instead of Q_1).

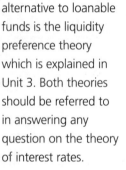

3.3 THE SUPPLY OF INVESTMENT FUNDS

A society can only provide funds for investment through the process of saving. Saving requires consumption to be less than income as saving is the process of abstaining from consumption, and the rate of interest is the reward for this abstinence.

The richer a society is, the more funds will be available internally for investment.

There are two main theories of interest rate determination. The alternative to loanable funds is the liquidity preference theory which is explained in Unit 3. Both theories should be referred to in answering any question on the theory of interest rates.

3.4 THE LOANABLE FUNDS THEORY OF INTEREST RATE DETERMINATION

The loanable funds theory suggests that the rate of interest is endogenous to the supply and demand for loanable funds, where the demand for loans to build capital is one component of the total demand which includes mortgage loans, personal loans and other business loans. In Figure 2.73, Q_1 units of capital will be demanded at the equilibrium rate of interest r_1.

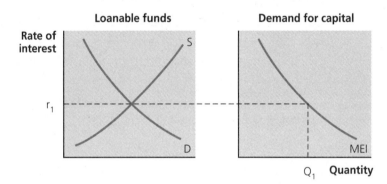

Figure 2.73

4 *The price of enterprise*

4.1 PROFIT

We have so far identified that the entrepreneur pays a single price to employ units of labour and capital.

We have also noted that the return on employing these factors is a downward-sloping MRP or MEI curve (Figure 2.74).

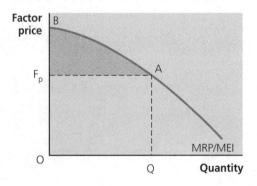

Figure 2.74

This surplus is the foundation of the socialist argument against capitalism.

The rectangle F$_p$AQO is the total cost of employing the factor and the shaded triangle F$_p$AB is the **surplus** earnt by the factor but not paid to the factor. This surplus is the reward to enterprise or profit.

AS

4.2 THE ROLE OF PROFIT

The uninsurable risk taken by entrepreneurs is rewarded by profits. This risk is very real as many failed entrepreneurs will agree. Only a small proportion of entrepreneurs are successful.

The uncertainties faced by entrepreneurs are all part of the process which allocates and **reallocates** resources. Productive factors are attracted to firms with rising profits and therefore expand the industry, while falling profits and losses cause an industry to contract.

5 The price of land

A2

5.1 FROM RENT TO ECONOMIC RENT

The price of land is once again established by the interaction of supply and demand. The term used to describe the price is **rent**.

As all land resources were originally free gifts of nature, any income derived from their ownership was considered to be a **surplus**.

This idea of a surplus reward was applied to all factors of production and the term **economic rent** was used to describe a situation where a productive factor earnt more than the minimum amount required to keep it in its present employment.

A2

5.2 ECONOMIC RENT AND TRANSFER EARNINGS

This should not be confused with a transfer payment which is income, like unemployment pay, which is received without the factor having to produce anything.

The minimum income required by a productive factor to keep it in its current employment was termed a **transfer earning**.

In a market place for a productive factor such as labour, economic rent and transfer earnings are identified (Figure 2.75).

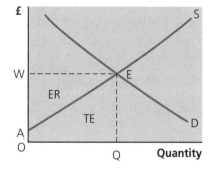

Figure 2.75

The trapezium shape OAEQ shows the minimum income required by labour to remain in this market while the triangle AWE is the surplus.

The slope of the supply curve shows the proportion of economic rent and transfer earnings received by a factor. If it becomes **vertical**, the whole area is economic rent (Figure 2.76).

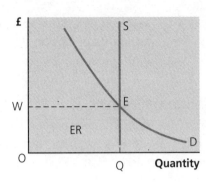

Figure 2.76

If the supply curve is **horizontal**, the whole area is a transfer earning (Figure 2.77).

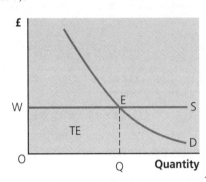

Figure 2.77

In the case of the entrepreneur, **normal profit** is equivalent to a transfer earning while any **excessive profit** is economic rent.

A2

5.3 ECONOMIC RENT AND QUASI-RENT

Because demand can change quickly while the supply of productive factors adjusts more slowly, there may be a time when productive factors can earn a **temporary** economic rent or quasi-rent.

For example, when the NHS was set up there was a sudden increase in the demand for doctors and dentists as consumers raised consumption to the point where **marginal utility was zero**. As it takes 6 or more years to qualify, there were opportunities for those already qualified to increase their incomes. Gradually over time some of this surplus income was eroded.

Strictly, **economic rent** is permanent and usually refers to unique talents which are difficult to **substitute**.

How many other, more recent, examples can you think of where labour became short in supply for a period of time?

In Unit 2 we looked at economics from the perspective of the flow of goods. We are now going to look at the flow which goes in the opposite direction, namely money. This unit has only a minor role in the economics syllabus, but it is nevertheless important to understand that money is the lubricant for the economic system and we are going to focus on both money and the institutions through which it flows.

The unit is subdivided into the following major headings:

A Money and its value
B The UK banking system

A Money and its value

1 The origin and development of money

A2

1.1 BEFORE MONEY

In prehistorical societies trade took place through **barter** which is the direct exchange of products. This system of trade had a number of drawbacks:
- the need for a **double coincidence of wants**
- the **indivisibility** of many products
- problems of **storing** products for future exchange
- each trade is unique with **no standard unit of account**

A2

1.2 THE INTRODUCTION OF MONEY

The origin of money can be found in generally acceptable products. Gradually people realised they could trade their surplus for products which could be passed on to other people in trade. The generally acceptable products were usually **useful** or **ornamental**, for example:
- hides
- furs
- tea
- salt
- shells

According to Adam Smith, dried cod was used as money in Newfoundland.

A2

1.3 THE CHARACTERISTICS OF AN EFFICIENT MONEY

Another of those definitions which can be used to impress people at parties.

Walker defined money as **'that which passes freely from hand to hand in full payment for goods, in final discharge of indebtedness, being accepted equally without reference to the character or credit of the person tendering it and without the intention on the part of the person receiving it to consume or enjoy or otherwise use it than passing it on sooner or later in exchange'.**

A good monetary medium needs to be:

- generally acceptable
- fairly durable
- divisible by value
- portable
- scarce, but not too scarce
- relatively stable over time

The first commodities to become universally acceptable as money were **silver** and **gold**.

1.4 MODERN TYPES OF MONEY

A2

Coins are nothing more than definitive amounts of metal whose weight and fineness are guaranteed by the issuing authorities' stamp.

Notes in their earliest form were 100% backed by real assets; however, modern notes are a **fiduciary** issue which has no backing by real assets.

When the notes became a fiduciary issue, then money had been created. The easiest way to see this is to look at the forerunners of modern banks, the goldsmiths.

The heyday of the goldsmiths was in the eighteenth century just after the Civil War when people who held surpluses mainly in the form of gold needed to store them safely. From this we can trace through the probable sequence of events that turned a goldsmith into a bank and money into a **fractionally backed currency.**

- Goldsmiths charge people to look after their gold.
- People holding goldsmiths' receipts can purchase goods and settle debts by transferring the ownership of the gold. This is done by passing on the receipt rather than physically transferring the gold.
- To facilitate this process, the goldsmith hands out receipts in various denominations and **bank notes** are thus introduced into the monetary system. **However, no new money has yet been created.** All notes are 100% backed by gold.
- A respected goldsmith now holds gold that no-one uses as the notes are passed from one person to another.
- The goldsmith observes that there are a lot of respectable people who occasionally need to borrow some money. Why not lend them some of the surplus gold?
- Now the people who borrow the money do not want gold – they are quite happy to accept notes from goldsmiths. At this point, there are more notes in circulation than gold backing.

New money has been created.

1.5 THE FUNCTIONS OF MONEY

A2

- medium of exchange
- unit of account
- store of wealth
- standard of deferred payment

Side notes:

Issuing authorities could not always be trusted to maintain the real value of a coin. Henry VIII debased coinage so much that during the period 1543–47 coins fell to 15% of their original value.

Understanding credit creation proves difficult for many students. As an introduction, read through this process. It should make the calculations that follow a little easier to understand.

Do not confuse these functions with the characteristics of money when you are answering examination questions.

A2

1.6 DISTINCTIONS AND DEFINITIONS

In order to comprehend a lot of monetary theory it is important to understand the difference between **money** and **cash**.

Cash includes tangible notes and coins whereas money includes cash and the claims on cash which were created by bank loans. **Therefore all cash is money but not all money is cash**.

In fact, of all the transactions that take place at one point in time using money, less than 10% could actually be carried out using cash.

Therefore, definitions of the **money supply** include more variables than cash. To simplify things, money is often referred to as **cash + credit**. However, the need to be more precise has led to a wide range of money supply definitions including the most commonly referred to:

- M_0 which is basically cash
- M_2 which is basically cash + sight deposits or chequeable accounts
- M_4 which is a broader monetary aggregate that includes M_2 + fairly liquid deposit accounts

As the monetary aggregates grow larger, so they incorporate more financial assets which are referred to as **near money**. These assets require some small changes before they can be used in a transaction, i.e. shifted from a deposit to a current account.

One final distinction to make is between **money** and **legal tender**. Any means that a debtor can legally compel a creditor to accept is termed legal tender. All notes issued by the Bank of England are legal tender in the UK and coins up to a specified amount. The most commonly used forms of money, the cheque and the credit card, are not legal tender.

A2

1.7 THE DEMAND FOR MONEY

There are three motives for demanding money, two are straightforward while one is often misunderstood. They are:

- **transactionary**
- **precautionary**
- **speculative**

The transactionary and precautionary demands for money are collectively known as **active balances**. They are easy to understand when you look at how much money you are carrying on your person. Usually it is enough to complete today's transactions and a little bit extra just in case. **Speculating** with money produces an **idle balance**. It is not using money to make money; it is anticipating a change in the value of money. For example, deferring the purchase of Christmas presents until the January sales is speculating with money. In December, money is worth less than it is in January.

A2

1.8 A SUMMARY OF THE CHANGING FACE OF MONEY

The principal stages in the development of money have been:

- precious metals by weight
- definitive weights of metal in the form of coins
- goldsmiths' receipts for deposits of gold

There are many more aggregates of money, which illustrates the difficulties involved in identifying exactly what is and what is not money.

Can you think why more than one pound's worth of 1p and 2p coins or five pounds' worth of 5p or 10p coins is not legal tender?

These distinctions are important in the development of Keynesian Liquidity Preference Theory.

Textbooks often make this seem a little more difficult than it is by using the inverse relationship between bond prices and interest rates.

- bank notes convertible into gold on demand
- inconvertible paper money
- cheques backed by cash
- credit cards backed by cash
- electronic transfers usually backed by credit cards, e.g. shopping on the Internet

Throughout its changes, money has gone from having two characteristics, namely **value in use** and **value in exchange**, to having only a value in exchange.

2 *The value of money*

2.1 EXPLAINING THE TERMS

A person's money is represented by a nominal number. Its real value is the quantity of products that can be purchased with a given amount of money.

The value of money and the average level of prices are inversely related: if prices go up the value of money goes down.

Over the centuries the value of money has fallen, although during the seventeenth century it increased slightly in value. The changes in value were slow until the twentieth century when governments took control over managing money and seem to have mismanaged its value.

2.2 MEASURING CHANGES IN THE VALUE OF MONEY

2.2a The difference between a change in relative prices and a change in average price

In a dynamic economy relative prices are changing all the time but this does not necessarily mean that the average level of prices changes. A change in the value of money requires the average level to rise (inflation) or fall (deflation).

2.2b The problem of choosing representative prices

It would not be possible to measure all price changes. Therefore statisticians concentrate on **retail** prices and from these they select a **key** products basket and monitor its prices.

2.2c The use of index numbers

A lot of statistics in economics are presented in index number form. A starting date is chosen and each item is given a base value of 100.

If we assume only three products and their price change over one year, then a raw index would look like Table 3.1.

> This is important to understand. If monetarists are right, then wage rises change relative prices but they cannot change the average level of prices. Therefore, they cannot cause inflation.

> 100 is chosen so that both rises and falls keep numbers positive.

Product	Year 1 Price	Year 1 Index no.	Year 2 Price	Year 2 Index no.
A	5p	100	10p	200
B	15p	100	18p	120
C	100p	100	75p	75
				395

395/3 = 131.67

Table 3.1

In Year 2, prices have risen on average by 31.67 %.

2.2d The use of weights

In the previous example there is an implicit assumption that equal amounts of money are spent on each product. If this is not the case, then each product needs to be weighted to reflect its relative importance.

If we assume 50 % of total consumer spending is devoted to Product A, 30 % to B and 20 % to C, weights can be allocated in the proportions 5:3:2. The price indices are multiplied by the weight and the average is obtained by dividing the total of these weighted indices by the **total number of weights** (not the number of products). Using the same example, we get Table 3.2.

Read this carefully – it is a common mistake to divide by the number of products.

Table 3.2

Product	Price	Index	Weight	Weighted index
		Year 1		
A	5p	100	5	500
B	15p	100	3	300
C	100p	100	2	200
				1000

1000/10 = 100

Product	Price	Index	Weight	Weighted index
		Year 2		
A	10p	200	5	1000
B	18p	120	3	360
C	75p	75	2	150
				1510

1510/10 = 151

In the actual index of retail prices, key products are changed each year. Recently out are: kippers, cup and saucer, men's vests and women's stockings. Recently in are: microwave meals, bottles of mineral water, leggings and satellite television.

On average, prices now show a rise of 51 %. This is because the product whose price went up the most is the most heavily weighted.

Having calculated the change in the index of retail prices, it is a small step to measuring the change in the value of money. Compared to the base year, money has now fallen in value by 33.8 %.

$$\frac{\text{Base year (or previous year)}}{\text{Current year}} \times 100 = \frac{100}{151} \times 100 = 66.2\% \text{ of last year's value}$$

B The UK banking system

1 Private sector banking

A2

1.1 THE COMMERCIAL BANKS

Until recently the Big Four commercial banks dominated the banking business for private customers. The building societies dominated the mortgage market. The restrictions imposed by building society legislation have led a number of large building societies to convert to banks. Now there are many more banks offering a far wider range of financial services than just **accepting deposits** and **making loans**.

A2

1.2 THE CONFLICT BETWEEN PROFITABILITY AND LIQUIDITY

> Cash does not derive any income for the bank.

The commercial banks are public limited companies which are owned by shareholders. Shareholders want dividends and dividends are paid out of profits. The most profitable thing to do is to hold as small a proportion of cash to total assets as is prudent.

The customers of the bank, who have made deposits and accepted loans, want to know that they have access to cash on demand or at relatively short notice. Therefore, there must be till money (cash) readily available at the bank.

How this conflict is solved can be seen by looking at a simplified balance sheet for a commercial bank.

Liabilities	Assets
Deposits from customers	Cash
	Other liquid assets
	Illiquid assets

> In the past, the amount of cash has been determined either by the anticipated demand from the customer or by the restrictions imposed on the bank by the Bank of England.

The bank has to hold enough cash to satisfy customer demand. Cash earns no interest.

It will hold other liquid assets which can be turned into cash at very short notice. These assets earn low interest.

The higher interest earning assets of a bank are not liquid and include loans to customers over fixed or variable periods of time.

A2

1.3 BANKS CREATING MONEY AND THE BANK CREDIT MULTIPLIER

We have already described how money, which had value in exchange, was created when goldsmiths started offering loans to customers. The idea of banks creating money has been a difficult concept for some students to grasp.

> 'Do banks create money?' is a common examination question.

Here is the simplest example of the bank credit multiplier based upon the following assumptions:
- There is only one bank with many branches.

- Customers are happy to use cheques and when a new cash deposit is made at the bank there is no cash drain to the public.
- The bank wishes to keep 10% of all its assets in cash.
- The only services the bank offers are accepting deposits and making personal loans to customers.

While digging in your garden you find a million pounds in coins which you deposit at the bank so that a balance sheet for your deposit looks like this:

Liabilities	Assets
£1 million	£1 million in cash

The bank's liabilities and assets increase by £1m because the cash can be used to make loans and earn interest, so it is an asset to the bank. However, the bank has a liability to the customer who owns the account.

The bank can now start making loans to customers. Each loan is double entered on the balance sheet and with no cash drain to the public and a 10% cash base the balance sheet will grow to:

Liabilities	Assets
£10 million	£1 million in cash
	£9 million in loans

The effect on the total assets of the bank including the original cash deposit of £1 million is 10 times the change in the cash base.

Sometimes this is written as:
1/cash base ratio =
$\dfrac{1}{10/100} = 10.$

In this example the bank credit multiplier is:

$$\frac{100\%}{\text{Required cash base}\%} \qquad \frac{100\%}{10\%} \;=\; 10$$

If the head office changed the cash base requirement to 20%, the multiplier would be:

$$\frac{100\%}{20\%} \;=\; 5$$

To prove to yourself that you understand this concept, answer the following question:

If your answer is £150,000, think about the question again until you arrive at the answer £90,000.

'Assume a bank wishes to keep 40% of its assets in cash and a £60,000 cash deposit is made at the bank. What value of **new loans** can be created in a banking system which comprises a single bank and no cash drain to the public?'

The process of money creation becomes a little more difficult to understand with cash drains to the public and other banks, but the fundamental rules apply.

A2

1.4 BANKING CRISES

Banking profits depend upon high interest earning loans to customers. However, the more loans are made, the less cash there is available to satisfy everyday customer demand.

Particularly in the past, banks were tempted to make more loans than could be serviced on a day-to-day basis. Default on loans and unexpectedly heavy demand for cash could damage customer confidence and if a run started on the bank, then the bank could collapse.

Confidence is still essential for modern banking systems to function efficiently.

A history of banking crises has led countries to develop a central bank system to support liquidity. We will now turn to just how it works in the UK.

2 *The Bank of England*

2.1 THE FUNCTIONS

The Bank of England fulfils the following functions:
- government's bank
- bankers' bank
- lender of last resort
- intervenes on the foreign currency market
- supervises other banks with legal power
- manages monetary policy
- seeks to achieve inflation target set by government
- manages note issue

2.2 THE STRUCTURE OF THE BANK

The Bank of England has two totally separate parts:

The Issue Department produces weekly accounts which show the issue of legal tender. It is concerned with the provision of liquidity to the banking system.

Monetarist economists consider this department responsible for much of the inflation suffered in the UK.

The Banking Department acts more like a bank in that it accepts loans and makes deposits. Its main customers are the commercial banks and the government.

2.3 THE MECHANICS OF MONETARY POLICY

2.3a Interest rates

Over recent years the Bank has conducted almost all of its monetary policy through controls over interest rates.

Interest rates have been raised to dampen down excessive demand or reduced if it looks as though the economy is moving into recession.

The Monetary Policy Committee meets regularly to determine interest rates, but the gap between decisions and the time lags involved in economic events have led to the criticism that its actions are often 'too little too late' or 'too much too early'.

2.3b Other techniques

In the past, the Bank has used a variety of techniques to pursue its monetary policy. Although it does not currently use any technique other than interest rates, the other options remain available. They include:
- **Open market operations:** selling government debt removes cash from the economy while buying back debt returns it.
- **Funding:** changes the structure of the National Debt by issuing more

long-term securities and fewer short-term securities. This reduces liquid assets in the banking system.

- **Quantitative controls:** previous governments have used ceilings to restrict bank lending.
- **Quantitative guidance:** the Bank could encourage banks to lend to exporters, but not lend for domestic consumption.
- **Special deposits:** a cash call from the Bank to the commercial bank – the account is frozen and cannot be included in the bank's liquid reserves.

2.4 THE TARGETS OF MONETARY POLICY

The main target of monetary policy is the level of monetary demand. This can be affected in one of two ways:

- by changing interest rates
- by changing the supply of money

There are two broadly opposed views to targeting monetary policy.

Keynesians argue that **fiscal** policy is the important target and monetary policy is not important on its own, but needs to accommodate the expenditure and taxation policy. Therefore, it is not necessary to have monetary targets, and interest rates only need to be adjusted in order to aid the financing of the **public sector borrowing requirement (PSBR)**.

Monetarists base their argument on the **Quantity Theory of Money** which was first popularised by **Irving Fisher**. The equation MV = PT where:

$$M = \text{money stock}$$
$$V = \text{velocity of circulation}$$
$$P = \text{average price level}$$
$$T = \text{number of transactions}$$

is the foundation of modern monetarism.

Crudely stated, M and V make up **monetary demand** while P and T could be translated into **national income**.

Monetarists argue that it is very important that the money supply does not grow out of phase with the growth of productivity/output in the economy. If it does, then **inflation** and **deflation** will damage the economy.

Among the monetarists there is an interesting debate. One side argues that the money supply must be managed by controls over **cash**. This will determine the money supply through the bank credit multiplier and interest rates can be established through market forces. The other side argues that the more direct and precise method of control is through managed **interest rates**.

2.5 KEYNESIAN LIQUIDITY PREFERENCE THEORY OF INTEREST RATE DETERMINATION

People's demand for money is their liquidity preference. As the rate of interest falls, demand for money will increase until the **liquidity trap**, at which point rates cannot be lowered further. The supply of money is determined by the Bank of England.

These ways are not totally independent as a change in interest rates will affect the money supply and vice versa.

Fiscal policy and debt financing are looked at in detail in Unit 4.

The modern exponents of monetarism include F. A. Hayek and M. Friedman.

Remember that there are two theories of interest rate determination, which are this one and loanable funds theory. Both may need to be explained in a question about interest rates.

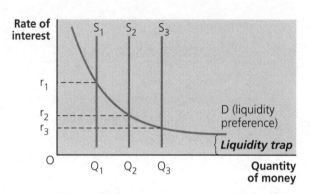

Figure 3.1

As the supply of money is increased, S_1–S_3 in Figure 3.1, so the rate of interest falls until the liquidity trap is reached.

2.6 AN INDEPENDENT BANK OF ENGLAND

On 6 May 1997, the Bank of England was given its independence and charged to maintain an **inflation target**.

Advantages

- Profile of monetary policy has been raised and will act as a discipline on government spending.
- From a monetarist perspective, the Bank is now being asked to manage the only thing it can control, i.e. inflation.
- The Bank will no longer have to follow the Treasury against its better judgement.
- Reconciling the conflict between monetary policy and managing the **National Debt** will be less of a problem. Previously, the PSBR and interest rate targets were often seen as incompatible with monetary and inflation targets.
- The commercial banks expect the Bank to maintain stability in the banking sector.

Disadvantages

- From the government's perspective, borrowing targets may have to be changed.
- The Keynesians will see a weakening of fiscal policy and the pursuit of demand management and difficulties in achieving employment level targets.
- The Bank may overreact on inflation targets and push the economy into recession.
- If cost-push inflation exists, the Bank may be helpless in its pursuit of an inflation target.

This unit usually appears in most textbooks under the heading of **macro-economics**. As well as looking at how the economy is measured and the theories associated with the circular flow of income, we will look at the large-scale problems of imbalance between **aggregate supply and aggregate demand**, and the way in which the government attempts to manage the economy.

The unit is subdivided into the following major headings:
- A Measuring the economy: the circular flow of income
- B Problems of imbalance
- C Problems of instability
- D Government and the economy

A Measuring the economy: the circular flow of income

1 Important definitions

These are just a few of the main terms used in measuring national income.

Gross national income: the sum total of income received by the factors of production, i.e. wages + profits + interest + rent.

(Net) national income: gross national income minus depreciation of capital stock at factor cost (see below). The net is in brackets to remind you that reference to national income is always net national income, not gross national income.

All of the aggregates are calculated over specific time periods, often 1 year.

Gross domestic product (GDP): the total value of all domestically produced goods and services.

Property refers to the ownership of a wide range of assets, i.e. land, buildings, shares, government securities.

Gross national product (GNP): GDP plus property income from abroad minus property income paid abroad.

Net national product: GNP minus depreciation of capital stock.

Total final expenditure: the total expenditure on domestic products by UK and foreign residents. Aggregate expenditure can be subdivided into:
- consumer expenditure
- government expenditure
- capital expenditure
- stockbuilding
- exports

All the above can be measured at:

Market price which includes indirect taxes but excludes subsidies.

Factor cost which excludes indirect taxes but includes subsidies.

This measure is used to show changes in output as it is adjusted for any price changes.

Constant prices which shows the value of output for each year in terms of the prices ruling in a base year.

2   *National income*

2.1 MEASUREMENT AND ITS PROBLEMS

Over a specific period of time the national income can be measured by adding up the value of its:

- output
- income
- expenditure

All three totals will be equal as they are measuring the same thing. In reality, the totals do not match exactly, so a **residual error** is indicated in the statistics. The main problems using and interpreting national income statistics are:

- **Real income:** national income statistics will need to be deflated to represent a real value:

$$\frac{\text{Index number Year 1}}{\text{Index number Year 2}} \times \text{National income Year 2}$$

- **Imperfect knowledge:** not everyone tells the truth to the taxman.
- **Public goods** do not have prices.
- **Double counting** takes place unless only value added is identified at each stage in the production process.
- **DIY** products do not provide an income to be measured.
- **Externalities:** to give a true value, costs should be removed from the total while benefits are added.
- **Depreciation** is not easy to value precisely.

2.2 USING NATIONAL INCOME STATISTICS TO COMPARE LIVING STANDARDS

2.2a Comparisons between countries

Different population sizes: national income figures are meaningless unless they are given as **per capita**.

Different currencies: ideally **purchasing power parities** would solve this problem, but the easily available **exchange rates** do not reflect purchasing power. There are also many countries whose currencies are not freely traded on markets.

Different methods of collection: some are more comprehensive than others. The UK, for example, includes goods and services while Russia only includes goods.

Different distributions of income and wealth: the more equal the distribution the higher is the average standard of living.

Differences in non-marketed resources: climate, scenery, political stability, etc.

Differences in leisure time: if two countries produce the same income per head, then the one that does it with less working time and more leisure has the higher standard of living.

Different defence budgets: more money spent on defence means less money spent on consumer products.

Externalities: Neither costs nor benefits would be measured in national income statistics.

It is very common in examination questions to come across the need to compare the usefulness of statistics in measuring welfare or standards of living. Remember in these questions to explain that standards of living and welfare involve more than just material things. For example, being free from religious, ethnic or political persecution will raise living standards but not in a way that can be measured by national income statistics.

A2

2.2b Comparisons over time in the same country

Population changes: statistics need to be offered in a **per capita** form.

Collection of statistics: this will change over time. In their current form, official national income statistics have only been compiled in the UK since 1941.

Changes in the value of money: throughout this century there have been inflations and deflations.

Balance of payments disequilibrium: a current account surplus depresses living standards and vice versa.

Distribution of income and wealth: this changes over time.

Changes in working conditions: improvement in non-pecuniary benefits, fewer hours worked.

Exceptional years: it would not be realistic to compare war years with other years.

Externalities: a rise in national income may be offset by a rise in external costs.

3   The theory of the circular flow of income

A2

3.1 SYMBOLS USED IN THE THEORY

Y   =   national income

C   =   consumption

MPC   =   marginal propensity to consume, i.e. $\dfrac{\Delta C}{\Delta Y}$

APC   =   average propensity to consume, i.e. $\dfrac{C}{Y}$

W   =   withdrawals
  S   =   savings
  M   =   imports
  T   =   taxation

J   =   injections
  I   =   investments
  X   =   exports
  G   =   government expenditure

AE   =   aggregate expenditure

K   =   the multiplier

> Delta is used throughout economics to record a change in any variable.

3.2 THE BASIC CIRCULAR FLOW MODEL

A2

3.2a The flow of income

Y is a continuous flow which is cut off at specified points in time when national income statistics are measured.

C is a continuous flow in Y. The main additions to this flow are the injections I, X and G. The main subtractions from the flow are the **matching** withdrawals S, M and T.

A2

3.2b The consumption function

Consumption is by far the largest component of aggregate expenditure. An estimate of the relationship between consumption and income is important in macroeconomic management.

Keynesians predict that rising income reduces **MPC** and raises the **marginal propensity to save (MPS)**.

Popularised by Milton Friedman.

The Permanent Income Hypothesis assumes a perception of permanent income which influences actual consumption. Therefore, if a change in income is not perceived as permanent, consumption will not change.

Popularised by Franco Modigliani and others.

The Life Cycle Hypothesis assumes that consumption is planned over a life so as not to pass debts on to future generations.

The last two theories of the consumption function distinguish between a **short-** and **long-run** effect on consumption of a change in income. There will be less of a reaction in the short run, C_1–C_2, and a greater reaction in the long run, C_1–C_3 (Figure 4.1).

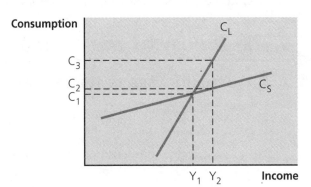

Figure 4.1

Changes in the consumption function can result from:
- changes in the distribution of income
- changes in attitude
- changes in access to credit
- the wealth effect

When asset values are rising, people feel happy about spending more money, and vice versa.

AS

3.2c AD/AS model of equilibrium in the circular flow of income

The aggregate demand curve (AD) comprises the following components: AD = C + I + G + (X − M). The aggregate supply curve represents the total output of the economy at a given point in time and at a given average level of prices. This curve will become vertical at a point where productive capacity is fully utilised, as illustrated in Figure 4.2.

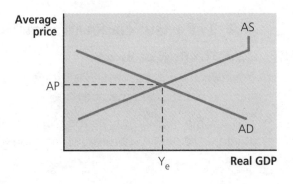

Figure 4.2

An extreme Keynesian diagram assumes that there is no relationship between average prices and changes in output until full employment is reached, as illustrated in Figure 4.3.

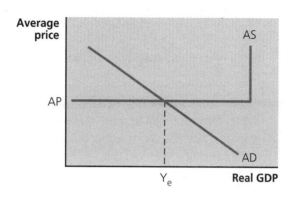

Figure 4.3

An extreme free market monetarist assumes that there is no relationship between output and shifts in aggregate demand curves so that the aggregate supply curve is perfectly inelastic, as illustrated in Figure 4.4.

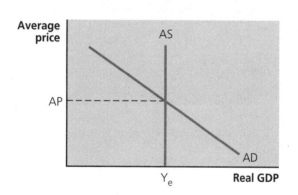

Figure 4.4

Make sure that you can distinguish carefully between shifts and movements in aggregate demand and aggregate supply curves. Apply the same principles that you used for market supply and demand curves.

Depending upon which diagram is thought to be correct, a shift to the right in the aggregate demand curve will:

- in Figure 4.2, produce inflation and an increase in output
- in Figure 4.3, produce an increase in output up to the point where all resources are fully employed, and then inflation
- in Figure 4.4, produce inflation only

3.2d The withdrawals/injections model of equilibrium in the circular flow of income

A less commonly used diagram, but one that is useful for illustrating a number of issues in macroeconomics, is the model constructed below.

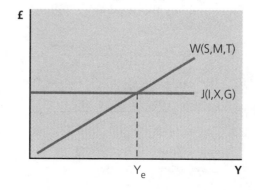

Figure 4.5

In Figure 4.5, real GDP is in equilibrium at Y_e, where the withdrawals from the flow equal the injections into the flow. S, M and T are assumed to be endogenous or induced inside the system, i.e. they change as real GDP changes. I, X and G are assumed to be exogenous or autonomous and are therefore unaffected by changes on the horizontal axis.

A2

3.2e Changes in equilibrium: the multiplier and the accelerator

The multiplier

A change in either the injections into or withdrawals from the circular flow will have a multiple effect on Y. The easiest way to illustrate this is to use the withdrawals injections model. An increase in injections will be illustrated by a shift from J–J_1 (Figure 4.6).

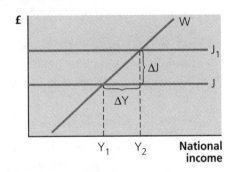

Figure 4.6

The multiplier $\quad K = \dfrac{\Delta Y}{\Delta J}$

The steeper the slope of W, the smaller is the multiplier and vice versa.

The algebraic calculation of this value in a one-sector model is:

$$\frac{1}{MPS} \quad \text{or} \quad \frac{1}{1-MPC} \quad \text{if} \quad \begin{array}{l} MPC = 0.8 \\ MPS = 0.2 \end{array}$$

$$\text{then} \quad \frac{1}{0.2} \quad = 5$$

In a two-sector model where government is added, the calculation is:

$$\frac{1}{MPS + MPT} \quad \text{if} \quad \begin{array}{l} MPS = 0.2 \\ MPT = 0.2 \end{array}$$

$$\text{then} \quad \frac{1}{0.2 + 0.2} = \frac{1}{0.4} = 2.5$$

In a three-sector model where international trade is added, the calculation is:

$$\frac{1}{MPS + MPT + MPM} \quad \text{if} \quad \begin{array}{l} MPS = 0.2 \\ MPT = 0.2 \\ MPM = 0.1 \end{array}$$

$$\text{then} \quad \frac{1}{0.2 + 0.2 + 0.1} = \frac{1}{0.5} = 2$$

The same calculation is used whether there is an increase or a decrease in injections or withdrawals.

The interesting point is that an increase or decrease in taxation and government expenditure of the same total produces a **balanced budget multiplier** which always has the value 1.

The obvious assumption is that the injection and withdrawal cancel each other out, but this is not the case. This is because all government expenditure is money spent while only a proportion of the money taxed would have been spent.

It is essential that you grasp the difference between the multiplier and the accelerator. An **autonomous** change in investment has a multiplier effect on Y, while a change in Y **induces** an acceleration in investment.

The accelerator

This is a response to a change in national income. If national income is constant from one year to the next, capital will be replaced at a constant rate. However, if national income is **accelerating**, new capital will have to be purchased.

To illustrate this point, assume there are 1000 units of capital in the economy of which 100 are replaced each year. Suppose national income doubles. For one year, investment in capital will rise from 100 to 1100 before setting back at 200 per year or 10%. This acceleration is necessary to maintain the same **capital output ratio**.

B Problems of imbalance

1 Introduction

An imbalance between the aggregate supply of products and the aggregate demand can produce problems which have encouraged government action.

These problems could be caused by either too much demand or too much supply.

2 Inflation

2.1 DIFFERENT TYPES OF INFLATION

Inflations are often described by the rate at which the **average level of prices rises**.

Creeping inflation is a few per cent a year.

Accelerating inflation is self-explanatory.

Hyperinflation ranges from hundreds to thousands to millions of per cent a year and usually leads to the downfall of the currency.

2.2 CAUSES OF INFLATION

Cost-push inflation results from rises in wages, raw materials, etc.

Demand-pull inflation occurs when aggregate demand exceeds aggregate supply at full employment.

Too much money chasing too few goods: monetarists argue that all inflations at any level of employment have a monetary cause.

Imported inflation: higher prices can be imported from foreign countries.

2.3 THE RESULTS OF INFLATION

Redistribution of wealth: holders of wealth in money contracts lose while holders of particular tangible assets gain.

Redistribution of income: some groups are better at protecting their real income so that a period of inflation produces winners and losers.

Redistribution from creditors and debtors: creditors lose as the value of their savings fall in real terms while the debtors gain as the real value of their debt falls.

Loss of business confidence: variable rates of inflation, interest, foreign exchange and profits disturb business sentiment.

Adjustment to exchange rates: usually a fall in the value of a domestic currency takes place if your rate of inflation is higher than your trading partners'.

There is the well-known story of how, in 1923 in Germany, a person took a barrow loaded with money to the shops. The first stop was to buy some bread and the person foolishly left the barrow load of money outside. When they came out of the shop, the barrow had been stolen. However, the money was still there. Between June and October 1923 prices rose by 5,882,352,900%.

Monetarists who believe that government is the sole cause of inflation like to point out that it is also the biggest debtor in the economy and therefore benefits by seeing a fall in the real value of the National Debt.

Adjustment to living standards: as well as the redistributions already described, growth rates slow and can become negative, particularly at high rates of inflation.

Social and political disorder: high rates of inflation have, arguably, caused revolutions in South American countries and brought down governments in other parts of the world.

2.4 SOME WAYS TO CONTROL INFLATION

A good way to illustrate an **inflationary gap** is to use the withdrawals/injections model (Figure 4.7).

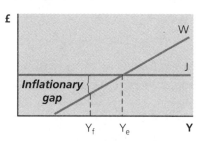

Figure 4.7

Y_e = equilibrium income

Y_f = full employment equilibrium

Solutions to inflation include **reducing aggregate demand** or **increasing aggregate supply**.

In the past, **incomes policies** have been used to control wage push while some economists have argued that **unemployment should be allowed to rise** to reduce wage pressure.

Monetarists see only one solution to inflation which is to stop the money supply from growing faster than the growth in output.

Some economists accept that inflation is inevitable and therefore argue that the solution is to control the harmful redistributive effects by **index linking** mainly public sector contracts.

3 Deflation

3.1 TERMINOLOGY

There is a problem with the term 'deflation' as it is the opposite of two words, namely inflation and reflation. We will take it to be the opposite of inflation and therefore define it **as a fall in the average level of prices**.

3.2 THE CAUSE OF DEFLATION

Throughout history, deficient aggregate monetary demand has been caused by:
- relative shortages of monetary metal
- banking collapses
- the Wall Street Crash
- slumps in world trade

Perhaps you could invent a word which is just the opposite of 'inflation'. When 'deflation' is taken to be the opposite of 'reflation', it means a reduction in aggregate demand irrespective of what is happening to prices. This produces a lot of potential for confusion.

A2

3.3 THE RESULTS OF DEFLATION

Falling prices and unemployment: falling prices squeeze profits and encourage employers to shed surplus labour.

Redistribution of wealth: away from the holder of tangible assets to the holder of contracts in money.

Redistribution of income: some groups are better at protecting themselves from falls in their nominal income.

Redistribution from debtors to creditors: loan contract values increase in real terms and therefore more has to be repaid to creditors.

Loss of business confidence: profits are squeezed and difficulties occur in trying to adjust factor prices.

Adjustment to exchange rates: this time there is a rise in the value of the domestic currency unless other countries are deflating faster.

Adjustment to living standards: redistributions and a likely overall fall.

Social and political disorder: look in the history books under the Great Depression.

A2

3.4 SOME WAYS TO CONTROL DEFLATION

The deflationary gap is illustrated in Figure 4.8 using the withdrawals/injections model.

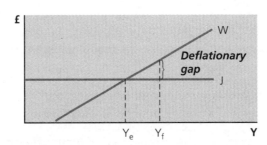

Figure 4.8

Y_e = equilibrium income

Y_f = full employment equilibrium

The solutions to deflation can be broadly divided into **pre-Keynesian and post-Keynesian**.

Pre-Keynesian tended to leave factor prices to fall so that the adjustment was to the supply side of the economy.

Post-Keynesian shifted the emphasis to boosting the demand side of the economy.

John Maynard Keynes had a significant influence on how policies were pursued after 1945.

4 *Unemployment*

4.1 IMPORTANT CONCEPTS

AS

4.1a Separating unemployment from deflation

Although most definitely related to periods of deflation, unemployment has risen during periods of inflation and as the result of policies aimed at reducing the rate of inflation or disinflation.

4.1b Full employment

Under the guidance of Keynesian economists, governments used to think that they could manipulate aggregate demand to achieve and maintain full employment. Empirical evidence from the 1970s seemed to disprove this view.

4.1c A natural level of unemployment

These may be legal, political or cultural.

This level is now commonly referred to as the non-accelerating inflation rate of unemployment (NAIRU).

Other economists believe that when prices are stable, any economy will settle at a level of unemployment which is determined by market forces and a range of institutional factors. The percentage of the workforce unemployed will vary from country to country and from time to time in the same country. These differences occur as the result of changes on the supply side of the economy. In the view of these economists, no amount of demand management can have any long-term effect on the natural level of unemployment.

4.2 Types of unemployment

Unemployed people are not part of a homogeneous grouping and economists have identified a number of distinct types:

- **casual:** irregular work, e.g. affected by weather
- **cyclical:** brought about by recession and depression in the trade cycle
- **disguised:** people are unemployed but there are no records
- **export:** decline in export markets
- **frictional:** said to exist when jobs are available in one area and people are unemployed in another
- **regional:** related to a particular part of the country
- **seasonal:** related to seasonal changes in climate
- **structural:** decline of a major industry
- **technical:** capital replacing labour
- **unemployable:** physically or mentally unable to work
- **voluntary:** chosen to and is able to live without work

The fact that there are many types suggests that there cannot be one solution to the unemployment problem.

4.3 Causes and solutions to unemployment

If unemployment is judged to be **demand deficient**, then boosting demand by budgeting for a deficit and lowering interest rates may be the solution.

Structural unemployment may need retraining and increased labour mobility.

Frictional unemployment requires improvements in mobility.

Supply-side restrictions may be distorting labour markets. Freeing these restrictions is the solution.

A short-term solution to unemployment caused by imports may be protection through **tariffs and quotas**.

Fixed currencies can cause a problem if they become overvalued. Devaluation or controlled depreciation may be a solution.

The poverty trap captures a number of people who judge there is no financial advantage to work. A solution may be **reverse income tax**.

4.4 IS THERE A RELATIONSHIP BETWEEN PRICE STABILITY AND THE LEVEL OF EMPLOYMENT?

A2

4.4a Phillips thought there was

From empirical evidence, A.W. Phillips established a relationship between the level of employment and the rate of change of wages. From this model a theoretical inverse relationship between inflation and unemployment was established and this underpinned much government policy during the 1960s and 1970s.

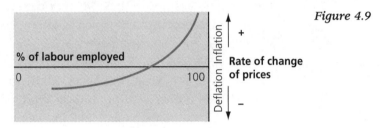

Figure 4.9

The model shown in Figure 4.9 predicts that above a certain level of employment, inflation will start to rise, whereas below a certain level, deflation will occur.

This opinion was voiced in a paper written by M. Friedman entitled 'Inflation and unemployment' for the 1976 Nobel Memorial Lecture.

A2

4.4b Friedman was not so sure

The Phillips curve does not predict what happened during the 1970s when both unemployment and inflation rose together. Some economists had their doubts about the model and M. Friedman suggested that although there may be some short-term relationship between higher levels of employment and **unanticipated** inflation, over the long term, the relationship was not as predicted. In fact, he suggested that both inflation and deflation had distorting effects on markets and could cause unemployment to rise.

C Problems of instability

1 Introduction

AS

Over time, economists have noticed fluctuations in economic activity, some more regular than others. An obvious example is the **trade cycle**.

Also over time, the peaks appear a little higher than last time and the troughs are not quite so low; in other words, the economy is growing. It may be that **economic growth** creates instability or that the instability fuels economic growth.

2 Fluctuations in economic activity

AS

2.1 THE TRADE CYCLE

2.1a Phases

Depression: the economy is characterised by high unemployment, stable or falling prices, profits and incomes.

Recovery: this sometimes starts in the capital goods sector. Demand rises, jobs are created, profits and incomes start to rise.

Boom: full employment, rising prices and profits.

Recession: profits and incomes are squeezed and unemployment begins to rise.

AS

2.1b Irregular fluctuations

The trade cycle is often associated with the nineteenth century. The twentieth century has been much more irregular and theorists tend to talk of fluctuations in economic activity in terms of **cumulative movements** where momentum builds up. The multiplier and accelerator fit in here. Then there are **tops and bottoms** from which a reversal of direction or a **turning point** is recorded.

Economists who try to predict the future are interested in cycles. **The Kondratief cycle** is spread over a period of 50 years whereas business cycles can be played out in less than 10 years.

A2

2.1c Theories of cyclical events

Under-production or over-consumption may cause the economy to reverse direction.

Business confidence may be jolted by real events; or rumours and uncertainties about the future may lead to a 'lemming' response.

Keynesians have their own theories related to the multiplier and accelerator.

Monetarists refer to supplies of money growing at rates which are different to output.

3 Economic growth

AS

3.1 WHAT IS ECONOMIC GROWTH?

One definition of economic growth is **an increase in the productive capacity per**

Not to be taken too seriously, but the American president Harry S. Truman said: 'It's a recession when your neighbour loses his job; it's a depression when you lose yours'.

capita over time. This is clearly distinct from a growth in output due to the increased use of existing capacity. Figure 4.10 shows the movement from X–Y as increased use of capacity while the production possibility boundary shifting outwards from AB to A_1B_1 is economic growth.

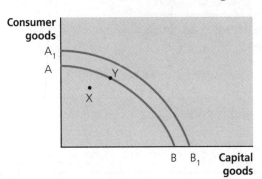

*Figure 4.10
Production possibility
boundaries*

A2

3.2 WHY IS ECONOMIC GROWTH DESIRABLE?

Over the next 45 years, if the world economy grows at only 2.5% per annum on average, its citizens will be three times better off than they are today.

Economic growth offers the prospect of reducing poverty without having to make some people worse off.

Economic growth allows people to increase their leisure time and their standard of living.

People have come to expect rising living standards and economic growth can fulfil all expectations.

A2

3.3 SOURCES OF ECONOMIC GROWTH

There are various sources of economic growth:

- invention and innovation
- improvements in quality of labour
- investment in capital stock
- increased mobility of productive factors
- more efficient allocation of resources
- from small- to large-scale production
- capitalism and the profit motive

Innovation is the role of the entrepreneur but, arguably, the single most important source of economic growth throughout history is invention.

3.4 THE COSTS OF ECONOMIC GROWTH

A2

The **opportunity cost** of resources allocated to economic growth is foregone consumption and lower living standards in the present.

The **social costs** of economic growth are described in many forms, e.g. rising incomes lead to more cars, more pollution and more congestion.

The **personal costs** of economic growth are that people need to be occupationally and geographically more mobile. This leads to disruption and unpleasant breaks in working life.

Link 3.2 to 3.4 and you have an answer to questions about the costs and benefits of economic growth.

3.5 ARE THERE LIMITS TO ECONOMIC GROWTH?

A2

3.5a The doomsday case

Some economists predict a growth-induced doomsday brought about by pressure on natural resources. It will result from:

- accelerating population growth
- a worldwide desire to raise living standards
- exhaustion of non-renewable resources within the next 50 years satisfying accelerating demand throughout the world
- damage to the ozone layer
- global warming
- flooding of low-lying areas
- increased pollution of the atmosphere, rivers and seas

Solutions involve:

- cutting back on use of natural resources
- reducing investment
- cleaning up the environment
- cutting the birth rate

As these are not likely to be forth-coming, the result will be doomsday sometime in the next century.

3.5b A reply to doomsday

Mistakenly, the doomsday case is based upon weak assumptions including:

- no technical progress
- no new resources discovered
- no old resources rendered usable by new techniques
- no substitution of non-renewable resources by renewable resources
- accelerating population growth

The other economists argue for technical developments, a world that can afford to clean up the environment and a **price mechanism** that will ensure that, as resources become scarce, prices will rise and make it profitable to utilise other resources and search for substitutes.

Who has seriously considered this possibility?

A final point often ignored by the scientists is that the **benefits** from global warming may far outweigh the **costs**.

D Government and the economy

1 Government's role

They need not necessarily be supplied by the state.

The role of government is to:

- **provide public goods:** there is almost universal agreement among economists that non-rival, non-excludable products must be bought by the state.
- **provide merit goods:** there is much debate as to whether health and education should be provided free, should be subsidised or should be left to the marketplace.
- **provide social security:** there is much debate about the level and way in which social security payments are made.
- **provide a legal framework to the economy:** this covers monopolies, mergers, restrictive practices, fair trade, factory acts, public health, etc.
- **influence resource allocation** to merit and demerit goods, imports and exports, capital goods and consumer goods.
- **regulate the overall level of economic activity** using fiscal and monetary policy.

2 Public finance and the budget

2.1 ONCE A YEAR

Under normal circumstances, the Chancellor of the Exchequer presents his annual budget to Parliament. It will review the past year and set out or reinforce guidelines for the future.

The budget can be analysed on two levels: first, it is how government expenditure is financed; and, second, it is how the budget is used as a technique for managing the overall level of economic policy. Using the budget in this way is referred to as carrying out **fiscal policy**.

2.2 GOVERNMENT EXPENDITURE

A large proportion of national income is spent, on your behalf, by the government. We have identified the need for spending on **public goods**, but much other spending by government is the basis for academic debate. The difficulty is how much government spending is necessary to promote an **optimum allocation of resources**.

In any year the government is concerned with maintaining the **current** level of service as well as changing, adding and improving which involves **capital** spending.

The pattern of government expenditure involves direct expenditure on products including public and merit goods, transfer payments as part of its welfare commitment, and servicing the National Debt.

2.3 TAXATION

2.3a The economist and taxes

The economist investigates the tax system in terms of its effect on **efficiency**. Questions of fairness, equity and justice are not the direct concern of economists. What is important is whether a tax produces a more or less efficient allocation of resources.

An economist may look at the likely impact of a number of taxes, all of which will bring about a less efficient allocation of resources but a more equitable distribution of income and wealth.

If the issue is between direct and indirect taxes or proportional and progressive taxes, then questions must be asked about their effect on the incentive to work, invest, save, or even stay in the country. And how will the tax affect demand, prices and employment?

In principle, taxes are based upon the following four canons:
- equity
- certainty
- economy
- convenience

Economists encouraged government to drop high marginal income tax rates as some estimates suggested they cost more to administer than the revenue they raised.

2.3b The structure of taxes

Progressive taxes are where higher income earners pay proportionally more of their income in tax.

Proportional taxes are where the same proportion of income is paid in tax by the different income groups.

Regressive taxes are where the lower income earners pay a higher proportion of their income in tax, and the higher income earners pay a lower proportion in tax.

2.3c Direct taxation

These taxes are paid to the **Inland Revenue**. They are levied on income and wealth and the burden of tax cannot be shared.

The main taxes are:
- income tax
- corporation tax
- petroleum taxes
- capital gains tax
- inheritance tax
- stamp duties

Food for thought – G. Gilder wrote that 'highly progressive tax rates do not redistribute incomes, they redistribute taxpayers'.

The advantages of income tax:
- progressive and redistributive
- large tax take
- PAYE is difficult to evade
- fairly precise estimates

The disadvantages of income tax:
- disincentive to work, particularly with high marginal rates of tax

Tax evasion is illegal while tax avoidance is legal.

- tax evasion among non-PAYE group
- resources wasted trying to avoid tax
- may reduce the potential savings of high income earners
- may encourage high earners to emigrate

The advantages of corporation tax:
- reduces potential dividends to high income earners
- does not affect costs, prices and resource allocation

The disadvantages of corporation tax:
- reduces profits and may discourage enterprise
- can be avoided by multinational companies

2.3d Indirect taxation

These taxes are paid to **Customs and Excise**. They are **expenditure taxes** and the burden can be shared between producer and consumer.

The main taxes are:
- VAT
- excise duties
- car tax
- tariffs
- miscellaneous licences

The advantages of indirect taxes are that they:
- can be used to discourage consumption, e.g. demerit goods, non-renewable resources
- can raise a large amount of revenue quickly
- are difficult to evade
- are relatively simple to collect
- do not make taxpayers feel forced to pay them
- can be used to manage the balance of payments current account

Quite a few so-called tax havens, which attract high income earners, have very high expenditure taxes.

The disadvantages of indirect taxes are that:
- they place a heavier burden on the poor because of their regressive nature
- differential rates are usually limited to products with inelastic demand curves
- they raise the cost of living and may affect inflation
- they could cause jobs to be lost

2.3e Some often asked questions

What effect do changes in expenditure taxes have on prices?

This depends mainly on the elasticity of demand for the product. Perfectly inelastic demand leads to the price rising by the amount of the tax (Figure 4.11), whereas perfectly elastic demand leads to no price change (Figure 4.12).

With a normal downward-sloping demand curve, the **tax incidence** will be shared between producer and consumer (Figure 4.13).

The producer pays a greater proportion of the tax if the demand curve is **elastic**, while the consumer pays the largest proportion if the curve is **inelastic**.

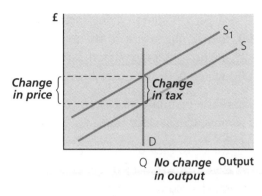

Figure 4.11

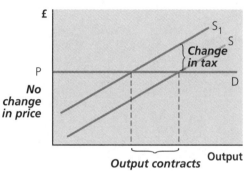

Figure 4.12

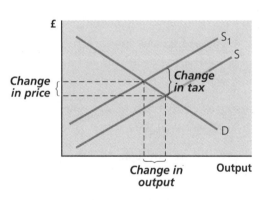

Figure 4.13

Why not tax wealth rather than income?

Wealth is very unevenly distributed compared with income, so it has been argued that the whole foundation of taxation should be changed from income to wealth.

There are a number of problems in using wealth:
- the source of wealth is difficult to distinguish
- it could create a disincentive to accumulate capital
- fragmentation of businesses and loss of economies of scale
- income is a stream, but wealth is a stock and therefore the source can be destroyed by the tax

Will negative (reverse) income tax help remove the poverty trap?

The poverty trap exists because people start paying tax below the poverty line as well as receiving benefits. Therefore, there is a range of income over which a further pound earned causes them to pay tax and lose entitlement to a welfare benefit. Only a relatively large jump in income can cross this trap.

The basic idea of negative income tax is to use the current system of tax collection to offer people financial assistance.

This means you can take away income and there is still more flowing through the system.

These people have been recorded as paying the highest implied marginal rate of tax on income.

Suppose a person starts paying income tax at £5,000 and the poverty line is £2,000, then a negative income tax of 40% will pay £2,000 to a person who receives no income. If the person earns £1,000, he or she will be entitled to 40% of 4,000 which is £1,600, totalling £2,600.

Each time the person earns more money he or she becomes better off, which helps remove the poverty trap.

What is the relevance of the Laffer curve?

Named after Professor Arthur Laffer, the Laffer curve has important implications for political decisions.

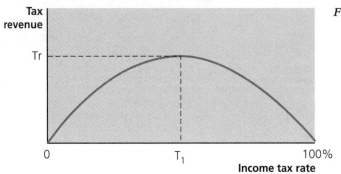

Figure 4.14

Laffer suggested that as the income tax rate rises, so the tax take will increase up to T_1 where maximum revenue will be achieved (Figure 4.14). After T_1, revenue will fall as tax rates rise.

Laffer suggested that many large government, high-tax countries had raised rates above T_1. There was thus scope to **lower tax rates** and **raise tax revenue**.

This is and has been a vote winner for governments in the UK and US.

What are the advantages of taxing demerit goods and subsidising merit goods?

An indirect tax on demerit goods will raise the price and reduce the consumption of a product to reflect its external **costs** to society (Figure 4.15).

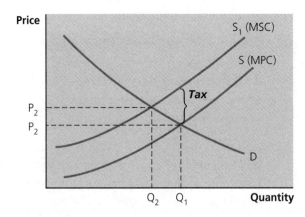

Figure 4.15
Demerit good

MSC = marginal social cost

MPC = marginal private cost

A subsidy on a merit good will lower the price and increase the consumption of a product to reflect its external **benefits** to society (Figure 4.16).

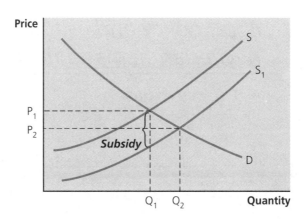

Figure 4.16
Merit good

Borrowing and the National Debt

3.1 THE PSBR/PSDR AND THE NATIONAL DEBT

In pursuit of fiscal policy the government may produce a deficit budget, in which case it will require a **public sector borrowing requirement**. If it achieves a budget surplus, it may make a **public sector debt repayment**.

These year-on-year debts and surpluses change the nominal size of the **National Debt**.

> This debt has been with us since the Bank of England was set up in 1694 by William III. By the end of his reign the debt was £49 million.

3.2 THE STRUCTURE OF THE NATIONAL DEBT

The National Debt is divided into two main parts:
- traded debt
- non-traded debt

The non-traded debt includes national savings, which are held until maturity, and the traded debt includes securities that can be bought and sold on the **stock market**.

The traded debt is further subdivided into:
- short: less than 5 years
- medium: 5 to 15 years
- long: more than 15 years
- undated: with no date for redemption

> This is described under the funding operation of the Bank of England.

Because some of the short debt, mainly **treasury bills**, are part of a commercial bank's liquid assets, the structure of the National Debt is an important element of **monetary policy**.

3.3 FINANCING THE BORROWING REQUIREMENT

This is important in the **monetarist** interpretation of cause and effect.

The PSBR can be financed in a **non-inflationary** way when debt is sold to the public and spending power is transferred to government. Alternatively, debt can be financed in an **inflationary** way when government securities are left unsold at the Bank and cash is printed to their value. According to the monetarists, the high inflation of the 1970s was caused by this process of money creation.

4 Fiscal policy and Keynesian demand management

AS

4.1 ASSUMPTIONS

The analysis is based upon the assumption that any economy has a **productive potential** which can only be reached at full employment of resources.

It is also assumed that the economy can settle at **under or over full employment equilibriums** where under is measured by unemployed labour and over by inflation.

To stabilise the economy at full employment, it is necessary to manage aggregate demand.

AS

4.2 UNDER FULL EMPLOYMENT AND THE BUDGET DEFICIT

If the economy is in equilibrium at Y_e in Figure 4.17, government can increase expenditure $J-J_1$ or reduce taxes $W-W_1$ to close the gap.

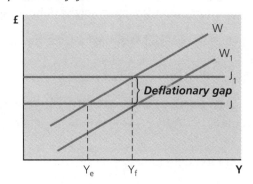

Figure 4.17

AS

4.3 OVER FULL EMPLOYMENT AND THE BUDGET SURPLUS

If the economy is undergoing inflation at full employment, taxes can be raised, $W-W_1$ in Figure 4.18, or expenditure reduced, $J-J_1$, to close the gap.

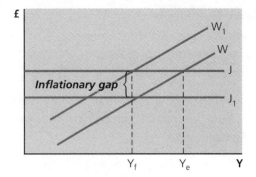

Figure 4.18

5 Free market monetarists vs Keynesians

AS

At the extreme, these two schools of thought produce opposing views.

Monetarists believe that the free market has a tendency to self-regulation through the forces of supply and demand which will cause it to settle at a high (natural) level of employment. The profit motive and private property rights will ensure

Strictly speaking, monetarism is only about the relationship between changes in the supply of money causing changes in nominal national income. However, monetarists are usually associated with free market capitalism, so our reference to monetarists will refer to this broader description.

economic growth. All that government needs to do is maintain the conditions under which the free market can function effectively. The money supply needs to be expanded in line with output and price stability will be maintained. They also believe that many problems like inflation are the result of misguided attempts to manage the economy.

At the other extreme, Keynesians believe the free market has weak self-regulatory powers and is prone to market failures that can cause under full employment equilibriums and low economic growth. Left to itself, the market will gradually be dominated by large firms which shift the balance of economic power towards the producer. Powerful unions and unfettered foreign exchange markets can cause cost-push inflation and large cyclical fluctuations in economic activity. To prevent these events, government must fine tune the economy using mainly fiscal policy supplemented by monetary policy.

The differences between these schools of thought are highlighted below:

Monetarists	Keynesians
Importance of money and monetary policy.	Importance of aggregate demand and fiscal policy.
A natural level of unemployment when prices are stable.	Under full employment equilibriums which can be managed away.
Unemployment can result from the monetary mismanagements which cause inflation and deflation.	Unemployment is caused by deficient aggregate demand and can be associated with cost-push inflation.
An excessive increase in the money supply will raise nominal national income and probably cause inflation.	A cost-push inflation needs an accommodating increase in money supply if deflation is to be avoided.
One cause of inflation.	Two causes of inflation.
Unemployment can be reduced by monetary stability and adjustments to the supply side of the economy.	Unemployment can be reduced by increasing demand and introducing income policies and import controls.

Aggregate supply and demand curves can be used to illustrate the difference.

Keynesians would argue that the aggregate supply function is perfectly elastic up to full employment and therefore demand management can be used to shift AD_1 to AD_2 (Figure 4.19).

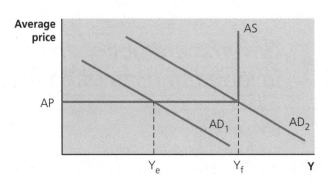

Figure 4.19

See section 6 below.

Monetarists argue that the aggregate supply function is vertical at the natural level of unemployment. AS can be shifted to the right, AS_1, by supply-side policies and prices will remain stable if monetary demand shifts in line with output $AD–AD_1$ (Figure 4.20).

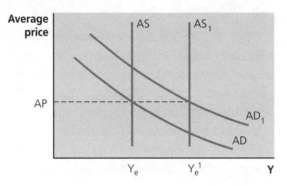

Figure 4.20

6 Replacing demand management by supply-side policies

The aim is to improve the workings of the market, increasing both competition and incentives, thus adding to the supply potential of the economy. There are three main policy groupings:

Market freedom:
- deregulation
- promotion of competition
- curbing monopoly power in labour markets
- privatisation
- remove barriers to the flow of capital
- reinforce private property rights

Incentives:
- tax reductions
- profit-related pay
- employee share ownership
- wider share ownership
- encouraging start-up business

Cost reductions:
- reductions in national insurance
- improvements in the quality of labour

7 Government policy and the difficulties involved in reconciling macroeconomic goals

Governments are usually referred to as having four main macroeconomic policy goals. They are:
- a high level of employment
- price stability

- economic growth
- balance of payments stability

Questions are often asked about the difficulty of reconciling these targets. For example:

- Achieving a higher level of employment, particularly using demand management techniques, may aggravate inflation and cause a current account deficit on the balance of payments.
- Stabilising prices may raise unemployment and slow economic growth.
- Boosting economic growth may destabilise prices and the current account balance.
- Removing a current account deficit may reduce employment levels and growth rates.

Textbooks often refer to 'developed' and 'developing'. These absolute standards mis-understand the nature of a dynamic world.

This unit looks at the way that countries trade across national boundaries, the growth of supranational organisations and the relationship between **more developed** and **less developed** countries.

The unit is subdivided into the following major headings:

A International trade
B The balance of payments
C Foreign exchange
D The less developed world

A International trade

1 The gains from trade

A2

The fundamental point about international trade is that **everyone benefits**. This is easy to see using examples where each country has an **absolute advantage**. It is harder to understand where a country has only **comparative advantage**.

Absolute advantage exists where, given the same resources, one country can produce more than the other.

Comparative advantage exists when a country has absolute disadvantage in its production but it has a lower **opportunity cost** for producing one product. Let us go through an example.

Suppose countries A and B both produce two products – wheat and barley – and, given the same amount of resources, they can produce the following totals:

m	Wheat	Barley
A	75,000	100,000
B	50,000	80,000

Country A has absolute advantage in the production of both wheat and barley.

Should the countries specialise? The answer is 'yes' if their opportunity costs are different.

To work out the opportunity cost of wheat, place the barley total **over** the wheat total. Remember that if statistics are given in the form of costs, then the opportunity cost would be found for wheat by placing the barley number **under** the wheat number.

	Opportunity cost of producing 1 unit of wheat	Opportunity cost of producing 1 unit of barley
A	$4/3$ B	$3/4$ W
B	$8/5$ B	$5/8$ W

The opportunity costs are different, so if each country specialises in the product for which it has comparative advantage, there will be gains from trade.

Opportunity costs are very important because not only do they tell us that A will specialise in wheat and B in barley, but they also provide the **limits to exchange** between which the **terms of trade** must lie for both countries to benefit. The terms of trade must lie between $\frac{5}{8}W$ and $\frac{6}{8}W$ for one unit of barley.

This could be written as 1 unit for wheat must trade between $\frac{4}{3}B$ and $\frac{8}{5}B$.

In any example of comparative advantage it is always possible to produce more of both products after specialisation. This may require some, not all, resources to be shifted to the product with the lower opportunity cost.

One final point is that if the opportunity costs are the **same**, then there is no way that resources can be reallocated to produce gains from trade. For example, if there was a very slight change to the previous example:

	Wheat	Barley
A	62,500	100,000
B	50,000	80,000

Country A still has absolute advantage in the production of wheat and barley, but the opportunity costs are now the same (check the calculation yourself). In this situation, there can be **no trade gains**.

2 Measuring the terms of trade

A2

Direct trade of wheat for barley gives rise to the **real terms of trade**. To measure the terms of trade given prices, the following calculation is used:

$$\text{Terms of trade} = \frac{\text{Index number for the change in export prices}}{\text{Index number for the change in import prices}} \times 100$$

Suppose, in Year 1, export prices rose by 10% and import prices by 25%. The terms of trade would be:

$$\frac{110}{125} \times 100 = 88$$

The fall in the terms of trade is described as **unfavourable** as more exports would have to be sold to buy the same quantity of imports.

In Year 2, suppose the export index rose to 125 while the import index rose to 130:

$$\frac{125}{130} \times 100 = 96.2$$

Remember that the terms of trade must rise to be described as favourable. It does not have to be above 100 unless a comparison is being made with a base year.

The rise from 88 to 96.2 is a **favourable** movement as less exports will have to be sold to buy the same quantity of imports.

3 Misleading terminology

A2

The terms of trade descriptions **favourable** and **unfavourable** can be misleading when one looks at the impact on the balance of payments.

This apparent confusion is a common source of examination questions.

A fall in export prices and a rise in import prices will bring about an **unfavourable fall in the terms of trade**. However, if the demand for both imports and exports is elastic, the lower price for exports will **increase** sales revenue from foreign countries while the higher price for imports will reduce the sales revenue going abroad. This can be described as having a **favourable effect on the balance of payments** as less sterling is being spent on foreign products and more foreign currency is being spent on UK products.

Alternatively, a **favourable** movement in the terms of trade, under these conditions, will have an **unfavourable** effect on the balance of payments.

4   *Free trade or protection*

A2

4.1 INTRODUCTION

At the beginning of Part A the theory of comparative advantage produces trade gains which are described as giving benefits to both trading partners in terms of higher output. Many economists argue that, in theory, the world economy would be most efficient if there was totally free trade and market forces allocated resources.

However, the reality is that the world trading model is a complex interaction of national economies which have created trade barriers against all countries, some countries, all products or some products.

A2

4.2   THE MAIN METHODS OF PROTECTION

Tariffs raise the price of imports either by a specific amount or by a percentage of the import price.

Quotas limit the imports from a certain country or a particular industry to a specific total per time period.

Domestic policies include a variety of options such as:
- subsidies to domestic industry
- legislation
- differential tax rates
- quality control
- minimum standards
- 'Buy British' campaigns

Dumping means a country sells its products abroad at below cost. This could be to clear an oversupply or it could be an attempt to bring down a domestic industry and penetrate a new market.

A2

4.3   THE CASE FOR PROTECTION
- Protection of infant industries.
- Protection of a senile industry while it regenerates.
- To counter unfair trading practices which may include dumping or protection from a foreign monopoly supplier.
- Protection against illegal imports, i.e. drugs.
- Protection of industries for national security reasons.
- To protect employment in industries sensitive to foreign competition.
- A source of revenue for government.

A2

4.4 THE CASE AGAINST PROTECTION

- Protecting inefficient industry becomes a permanent rather than a temporary misallocation of resources.
- Infant industries never grow up.
- Retaliation from other countries.
- Raises the cost of living.
- Restricts consumer choice.
- Ignores the theory of comparative advantage.

5 | *Supranational organisations*

A2

5.1 CUSTOMS UNION

This refers to a group of countries which remove trade barriers between themselves and **erect a common external barrier** against the rest of the world.

This is usually a movement towards freer trade, although technically it could be a move towards protection, depending upon the original position of the countries which join.

Agriculture is an exception that will be looked at on its own.

In the case of the European Union, the original set up produced freer trade not only by removing internal tariffs but also by attempting to create a common external tariff at the lowest level.

Advantages:
- Trade creation.
- Single large market.
- Industries can expand and take advantage of economies of scale.
- Theory of comparative advantage.
- Over the longer term more competition will have beneficial effects on enterprise and efficiency.

Disadvantages
- Trade-diverting effect.
- Advantages will not be evenly distributed.
- Countries located near the centre of the market will receive more benefits.
- Some industries in some countries will not survive the increased competition.

A customs union for less developed countries: the arguments for and against a customs union among less developed countries are similar with one important addition.

The EU is a very powerful union and individual, less developed countries find it difficult to act alone, but as a group of countries they will be able to protect themselves against EU policies that they may see damaging their economies.

A2

5.2 A SINGLE EUROPEAN MARKET

This is one stage further on from a customs union. All the rules of the customs union apply plus:
- complete freedom of movement for productive factors
- no customs hold-ups

More on this in Part C.

- common commercial laws
- single European currency
- standardised quality control
- open tender for public contracts

A2 5.3 A FREE TRADE AREA

This is different from a customs union in that each country maintains its own external barrier against the rest of the world while removing barriers to those countries which are members. An example is **EFTA (European Free Trade Area)**.

With no common external tariff it is necessary to have a **re-export tariff**. For example, if country A has a 50% tariff on one product while country B has a 10% tariff, then a 40% re-export tariff will be necessary in B to stop products entering the free trade area and breaching A's tariff.

Other differences are that only goods move freely in a free trade area and there is no centralised political structure.

A2 5.4 A EUROPEAN UNION PROBLEM: THE CAP

The only industry within the EU that has its own set of rules and does not abide by the rules of a customs union is agriculture.

The Common Agricultural Policy (CAP) has a minimum pricing policy for 90% of its products which, as described in Unit 2, Part E, distorts the free market.

Advantages
- Unified a hotchpotch of national controls.
- Stabilised farm incomes.
- Expanded agricultural output.
- Reduced fluctuations in output.
- Created surpluses to be used in bad years.

Disadvantages
- Most prices are above market clearing levels.
- Surpluses are not cleared and are costly to sustain.
- Consumers face higher prices.
- Consumers face less choice.
- Consumers pay higher taxes.
- Non-EU farmers are denied a competitive marketplace through import levies.
- Non-EU countries have products dumped on them through export subsidies.

A simple solution?
Observe the rules of a customs union, support farm incomes, but leave prices alone and let them clear at the free market level.

B The balance of payments

1 Some definitions

Balance of payments: the difference between the total payments into and out of a country measured in domestic currency over a given time period.

Balance of payments current account: this is usually referred to as the **current balance** – the difference between the total value of **goods** and **services** exported and imported over a given time period.

Visible balance of trade: the difference between the total value of **goods** exported and imported over a given time period.

Invisible balance: the difference between the total value of **services** exported and imported over a given time period.

Capital account: since the introduction of new accounting rules in 1998, this account only includes details of transactions in fixed and non-financial assets. Its main component is asset transfers by migrants and it is now a very small component of the balance of payments.

Financial account: this includes almost all the components that were originally in the pre-1998 capital account except those items that appear above in the new capital account. It includes all unofficial movements in terms of the sale and purchase of companies and portfolio investment, as well as the official flows mainly from and to the foreign exchange reserves.

Official financing: this is a part of the capital account which offsets the positive or negative currency flow generated by all other parts of the balance of payments.

Net errors and omissions: originally the balance item, this represents an estimate of the sum of errors and omissions in the accounts. It has a value such that what has been paid for is equal to what has been imported.

Exports or imports FOB: this means free on board and is a value of tangible goods excluding the cost of insurance and transport.

Exports or imports CIF: this measures the value of goods including a contract for the cost of insurance and freight.

Financial news items often concentrate on this account which is somewhat misleading as the **current balance** is much more significant as an indicator of the well-being of the economy.

2 Why does the balance of payments always balance?

Quite simply, it is an accounting identity. Any negative or positive currency flow which results from current balance and unofficial financial account and capital account transactions will be offset by official financing. For example, if there is a current account deficit of −£10 million and a deficit on the unofficial capital account of −£15 million, the currency flow is −£25 million and this will be financed officially by running down the foreign exchange reserves by +£25 million.

A positive currency flow will produce an equal and opposite negative official financing figure. In this case, foreign exchange reserves will be increased.

Because official financing is part of the financial account, it is often said that a current account deficit will equal a financial account surplus and vice versa.

3 *Equilibrium and disequilibrium on the current balance*

A2

Disequilibrium on the current account can be either a deficit or a surplus which is persistent. Statistically, every month is likely to be a temporary disequilibrium as the likelihood of the current balance being zero is very improbable. Therefore equilibrium exists when the surpluses tend to be offset by deficits over a significant time period.

When currencies are **floating** there is an inbuilt corrective mechanism to persistent disequilibrium. The currency will tend to **depreciate** as a deficit reduces the demand for a currency relative to its supply, and **appreciate** with a surplus.

A disequilibrium requires corrective action when a currency is **fixed** against other currencies. The options we will consider are:
- **devaluation** of the currency
- **revaluation** of the currency
- **reflation** of domestic demand
- **deflation** of domestic demand

The choice of policy will depend upon whether the economy is at
- full employment
- under full employment
- over full employment

and it will be assumed that the sum of demand elasticities for imports and exports is greater than one. The reason for this is explained by the **Marshall-Lerner Condition**.

A persistent surplus at under full employment: this will require a **reflation** of domestic demand which will increase output and employment, increase the demand for imports and redirect some potential exports into the home market.

A persistent surplus at over full employment: this will require a **revaluation** of the currency which will relieve the pressure of demand on domestic products through lower import prices and higher export prices.

A persistent surplus at full employment: this will require a little **revaluation** to correct the current account imbalance and a little **reflation** to maintain full employment.

A persistent deficit at under full employment: this will require a **devaluation** to reduce the price of exports, raise the price of imports and boost demand for domestic products.

A persistent deficit at over full employment: this will require a **deflation** of demand to control inflation, reduce demand for imports and switch some unsold domestic products into export markets.

A persistent deficit at full employment: this will require a little **devaluation** to correct the current account imbalance and a little **deflation** to maintain full employment.

Finally, it should be noted that small imbalances can be dealt with by microeconomic policies which may involve adjustments to taxes or tariffs among other things.

Remember that reference to a floating system means change through appreciation and depreciation, while a fixed system requires a change from one agreed point to another and is termed revaluation or devaluation.

Knowing the correct changes is not so easy in practice.

4 Can a country run a persistent disequilibrium on current balance?

A2

Countries like the UK and USA have run deficits on current account for long periods of time while countries like Japan have run surpluses for similar periods. Can this continue indefinitely? Although reality may contradict this, the theoretical answer is 'no'.

A persistent deficit would require a country to have unlimited gold and foreign exchange reserves or an ability to borrow foreign currency indefinitely from the rest of the world. Given a fixed rate, speculators are able to force a currency devaluation, as occurred in the UK in 1967 and 1992. When currencies are floating, depreciation seems to allow the deficit to continue for a longer period.

A persistent surplus is less of a problem for the country concerned but, by definition, other parts of the world must be in deficit and it is likely that these countries will apply pressure on the surplus country to revalue, reflate or allow an upward float. Japan has certainly felt such pressure, particularly from the US.

5 Disequilibrium and the Marshall-Lerner Condition

A2

'One' is often written as 'unity' in economics, so do not be confused.

The Marshall-Lerner Condition states that for a devaluation to be successful the sum of the demand elasticities for imports and exports must be **greater than one**. If the sum is equal to one, a change in the rate of exchange will leave the balance unchanged in percentage terms; if the sum is less than one, a devaluation will worsen the balance.

The example below illustrates how a devaluation in the UK will have no effect on the balance in percentage terms.

In percentage terms the change will be the same; in real terms it will differ if the value of imports and exports differ to begin with:

(1) 100 − 100 = 0
    A 10% change
    in both and
    110 − 110 = 0.

(2) 200 − 100 = 100
    A 10% change
    in both and
    220 − 110 = 110.

A devaluation of 3%			
Price elasticity	Price change	Change in demand	Change in revenue
0.25	**Exports** Domestic output prices unchanged in sterling, 3% depreciated in foreign currency	+ 0.75%	+ 0.75%
0.75	**Imports** Import prices rise by 3% in terms of sterling	− 2.25%	+ 0.75%

The result of the above is that the change in sterling revenue received from exports and the change in sterling expenditure on imports rise by the same amount. The balance therefore remains unchanged.

If this example is repeated for a price elasticity sum which is less than one, the balance worsens. It only improves if the sum is greater than one.

C Foreign exchange

1 AS PPP: the earliest theory of exchange rates

Purchasing power parity between exchange rates is said to exist when equivalent amounts of the currencies have identical purchasing power in their respective countries.

It is a fact that exchange rates do not equalise purchasing power. Supporters of the theory say this is because there is not a free market and the rate cannot settle where purchasing power is equalised.

The most powerful argument against PPP as a theory of exchange rate determination is that the supply and demand for currency is only determined by those current and capital account items that are traded across international boundaries. Those products which are not traded internationally and have different prices will still be included in any measure of PPP.

2 AS Simple exchange rate theory

Students are often confused by the fact that it is demand that causes both the supply and demand for a currency, i.e. the demand for imports and the demand for exports.

The demand for a currency is determined by the **demand** for exports.

The supply of a currency is determined by the **demand** for imports.

The price of a currency in a free market is determined by the interaction of supply and demand, as illustrated in Figure 5.1.

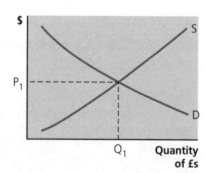

Figure 5.1 Price of sterling

P_1Q_1 is the market clearing equilibrium. It is important to note that you can only measure the price of **one currency** in units of **another currency**. In this case sterling is measured in dollars.

A2 **The elasticity complication:** in fact in Figure 5.1 the supply curve is drawn on the assumption that the demand for imports is elastic – this means that as the price of imports falls, more currency is supplied to buy more imports.

Refer back to Unit 2 (C, 4.4) which looks at the relationship between revenue and elasticity.

However, the same amount of currency would be provided to buy more imports if demand is **unitary**, and less currency would be supplied to buy more imports if demand is **inelastic**.

Although the demand for currency is **always** downward sloping from left to right, the supply curve could be as illustrated in Figure 5.2.

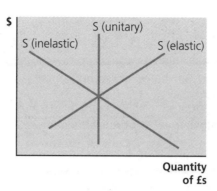

Figure 5.2
Supply of sterling
given different demand
elasticities for imports

Changes in the equilibrium rate of exchange will result from **shifts** in either the supply or demand curve for a currency. Common causes are:

- change in world prices
- development of an import substituting industry
- differential rates of inflation
- changes in interest rates
- other changes in capital flows not caused by interest rates
- economic growth
- government policies

3 Fixed or floating rates of exchange

3.1 THE CASE FOR FLOATING RATES

The free market does it best. One argument suggests that in a dynamic world economy, exchange rates have to change and, left to market forces, these will occur as required.

Fluctuating exchange rates have often been criticised for disturbing and distorting economies. Some economists, however, say that these fluctuations are just a symptom of deeper-seated economic problems, and therefore the floating exchange is not the cause.

Floating-rates reduce the chance of a currency becoming significantly over- or under-valued. This means that the massive speculations associated with fixed rates cannot occur.

Speculation under a fixed rates system is sometimes referred to as a speculator's 'paradise', i.e. a no-lose situation.

3.2 THE CASE FOR FIXED RATES

If floating rates cause instability, then fixed rates create the **stability** that traders require. A businessman agreeing to buy a foreign product for future delivery will be guaranteed the sterling price under a fixed rate system.

Monetarist economists have argued that a fixed exchange rate imposes a monetary discipline upon governments which might otherwise be inclined to fiscal excess.

3.3 THE DIFFERENCE BETWEEN FIXED AND FLOATING CURRENCIES

Both fixed and floating currencies have their prices determined by **market forces**. The only difference between them is that a **free float** involves no intervention

by government. A fixed system is only fixed in the sense that government says **overtly** that it will intervene in the markets and buy or sell currency to maintain a target or par value for that currency. Some market movement will be allowed either side of par before intervention takes place.

> Often a government will intervene if the exchange value moves close to what it considers to be a sensitive number.

In fact, in most countries where currencies float it is not a free float but a **managed float**. Here governments intervene **covertly** as they have no set target for a par value but they do have preferred numbers.

3.4   THE PRACTICE OF FOREIGN EXCHANGE

3.4a   A brief history

A gold standard existed during the nineteenth century and any net deficits or surpluses on trade were settled with a transfer of gold between countries. This had an automatic **reflationary or deflationary** effect on domestic demand and brought about a correction to the balance of payments.

The gold standard was abandoned during the First World War and only partially resurrected after a meeting at Bretton Woods in 1944 when the **Gold Exchange Standard** was used as the basis for fixed rates of exchange. The central bank of each country could settle debts in either gold or dollars which were transferable into gold at an official level. **Devaluations** and **revaluations** were also acceptable ways of adjusting the value of a currency that became over- or under-valued.

During the 1970s monetary mismanagement and an ever-increasing gap between the market price and official price of gold led to most countries adopting a floating system for their exchange rates, although Europe tried to maintain some degree of control over currency exchange which ultimately led to 1999 and the **single European currency**.

3.4b The single European currency

There is still a significant question mark about whether the UK should join a system that will fix the value of sterling irrevocably to the **euro** and the euro will be expected gradually to replace sterling in all transactions.

In favour

> Many economists consider this to be a considerable political overestimate.

A report from the EU commission stated that the **efficiency gain** from removing currency uncertainty and exchange rate costs may be worth as much as 10 % of GNP.

There will be **cost advantages** as changing currencies is time-consuming and costly.

A single currency will remove an artificial restriction to free trade within Europe and bring about a more **efficient allocation of resources**.

The euro will create more **price stability** in individual countries by removing any opportunity to speculate on price movements in their currency.

Traders in Europe will be **certain of the price** they agree under contract for future delivery.

Analysis of monetary and price stability throughout Europe since 1945 shows the UK lagging behind the other main countries, particularly Germany. It may therefore be an advantage to join a system whose members have a **better track record**.

The **monetary discipline** imposed upon the UK government will act as a discipline on fiscal policy, particularly in the run-up to a new election.

Against

Some economists estimate the cost advantages of joining as less than 0.1% of GNP which has to be measured against considerable **private and external costs** involved in the transition to a single currency.

Price stability is not guaranteed under the European Central Bank. It will be run by a cartel, and history has shown that when decisions are made by a group of people with different political agendas and target numbers, it is likely they will agree on the **larger number**.

As each economy is likely to grow at a different rate, there is support for flexibility in exchange rate and interest rate policy. Arguably, any adjustments to these variables can solve certain problems by affecting everyone a little rather than a few people a lot if **unemployment** results.

The UK will no longer be able to use its Keynesian fiscal policy to manage the overall level of economic activity.

An often forgotten problem is the rate at which sterling is irrevocably fixed to the euro. As long as there are interest rate differentials, it is likely that the currency value is distorted, and once a decision is made there is no going back.

A2 3.4c The foreign exchange market (FOREX)

The FOREX provides traders, tourists and investors with the facility to **exchange currencies**. Because there are a large number of operators in the market, uniform products and quick responses to price differences, the FOREX is often used as an example of a **near perfect market**.

The FOREX is subdivided into three main markets:
- spot
- forwards
- futures

The spot market is for current deals which are made at today's price for delivery today.

These became important after June 1972 when the UK moved from a fixed to a floating rate.

Forward deals offer traders certainty in an uncertain market in as much as they can agree today a price for currency delivered in the future.

Speculators rather than traders tend to use options.

Futures are contracts where an **option** to buy currency in the future is purchased. If the option is not exercised by a certain date, it becomes void.

A2 3.4d The eurocurrency market

This market is **quite distinct** from the FOREX. It is not a market for buying and selling currencies but a market for accepting deposits and making loans in foreign currency.

Bank deposits are made in a currency other than the national currency by a non-resident of the country.

For example, if dollars were deposited in Germany by an English company, is it the responsibility of the Federal Reserve, Bundesbank or Bank of England?

The market developed to circumnavigate national regulations. It only accepts large deposits and it makes loans on flexible terms with few formalities.

It is now a very large market and an important source of loans for capital projects. As there is no central authority controlling its activities, there is uncertainty surrounding the division of responsibility in the case of heavy losses. Does the responsibility rest with the country where the deposit was made, the country whose national made the deposit, or the country whose currency is being used?

D The less developed world

1 A real difference

A2

It is difficult to contemplate the fact that half the world's population live in low income countries where subsistence is the order of the day, famine is the result of a marginal change in weather conditions and disease is an ever-present risk.

These generalisations need to be tempered by the thought that there are many rich people in poor countries and many poor people in rich countries.

2 The characteristics of less developed countries (LDCs)

A2

- high population growth
- higher birth and death rates
- lower average age
- higher levels of illiteracy
- few middle income earners
- mainly work in agriculture and extractive industries
- low skill levels
- subsistence incomes
- undeveloped social infrastructure
- few public and merit goods
- immature financial structure
- unsound currency

3 Causes

3.1 POPULATION GROWTH

A2

Fast population growth is often the antithesis of economic growth which, by definition, is of a per capita nature.

Somewhat offensively, inhabitants of LDCs tend to be portrayed as illiterate peasants incapable of determining what is in their best interest. Sterilisation and restriction of family size need to be imposed, so the argument goes.

3.2 LACK OF NATURAL RESOURCES

A2

Oil made the Middle East rich. However, natural resources do not always ensure high incomes in the same way that the lack of natural resources does not always ensure low incomes, although it is often a contributing factor.

3.3 LACK OF PHYSICAL CAPITAL

A2

It is a **necessary** though not **sufficient** condition of high income countries that they have high capital labour ratios. Less developed countries have much less physical capital per head of population.

A rational explanation of large families is that in the absence of pensions and welfare benefits and with high child mortality, many children are a good security against old age and infirmity.

3.4 IMMATURE FINANCIAL STRUCTURE

To facilitate the growth of physical capital it is necessary to have a sophisticated financial system which can bring together **savers** and **investors**.

3.5 SOCIAL CAPITAL

An infrastructure of transportation and communication networks is necessary for the development of trade.

3.6 HUMAN CAPITAL

Without the resources to devote to education and health, the workforce in LDCs is less productive in similar jobs and less able to do more productive jobs.

3.7 CULTURE AND TRADITION

> Officially this does not exist but in reality there is still much evidence of labour immobility.

Arguably many LDCs have been held back by various institutional factors. The caste system in India did not allow the labour mobility that would bring about an efficient distribution of labour skills. Many religions do not embrace the ideals of capitalism, economic growth and secular prosperity. Societies which do not encourage **equal rights for women** will also languish down the economic league table.

4   *Solutions*

4.1 GROWTH BY TRADE IN PRIMARY PRODUCTS

Advantages
- Uses traditional skills.
- Provides basic raw materials.
- Requires low level skills.

Disadvantages
- Output of renewable resources is variable, e.g. agriculture.
- Output of non-renewable resources can receive a price shock by a new discovery.
- The country may be over-reliant on one product.
- Primary product prices are volatile as supply and demand curves are relatively inelastic.

> A solution to this has been the use of buffer stocks to stabilise prices.
>
> Politically, import substitution attracts more votes as the country is trying to produce, at home, the products it wants to use. However, working long hours with low wages to produce goods for rich

4.2 GROWTH BY TRADE IN MANUFACTURED PRODUCTS

Import substitution: the collapse of world trade in the 1930s led many countries to distrust the stability of export earnings and consider the possibility of import substitution behind quota and tariff barriers.

These countries seem to have been less successful than those which chose:

Export-led growth: following the success of Japan, many other countries, particularly in SE Asia, have grown at relatively fast rates through selling consumer durables to the more developed world.

consumers in other parts of the world seems to have been the best solution.

A2

4.3 Development through borrowing

In retrospect, this seems to have been a very dangerous way of bringing about economic expansion. Many less developed countries have found themselves in **debt crises** as the result of unexpectedly high interest rates, oil price shocks and fluctuating demand for their exports.

A2

4.4 Development through aid

Aid has been criticised as a scheme which produces a culture of **dependency**. At its worst, aid has been described as 'the poor people in rich countries giving money to the rich people in poor countries'.

Over recent years there has been growing support for the **'trade not aid'** approach. More developed countries are being encouraged to open up their markets to LDCs. There are many difficult barriers, especially those associated with the Common Agricultural Policy.

It has been said that many LDCs would forego all aid for a free crack at the **consumers** of the more developed world.

A2

4.5 Concluding points

In theory, a straightforward solution to inequality would be the free migration of peoples from the poor to the rich countries. This would increase the land and capital per head of the remaining population.

It is interesting to note, however, that immigrants have rarely been a burden to the host society, and there are many examples of them being the most productive group in their new country.

In reality, there are two problems. First, the people who leave may be the young and enterprising. Second, the more developed world has established sophisticated welfare and benefit systems which they protect through immigration barriers. The fear is that settlers from the LDCs would flood the system and make it unworkable.

5 | *Models of economic development*

A2

5.1 Rostow's model

This divides the growth model into five stages:
- traditional society
- pre-conditions for take-off
- the take-off
- the drive to maturity
- mass consumption

A2

5.2 The Harrod–Domar model

A one-sector growth model which, in the Keynesian tradition, looks at the role of savings and investment in terms of:
- capital accumulation
- aggregate demand
- aggregate supply
- the accelerator

5.3 THE LEWIS-FEI-RANIS MODEL

Put forward by A. Lewis in the 1950s, and developed by Fei and Ranis in the 1960s, this model assumes a dual economy with a subsistence agricultural sector and a developing industrial (manufacturing) sector. The industrial sector is the engine of growth that absorbs the surplus agricultural workers.

5.4 DEPENDENCY THEORIES

A group of theories which look at the relationship between the more developed world and the less developed world, and how the trade in ideas as well as products promotes economic development. Alternatively referred to as a dependency that leads to the development of peripheral capitalism.

5.5 BALANCED AND UNBALANCED GROWTH THEORIES

There is a debate between those economists who consider growth is more likely to take place when real variables grow at the same constant rate and those who consider that it is the very nature of imbalance in an economy that is likely to bring about a more efficient reallocation of resources.

PREFACE

O N RARE OCCASIONS books from the past emerge which are crying out to be reprinted in a way which makes them accessible to the interested general public. This is such a book.

The original, by LEO H. GRINDON, with it's rather dull title of *Lancashire: Brief Historical and Descriptive Notes*, published in the 1880s, was re-discovered recently at a second-hand book fair in Rawtenstall, Lancashire. It is an unwieldy, over-sized book, nicely bound, and well written, but it's most outstanding feature has to be the number of perfect, original etchings and vignettes included which we have tried to reproduce as closely as possible here.

The price of the original copy, like so many of our historical texts, alongside problems of availability, would put it outside the reach of many people who would derive great enjoyment from reading it. It is a book of miscellany in many ways, incorporating views of the great north-western cities of Liverpool and Manchester, but also introducing us to the scenic beauty of the Lake District, the stories associated with the production of cotton, once Lancashire's greatest industry, and informing us of the numerous historical buildings in the area.

This book is a faithfully reproduced facsimile copy of the original, highly readable, in a format and at a price that makes the history of Lancashire and the north west available to all.

There is a great deal to be learned from Leo Grindon. The chapters were originally written for the *Portfolio* of 1881 where they appeared monthly, and were seen by the author as simply a taster of that which is Lancashire. Mr Grindon himself was a native of Bristol, who spent forty years of his life in Manchester. He was the author of several other tracts on Manchester.

It is hoped that this *Aurora* edition of this wonderful text brings pleasure to many people.

DAWN ROBINSON-WALSH

EMIGRANTS AT LIVERPOOL. *By G. P. Jacomb Hood*

CONTENTS.

PAY-DAY IN A COTTON MILL. By G. P. Jacomb Hood

ILLUSTRATIONS OF LANCASHIRE.

I.

Leading Characteristics of the County.

DIRECTLY connected with the whole world, through the medium of its shipping and manufactures, Lancashire is commercially to Great Britain what the Forum was to ancient Rome—the centre from which roads led towards every principal province of the empire. Being nearer to the Atlantic, Liverpool commands a larger portion of our commerce with North America even than London : it is from the Mersey that the great westward steamers chiefly sail. The biographies of the distinguished men who had their birthplace in Lancashire, and lived there always, many of them living still, would fill a volume. A second would hardly suffice to tell of those who, though not natives, have identified themselves at various periods with Lancashire movements and occupations. No county has drawn into its population a larger number of individuals of the powerful classes, some taking up their permanent abode in it, others coming for temporary purposes. In cultivated circles, in the large towns, the veritable Lancashire men are always fewer in number than those born elsewhere, or whose fathers did not belong to Lancashire. No trifling item is it in the county annals that the immortal author of the 'Advancement of Learning' represented, as member of Parliament, for four years (1588-1592) the town which in 1809 gave birth to William Ewart Gladstone, and which, during the boyhood of the latter, sent Canning to the House of Commons.* In days to come England will point to Lancashire as the cradle also of the Stanleys, one generation after another, Sir Robert Peel, and John Bright. The value to the country of the several men, the soundness of their legislative policy, the consistency of their lines of reasoning, is at this moment not the question. They are types of the vigorous, constructive genius which has made England great and free, and so far they are types of the aboriginal Lancashire nature. Lancashire has been the birth-place also of a larger number of mechanical inventions, invaluable to the human race, and the scene of a larger number of the applications of science to great purposes, than any other fragment of the earth's surface of equal dimensions. It is in Lancashire that we find the greater portion of the early history of steam and steam-engines, the first railway forming a part of it. The same county had already led the way in regard to the English canal system. Here, too, we have the most interesting part of the early history of the use of gas for lighting purposes. In Lancashire, again, were laid the foundations of the whole of the stupendous industry represented in the cotton manu-facture, with calico-printing and the arts of pattern-design. The literary work of Lancashire has run abreast of the county industry and scientific life. Mr. Sutton's 'List of Lancashire Authors' contains the names of nearly 1250, three-fourths of whom, he tells us, were born within the frontiers—men widely various, of necessity, in wit and aim, more various still in fertility, some never going beyond a pamphlet or an 'article,'—useful, nevertheless, in their generation, and deserving a place in the honourable catalogue. Historians, antiquaries, poets, novelists, biographers, financiers, find a place in it, with scholars, critics, naturalists, divines. Every one acquainted with books knows that William Roscoe wrote in Liverpool. Bailey's 'Festus,' one of the most remarkable poems of the age, was originally published in Manchester. The standard work upon British Bryology was produced in Warrington, and, like the life of Lorenzo de Medici, by a solicitor,—the late William Wilson. Nowhere in the provinces have there been more conspicuous examples of exact and delicate philosophical and mathematical experiment and observation, than such as in Manchester enabled Dalton to determine the profoundest law in chemistry ; and Horrox, the young curate of Hoole, long before, to be the first of mankind to watch a transit of Venus, providing thereby, for astronomers, the means towards new departures of the highest moment. During the

---

* *Vide* Blue Book, 1878, Part I. p. 423. The first return of Bacon for St. Albans was not until 1601. Roger Ascham, whose influence upon education was even profounder than Bacon's, sat for another Lancashire town—Preston—in the Parliament of 1563.

Franco-Prussian war, when communication with the interior of Paris was manageable only by the employment of carrier-pigeons and the use of micro-photography, it was again a Lancashire man who had to be thanked for the art of concentrating a page of newspaper to the size of a postage-stamp. Possibly there were two or three contemporaneous inventors, but the first to make micro-photography—after the spectroscope, the most exquisite combination of chemical and optical science yet introduced to the world—public and practical, was Mr. J. B. Dancer, of Manchester.

Generous and substantial designs for promoting the education of the people, and their enjoyment,—habits also of thrift and of self-culture, are characteristic of Lancashire. Some have had their origin upon the middle social platform ; others have sprung from the civilised among the rich.* The Co-operative system, with its varied capacities for rendering good service to the provident and careful, had its beginning in Rochdale. The first place to copy Dr. Birkbeck's Mechanics' Institution was Manchester, in which town the first provincial School of Medicine was founded, and which to-day holds the head-quarters of the Victoria University. Manchester, again, was the first town in England to take advantage of the Free Libraries Act of 1850, opening on September 2nd, 1852, with Liverpool in its immediate wake. The famous Chetham Free Library had already existed for 201 years, conferring benefits upon the community which it would be difficult to over-estimate. Other Lancashire towns have latterly possessed themselves of capital libraries, so that, including the fine old collection at Warrington, the number of books now within reach of Lancashire readers, *pro rata* for the population, certainly has no parallel out of London. An excellent feature in the management of several of these libraries consists in the effort made to attain completeness in special departments. Rochdale aims at a complete collection of books relating to wool ; Wigan desires to possess all that has been written about engineering ; the Manchester library contains nearly eight hundred volumes having reference to cotton. In the last-named will also be found the nucleus of a collection which promises to be the finest in the country, of books illustrative of English dialects. The Manchester libraries collectively, or Free and Subscription taken together, are peculiarly rich also in botanical and horticultural works—very many of them magnificently illustrated and running to several volumes—the sum of the titles amounting to considerably over a thousand. Liverpool, too, is well provided with books of this very beautiful description, counting

among them that splendid Lancashire work, Roscoe's 'Monandrian Plants,' the drawings for which were chiefly made in the Liverpool Botanic Garden—the fourth in England, or first after Chelsea, Oxford, and Cambridge, and specially interesting in having been set on foot, in 1800, by Roscoe himself.

The legitimate and healthful recreation of the multitude is in Lancashire, with the thoughtful, as constant an object as their intellectual succour. The public parks in the suburbs of many of the principal Lancashire towns, with their playgrounds and gymnasia, are unrivalled. Manchester has no fewer than four, perfect in every way. There are very fine ones also at Blackburn, Preston, Oldham, Lancaster, Wigan, and Southport.

In Lancashire have always been witnessed the most vigorous and persistent struggles made in this country for civil and political liberty, and the amendment of unjust laws. Sometimes, unhappily, they have seemed to indicate disaffection; and enthusiasts, well-meaning, but extremely unwise, have never failed to obtain plenty of support, often prejudicial to the very cause they sought to vindicate. But the ways of the people have invariably been honest and right-minded. Deducting the intemperate and the zealots, Lancashire has always been patriotic, and determined to uphold the throne. 'The modern Volunteer movement,' according to Mr. Picton, 'may be fairly said to have originated in Liverpool,' the First Lancashire Rifles, which claims to be the oldest Volunteer company, having been organized there in 1859. In any case, the promptitude of the act showed the vitality of that fine old Lancashire disposition to defend the right, which, at the commencement of the Civil Wars, rendered the county so conspicuous for its loyalty. It was in Lancashire that the first blood was shed on behalf of Charles the First, and that the last effort, before Worcester, was made in favour of his son—this in the celebrated battle of Wigan Lane. It was the same loyalty which in 1644 sustained Charlotte de la Tremouille, Countess of Derby, in the famous three-months' successful defence of Lathom House when besieged by Fairfax. Charlotte, a lady of French extraction, might be supposed to have had less care for the king than an Englishwoman ; in the Earl's own devotedness she nevertheless took perfect share. The faithfulness to great trusts which always marks the noble wife, however humble her position, however exalted her rank and title, doubtless lay at the foundation of Charlotte's personal heroism. But even this would have availed nothing had her Lancashire garrison not been true. Lancashire men have always made good soldiers. Several were knighted 'when the fight was done' at Poitiers and Agincourt. The Middleton archers distinguished themselves at Flodden. The gallant 47th—the 'Lancashire Lads'—were at the Alma,

---

* It is necessary to say the 'civilised,' because in Lancashire, as in all other industrial communities, especially manufacturing ones, there are plenty of selfish and vulgar rich.

and at Inkerman formed part of the 'thin red line.' There is equally good promise for the future, should occasion arise. At the great Windsor Review of the Volunteers in July 1881, when 50,000 were brought together, it was unanimously allowed by the military critics that, without the slightest disrespect to the many other fine regiments upon the ground, the most distinguished for steadiness, physique, and discipline, as well as the numerically strongest, was the 1st Manchester. So striking was the spectacle that the Queen inquired specially for the name of the corps which reflected so much honour upon its county. The efforts made in Lancashire to obtain changes for the better in the statute-book had remarkable illustration in the establishment of the Anti-Corn-Law League, the original idea of which was of much earlier date than is commonly supposed, having occupied men's minds, both in Manchester and Liverpool, as far back as the year 1825. The celebrated cry, six years later, for Reform in the representation, was not heard more loudly even in Birmingham than in the metropolis of the cotton trade.

The pioneers of every kind of religious movement have, like the leaders in civil and political reform, always found Lancashire responsive; and, as with practical scientific inventions, it is to this county that the most interesting part of the early history of nonconforming bodies very generally pertains. George Fox, the celebrated founder of the 'Society of Friends,' commenced his earnest work in the neighbourhood of Ulverston. 'Denominations' of every kind have also in this county maintained themselves vigorously, and there are none which do not here still exist in their strength. The 'Established Church,' as elsewhere, holds the foremost place, and pursues, as always, the even tenour of its way. During the thirty-two years that Manchester has been the centre of a diocese, there have been built within the bishopric (including certain rebuildings on a larger scale) no fewer than 226 new churches, at an estimated cost of 1,220,000*l.* Bishop Fraser, the tireless and unhesitating, has, in the course of his own eleven years' exercise of the episcopal function, 'confirmed' young people at the rate of 11,000 every year. The strength of the Wesleyans is declared by their contributions to the great Thanksgiving Fund, which amounted, on November 15th, 1880, to nearly a quarter of the entire sum then subscribed, viz. to about 65,000*l.*, out of the 293,000*l.* They possess a college at Didsbury; not far from which, at Withington, the Congregationalists likewise have one of their own. The long standing and the power of the Presbyterians is illustrated in their owning the oldest place of worship in Manchester next to the 'Cathedral'—a building which dates from the early part of the fifteenth century. The sympathy of Lancashire with the Church of

Rome has been noted from time immemorial;— perhaps it would be more accurately said that there has been a stauncher allegiance here than in many other places to hereditary creed. The Catholic diocese of Salford (in which Manchester and several of the neighbouring towns are included) claimed, in 1879, a seventh of the entire population.* Stonyhurst, near Clitheroe, is the seat of the most celebrated of the provincial Jesuit colleges. Lastly, it is an interesting concurrent fact, that of the seventy Societies or Congregations in England which profess the faith called the 'New Jerusalem,' Lancashire contains no fewer than twenty-four.

The historical associations offered in many parts of Lancashire are by no means inferior to those of other counties. One of the most interesting of the old Roman roads crosses Blackstone Edge. Names of places near the south-west coast tell of the Scandinavian Vikings. In 1323, Robert Bruce and his army of Scots ravaged the northern districts, and nearly destroyed Preston. The neighbourhood of that town witnessed the chief part of the Stuart enterprise of 1715, and of Prince Charles Edward's march through the county in 1745 many memorials still exist.

The ruins of two of the most celebrated of the old English abbeys are also here — Whalley, with its long record of benevolence, and Furness, scarcely surpassed in manifold interest even by Fountains. One of the very few remaining examples of an ancient castle belongs to the famous old town from which John o' Gaunt received his title.† Parish churches of remote foundation, with sculptures and lettered monuments, supply the antiquary with pleasing variety. Old halls are very numerous; and connected with these, the abbeys, and other relics of the past, we find innumerable entertaining legends and traditions, often rendered so much the more attractive through preserving, in part, the quaint county dialect. The Lancashire dialect, still heard among the rustics, is well known to be peculiarly valuable to the student of the English language. 'Our South Lancashire speech,' says its most accomplished interpreter, 'is second to none in England in the vestiges which it contains of the tongue of other days. . . . To explain Anglo-Saxon there is no speech so original and important as our own South Lancashire *patois.*' ‡

In the sports, manners and customs, which still

---

* Namely, 209,480 Catholic, as against 1,437,000 non-Catholic.

† . . . . 'Next to whom
Was John of Gaunt, the Duke of Lancaster.'
King Henry VI., Part 2nd, ii. 2.
The *first* Duke of Lancaster was Henry, previously Earl of Derby, whose daughter Blanche was married by John of Gaunt, the latter succeeding to the title.

‡ 'On the South Lancashire Dialect.' By Thomas Heywood, F.S.A. Chetham Society. Vol. lvii. pp. 8, 36.

linger where not superseded by modern ones, there is yet further curious material for observation, and the same may be said of the recreations of the thoughtful and quiet among the Operative classes. It is in Lancashire that 'science in humble life' has always had its most numerous and remarkable illustrations. Natural history, in particular, forms one of the established pastimes in the cotton districts and among the men who are connected with the daylight work of the collieries. Many of the working-men botanists are banded into societies or clubs, which often possess libraries, and were founded before any living can remember. Music, especially choral and part singing, has been cultivated in Lancashire with a devotion equalled only, perhaps, in Yorkshire, and certainly nowhere excelled. Both the air and the words of the finest Christmas hymn in use among Protestants, 'Christians, awake!' were composed within the sound, or nearly so, of the Manchester old church bells. The verses were written by the celebrated Dr. Byrom; the music, which compares well with the grand 'Adeste Fideles' itself—the song of Christmas with others, was the production of John Wainwright. On a lower level we find the far-famed Lancashire Hand-bell Ringers. The facilities provided in Lancashire for self-culture have already been spoken of. That private education and school discipline are effective may be assumed, perhaps, from the circumstance that, in October 1880, the girl who at the Oxford Local Examinations stood highest in all England belonged to Liverpool.*

Not without significance either is it that the coveted distinction of 'Senior Wrangler' has been won by a Lancashire man on five occasions within the twenty years now just expired. Three of the victors went up from Liverpool, one from Manchester, and one from Wigan. Lancashire may well be proud of such a list as this; feeling added pleasure in knowing that the gold medal, with prize of ten guineas, offered by the Council of Trinity College, London, for the best essay on 'Middle-class Education, its Influence on Commercial Pursuits,' was won, in 1880, by a Lancashire lady—Miss Agnes Amy Bulley, of the Manchester College for Women.

The scenery presented in many portions of the county vies with the choicest to be found anywhere south of the Tweed. The artist turns with reluctance from the banks of the Lune and the Duddon. The largest and loveliest of the English lakes, supreme Winandermere, belongs essentially to Lancashire. Peaceful Coniston and lucid Esthwaite are entirely within the borders, and close by rise some of the loftiest of the English mountains. The top of 'Coniston Old Man'— alt maen, or 'the high rock'—is 2577 feet above the sea. The part which contains the lakes and mountains is detached, and properly belongs to the Lake district, emphatically so called, being reached from the south only by passing over the lowermost portion of Westmoreland, though accessible by a perilous way, when the tide is out, across the Morecambe sands. Still it is Lancashire, a circumstance often surprising to those who, very naturally, associate the idea of the 'Lakes' with the homes of Southey and Wordsworth, with Ambleside, and Helvellyn, and Lodore.

The geological character of this outlying piece being altogether different from that of the county in general, Lancashire presents a variety of surface peculiarly its own. At one extremity we have the cold, soft clay so useful to brickmakers; on reaching the lakes we find the slate rocks of the very earliest ages. Much of the eastern edge of the county is skirted by the broad bare hills which constitute the central vertebræ of the 'backbone of England,' the imposing 'Pennine range,' which extends from Derbyshire to the Cheviots, and conceals the three longest of the English railway tunnels, one of which both begins and ends in Lancashire. The rock composing them is millstone-grit, with its customary grey and weather-beaten crags and ferny ravines. Plenty of tell-tale gullies declare the vehemence of the winter storms that beat above, and in many of these the rush of water never ceases. Those who seek solitude, the romantic, and the picturesque, know these hills well; in parts, where there is moorland, the sportsman resorts to them for grouse.

In various places the rise of the ground is very considerable, far greater than would be anticipated when first sallying forth from Manchester, though on clear days, looking northwards, when a view can be obtained, there is pleasant intimation of distant hills. Rivington Pike, not far from Bolton, is 1545 feet above the sea-level. Pendle, near Clitheroe, where the rock changes to limestone, is 1803. The millstone-grit reappears, intermittently, as far as Lancaster, but afterwards limestone becomes predominant, continuing nearly to the slate rocks. It is to the limestone that Grange, one of the prettiest places in this part of the country, owes much of its scenic charm as well as salubrity. Not only does it give the bold and ivied tors which usually indicate calcareous rock. Suiting many kinds of ornamental trees, especially those which retain their foliage throughout the year, we owe to it in no slight measure the innumerable shining evergreens which at Grange, even in mid-winter, constantly tempt one to exclaim with Virgil, caressing his beloved Italy, 'Hic ver assiduum!'

The southernmost part of the county has for its surface-rock chiefly the upper new red sandstone, a formation not favourable to fine hill-scenery, though the long ridges for which it is distinguished, at all

---

* Miss Seward, of Blackburne House.

events in Lancashire and Cheshire, often give a decided character to the landscape. The highest point in the extreme south-west, or near Liverpool, occupied by Everton church, has an elevation of no more than 250 feet, or less than a tenth of that of 'Coniston Old Man.' Ashurst, between Wigan and Ormskirk, and Billinge, between Wigan and St. Helens, make amends, the tower upon the summit of the latter being 633 feet above the sea. The prospects from the two last named are very fine. They are interesting to the topographer as having been first resorted to as fit spots for beacons and signal-fires when the Spanish Armada was expected, watchers upon the airy heights of Rivington, Pendle, and Brown Wardle, standing ready to transmit the intelligence further inland. It is pleasing to recall to mind that the news of the sailing of the Armada, in the memorable August of 1588, was brought to England by one of the old Liverpool mariners, the captain of a little vessel that traded with the Mediterranean and the coast of Africa.

Very different is the western margin of this changeful county, the whole extent from the Mersey to Duddon Bridge being washed by the Irish Sea. But, although maritime, it has none of the prime factors of seaside scenery, broken rocks and cliffs—not, at least, until after passing Morecambe Bay. From Liverpool onwards there is only level sand, and, to the casual visitor, apparently never anything besides, for the tide, which is swift to go out, recedes very far, and seldom seems anxious to come in. Blackpool is exceptional. Here the roll of the water is often glorious, and the dimples in calm weather are such as charmed old Æschylus. On the whole, however, the coast must be pronounced monotonous, and the country that borders on it uninteresting. But whatever may be wanting in the way of rocks and cliffs, the need is fully compensated by the exceeding beauty, in parts, of the sand-hills, especially near Birkdale and St. Anne's, where for miles they have the semblance of a miniature mountain chain. Intervening there are broad, green, peaty plateaux, which, becoming saturated after rain with useful moisture, allow of the growth of countless wild-flowers. Curious orchises of two or three sorts; the immaculate Parnassia; the pyrola, that imitates the lily of the valley, all come to these pathless sand-hills to rejoice in the breath of the ocean, which, like that of the heavens, 'smells wooingly.' Looking seawards, though it is seldom that we have tossing surge, there is further compensation, very generally, in the inexpressible beauty of sunset—the old-fashioned but inestimable privilege of the western coast of our island—part of the 'daily bread' of those who thank God reflectingly for His infinite bounty to man's soul as well as body, and which no people in the world command more perfectly than the inhab-

itants of the coast of Lancashire. Seated on those quiet mounds, on a calm September evening, one may often contemplate, on the trembling water, a path of crimson light, more beautiful than the velvet laid down for the feet of a queen.

At the northern extremity of the county, as near Ulverston, there are rocky and turf-clad promontories; but even at Humphrey Head, owing to the flatness of the adjacent sands, there is seldom any considerable amount of surf.

The most remarkable feature of the sea-margin of Lancashire consists in the number and the magnitude of its estuaries. The largest of these form the outlets of the Ribble and the Wyre, at the mouth of the last of which is found the comparatively new port of Fleetwood. Next comes the estuary of the Lune, encumbered, like all the others, by sand-banks, these nowhere more remarkable than at the mouth of the Leven. The estuary of the Mersey (the southern shore of which belongs to Cheshire) is peculiarly interesting, on account of the seemingly recent origin of most of the lower portion. Ptolemy, the Roman geographer, writing about A.D. 130, though he speaks of the Dee and the Ribble, makes no mention of the Mersey, which, had the river existed in its present form and width, he could hardly have overlooked.* No mention is made of it either in the Antonine Itinerary; and as remains of old oaks, five or six feet round, which had evidently grown *in situ*, were not very long ago distinguishable on the northern margin when the tide was out, near where the Liverpool people used to bathe, the conclusion is quite legitimate that the level of the bed of the estuary must in the Celtic times, at the part where the ferry steamers go, have been very considerably higher, and the stream proportionately narrow, perhaps a mere brook, with a salt-marsh right and left. 'Liverpool' was originally the name, simply and purely, of the estuary, indicating, in its derivation, not a town, or a village, but simply water. How far upwards the brook, with its swamp or morass extended, it is not possible to tell, though probably there was always a sheet of water near the present Runcorn. Depression of the shore, with plenty of old tree-stumps, vestiges of an extinct forest, is plainly observable a few miles distant on the Cheshire coast, just below New Brighton.

In several parts of Lancashire, especially in the extreme south-east, the surface is occupied by wet and dreary wastes, composed of peat, and locally called 'mosses.' That they have been formed since

---

* Unless, possibly, as contended by Mr. T. G. Rylands, in the 'Manchester Literary and Philosophical Society's Proceedings' for 1878, vol. xvii., p. 81, following Horsley and Keith Johnston, Pliny intended the Mersey by his 'Belisama.' But West, Professor William Smith, and authors in general, consider that the 'Belisama' was the modern Ribble.

the commencement of the Christian era, there can be little doubt, abundance of remains of the branches of trees being found near the clay floor upon which the peat has gradually arisen. The most noted of these desolate flats is that one called Chat, or St. Chad's, moss, the scene of the special difficulty in the construction of the original Liverpool and Manchester Railway. Nothing can exceed the dismalness of the mosses during nine or ten months of the year. Absolutely level, stretching for several miles, treeless, and with a covering only of brown and wiry scrub, Nature seems expiring in them. June kindly brings a change. Everything has its festival some time. For a short period they are strewed with the lovely summer snow of the cotton-sedge,—the 'cana' of Ossian, 'Her bosom was whiter than the down of cana;' and again, in September, they are amethyst-tinted for two or three weeks with the bloom of the heather. During the last quarter of a century the extent of these mosses has been much reduced, as in north-east Cheshire, where peat-bogs are also frequent, by draining and cultivation at the margins, and in course of time they will probably disappear.

Forests were once a particular feature of a good deal of Lancashire. Long subsequently to the time of the Conquest, much of the county was still covered with trees. The celebrated ' *Carta de Foresta*,' or ' Forest Charter,' under which the clearing of the ground of England for farming purposes first became general and continuous, was granted only in the reign of Henry III., A.D. 1224, or contemporaneously with the uprise of Salisbury Cathedral, a date thus rendered easy of remembrance.

Here and there the trees were allowed to remain; and among these reserved portions of the original Lancashire 'wild wood' it is interesting to find West Derby, the 'western home of wild animals,' thus named because so valuable as a hunting-ground.* No forest, in the current sense of the word, has survived in Lancashire to the present day. Even single trees of patriarchal age are almost unknown. Agriculture, when commenced, proceeded vigorously, chiefly, however, in regard to meadow and pasture; corn-fields have never been either numerous or extensive, except in the district beyond Preston called the Fylde.

Such, in brief, is the character and complexion of the English county we propose to illustrate. Many subjects in addition to those alluded to will receive attention. We have to deal with the particular forms of the local industry; also with the architectural enrichment of the large towns, with the palæontology, and the natural history. Precedence is taken naturally by Liverpool and its noble river, seeing that commerce and enterprise, no less than industry and frugality, have been factors in the greatness of modern Lancashire.

---

* Retained to this day as the name of one of the principal Lancashire ' Hundreds,' it is West Derby which gives title to the Earls of the house of Stanley, and not, as often supposed, the city in the midland counties.

SHIPPING ON THE MERSEY. *By A. Brunet-Debaines*

II.

Liverpool.

THE situation of this great city is in some respects one of the most enviable in the country. Stretching along the upper bank of a magnificent estuary, 1200 yards across where narrowest, and the river current of which flows westwards, it is near enough to the sea to be called a maritime town, yet sufficiently far inland never to suffer any of the discomforts of the open coast. Upon the opposite side of the water the ground rises gently. Birkenhead, the vigorous new Liverpool of the last forty years, covers the nearer slopes; in the distance there are towers and spires, with glimpses of trees, and even of windmills that tell of corn-fields not far away.

Liverpool itself is pleasantly undulated. Walking through the busy streets there is constant sense of rise and fall. An ascent that can be called toilsome is never met with; nor, except concurrently with the docks, and in some of the remoter parts of the town, is there any long continuity of flatness.

Compared with the other two principal English seaports, London and Bristol, the superiority of position is incontestable. A town situated upon the edge of an estuary must needs have quite peculiar advantages. London is indebted for its wealth and grandeur more to its having been the metropolis for a thousand years than to the service directly rendered by the Thames; and as for Bristol, the wonder is that with a stream like the Avon it should still count with the trio, and retain its ancient title of Queen of the West. Away from the waterside, Liverpool loses. There are no green airy downs and delicious woods, reached in half-an-hour from the inmost of the city, such as give character to Clifton; nor, upon the whole, can the scenery of the neighbourhood be said to present any but the very mildest and simplest features. Only in the district which includes Mossley, Allerton, Toxteth, and Otterspool, is there any approach to the picturesque. Hereabouts we find meadows and rural lanes; and when, a few miles up the stream, the Cheshire hills begin to show plainly, the views, looking across, are sometimes delightful.

Not far from the agreeable neighbourhood called 'Prince's Park,' there is a little dell that aforetime, when further away from the borough boundaries, and when the name was given, would seem to have been another Kelvin Grove,—

'Where the rose, in all its pride,
Paints the hollow dingle side,
And the midnight fairies glide,
Bonnie lassie, O!'

Fairyland, tram-cars, and the hard facts of a great city, present few points of contact—Liverpool unites them in 'Exchange to Dingle, 3*d.* inside.' Among the charming poems left us by Roscoe, who had an exquisite perception of natural beauty, there is one upon the disappearance of the brooklet which, descending from springs now dried up, once babbled down this pretty dell with its tribute to the river.

To the stranger approaching Liverpool by railway, these inviting bits of the adjacent country are, unfortunately, not visible. When, after passing through the town, he steps upon the Landing-stage and looks out upon the heaving water, with its countless craft, endless in variety, and representing every nation that possesses ships, he is compensated. The whole world does not present anything in its way more fresh and striking. A third of a mile in length, broad enough for the parade of troops, imperceptibly adjusting itself to every condition of the tide, the Liverpool Landing-stage, regarded simply as a work of constructive art, is a wonderful sight. It is the scene of the daily movement of many thousands of human beings, some departing, others just arrived; and, above all, there is the fascinating prospect.

Thoroughly to appreciate the nobleness, the capacities, and the use made of this magnificent river, a couple of little voyages should be undertaken, one towards the entrance, where the tall white shaft of the lighthouse comes in view; the other, ascending the stream, as far as Rock Ferry. By this means the extent of the docks and the magnitude of the neighbouring warehouses may in some degree be estimated. Up the river and down, from the middle portion of the Landing-stage, without reckoning Birkenhead, the line of sea-wall measures more than six miles. The water area of the docks approaches 270 acres; the length of surrounding quay-margin is nearly twenty miles. The double voyage gives opportunity, also, for observation of the many majestic vessels which are either moving or at anchor in mid-channel. Merchant-men predominate, but, in addition, there are almost invariably two or three of the superb steamers which have their proper home upon the Atlantic, and in a few hours will be away. The great Companies whose names are so familiar, the Cunard, the Allan, the White Star, the Inman, and five or six others, de-spatch between them no fewer than ten of these splendid vessels every week, and fortnightly, two extra, the same number arriving at similar inter-vals. Columbus' largest ship was about ninety tons; the steamers spoken of are from 2000 to 5000 tons, and four are now in course of building of 8000

must be dark and dreary.' At times it is scarcely possible for the ferry-boats to find their way across, and not a sound is to be heard except to convey warning or alarm. But the gloomy hours, fortunately, do not come often. The local meteorologists acknow-ledge an excellent average of cheerful weather—the prevailing kind along the whole extent of the lower Lancashire coast, the hills being too distant to arrest the passage of the clouds—and the man who misses it two or three times running must indeed be unlucky. Nothing, on a sunshiny day, can be more exhilarating than three or four hours upon the Mersey. Liverpool, go where we may, is, in the better parts, a place em-phatically of exhilarations. The activity of the river-

AMERICAN WHEAT AT LIVERPOOL.

to 9000 tons. Besides these there are the South Americans, the steamers to the East and West Indies, China, Japan, and the West Coast of Africa, the weight varying from 1500 to 4000 tons, fifty-four going out every month, and as many coming in. The aggregate to the United States and Canada, away and home, is twenty-two weekly; and to other ports out of Europe, away and home, twenty-seven weekly. The total number of ships and steamers actually *in* the docks, Birkenhead included, on the 6th of Decem-ber, 1880, was 438.

A fairly fine day, a sunshiny one if possible, should be selected for these little voyages, not merely because of its pleasantness, but in order to observe the aston-ishing distance to which the river-life extends. Like every other town in our island, Liverpool knows full well what is meant by fog and rain. 'Some days

life is prefigured in the jauntiness of the movement in the streets; the display in the shop-windows, at all events where one has to make way for the current of well-dressed ladies, which at noon adds in no slight measure to the various gaiety of the scene, is a constant stimulus to the fancy—felt so much the more if one's railway-ticket for the day has been purchased in homely Stockport, or quiet Bury, or unadorned Mid-dleton, or even in thronged Manchester—still it is upon the water that the impression is most animating. High up the river, generally near the Rock Ferry pier, a guardship is stationed, usually an ironclad. Beyond this we come upon four old men-of-war used as training-ships. The *Conway*, a naval school for young officers, accommodates 150, including many of good birth, who pay 50*l.* a-year apiece. The *Inde-fatigable* gives gratuitous teaching to the sons of sailors, orphans, and other homeless boys. The *Akbar* and the *Clarence* are Reformatory schools, the first for misbehaving Protestant lads, the other for Catholics. The good work done by these Reformatories is immense. During the three years 1876 to 1878, the number passed out of the two vessels was 1890, and of these no fewer than 1420 had been converted into capital young seamen.*

Who will write us a book upon the immeasurable *minor* privileges of life, the things we are apt to pass by and take no note of, because 'common'? Sailing upon this glorious river, how beautiful overhead, the

number of vessels they contain when full is proportionately greater than is possible in the largest of the Liverpool. But in London there are not so many, nor is there so great a variety of cargo seen on the quays, nor is the quantity of certain imports so vast. In the single month of October 1880, Liverpool imported from North America, of apples alone, no fewer than 167,400 barrels. Most of the docks are devoted to particular classes of ships or steamers, or to special branches of trade. The King's Dock is the chief scene of the reception of tobacco, the quantity of which brought into Liverpool is second

RUN AWAY TO SEA.

gleam, against the azure, of the sea-gulls! Liverpool is just near enough to the salt water for them to come as daily visitants, just far enough for them to be never so many as to spoil the sweet charm of the unexpected : for the moment they make one forget even the ships. Man's most precious and enduring possessions are the loveliness and the significance of Nature. Were all things valued as they deserve, perhaps these cheery sea-birds would have their due.

The Liverpool docks are more remarkable than those even of London. Some of the vast receptacles fed from the Thames are more capacious, and the

only to the London import ; while the Brunswick is chiefly devoted to the ships bringing timber. The magnificent new Langton and Alexandra docks, opened in September 1881, are designed for the ocean steamers, which previously had to lie at anchor in the channel, considerably to the disadvantage of all concerned, but which henceforth will enjoy all the privileges of the smallest craft. At intervals along the quays, there are huge cranes for lifting ; and very interesting is it to note the care taken that their strength, though herculean, shall not be overtaxed, every crane being marked according to its power, ' Not to lift more than two tons,' or whatever other weight it is adapted to. Like old Bristol, Liverpool holds her docks in her arms. In London, as an

* *Vide* Mr. Inglis' Twenty-third Report to Government on the Certified and Industrial Schools of Great Britain, Dec. 1880.

entertaining German traveller told his countrymen some forty years ago, a merchant, when he wants to despatch an order to his ship in the docks, 'must often send his clerk down by the railroad ; in Liverpool, he may almost make himself heard in the docks out of his counting-house.'* This comes mainly of the town and the docks having grown up together.

The 'dockmen' are well worth notice. None of the loading and unloading of the ships is done by the sailors. As soon as the vessel is safely 'berthed,' the consignees contract with an intermediate operator called a stevedore,† who engages as many men as he requires, paying them 4s. 6d. per day, and for half-days and quarter-days in proportion. Nowhere do we see a better illustration than is supplied in Liverpool of the primitive Judean market-places, 'Why stand ye here all the day idle ? Because no man hath hired us.' Work enough for all there never is, a circumstance not surprising when we consider that the total number of day-labourers in Liverpool is estimated at 30,000. The non-employed, who are believed to be always about one half, or 15,000, congregate near the water ; a favourite place of assembly appears to be the pavement adjoining the Baths. The dockmen correspond to the male adults· among the operatives in the cotton-mill districts, with the great distinction that they are employed and paid by time, and that they are not helped by the girls and women of their families, who in the factories are quite as useful and important as the rougher sex. They correspond also to the 'pitmen' of collieries, and to journeymen labourers in general. Most of them are Irish—as many, it is said, as nine-tenths of the 30,000 —and as usual with that race of people, they have their homes near together. These are chiefly in the district including Scotland Road, where a very different scene awaits the tourist. Faction-fights are the established recreation ; the men engage in the streets, the women hurl missiles from the roofs of the houses. Liverpool has a profoundly mournful as well as a brilliant side. Canon Kingsley once said that the handsomest set of men he had ever beheld at one view was the group assembled within the quadrangle of the Liverpool Exchange. The income-tax assessment of Liverpool amounts to nearly 16 millions sterling. The people claim to be 'Evangelical' beyond compare ; and that they have intellectual power none will dispute. Behind the scenes the fact remains that nowhere in our island is there deeper destitution and profounder spiritual darkness.‡ When the famished and ignorant have to be dealt with, it is better to

begin with supply of good food than with aëriform benedictions. All along the line of the docks it is gratifying to observe that there are now 'cocoa-shops,' some of them upon wheels, metallic tickets, called 'cocoa-pennics,' giving access. Lady Hope (née Miss Elizabeth R. Cotton) has shown that among the genuine levers of civilisation there are none more substantial than good warm coffee and cocoa. Liverpool, in imitation, is giving a lesson to the philanthropic all over England, which, if discreetly taken up, cannot fail to tell immensely on the morals, as well as the physical needs, of the poor and destitute.

Liverpool is a town of comparatively modern date, being far younger than Warrington, Preston, Lancaster, and many another which commercially it has superseded. The name does not occur in Domesday Book, compiled A.D. 1086, nor till the time of King John does even the river seem to have been much used. Commerce, during the era of the Crusades, did not extend beyond the ports of continental Europe, the communications with which were confined to London, Bristol, and a few inconsiderable places on the southern coasts. Passengers to Ireland went chiefly by way of the Dee, and upon the Mersey there were only a few fishing-boats. At the commencement of the thirteenth century came a change. The advantages of the Mersey as a harbour were perceived, and the fishing village upon the northern shore asked for a charter, which in 1207 was granted. Liverpool, as a borough, is thus now in its 674th year. That this great and opulent city should virtually have begun life just at the period indicated is a circumstance of singular interest, since the reign of John, up till the time of the famous gathering at Runnymede, was utterly bare of historical incident, and the condition of the country in general was poor and depressed. Cœur de Lion, the popular idol, though scarcely ever seen at home, was dead. John, the basest monarch who ever sat upon the throne of England, had himself extinguished every spark of loyal sentiment by his cruel murder of Prince Arthur. Art was nearly passive, and literature, except in the person of Layamon, had no existence. Such was the age, overcast and silent, in which the foundations of Liverpool were laid. Contemplating the times, and all that has come of the event, one cannot but think of acorn-planting in winter, and of the grand line in 'Faust,'—

'Ein Theil der Finsterniss die sich das Licht gebar.'
(Part of the darkness which brought forth Light !)

The growth of the new borough was for a long period very slow. In 1272, the year of the accession of Edward I., Liverpool consisted of only 168 houses, occupied (computing on the usual basis) by about 840 people ; and even a century later, when Edward III. appealed to the nation to support him

* J. G. Kohl. 'England, Scotland, and Ireland,' vol. iii. p. 43. 1844.

† For the derivation of this curious word see 'Notes and Queries,' Sixth Series, vol. ii. pp. 365 and 2. 1880.

‡ Vide 'The Dark Side of Liverpool.' the Rev. R. H. Lundie. 'Weekly Review,' Nov. 20, 1880, p. 113.

ST. NICHOLAS CHURCH, LIVERPOOL. *By H. Toussaint*

The Exchange, Liverpool. By R. Kent Thomas

in his attack upon France, though Bristol supplied 24 vessels and 800 men, Liverpool could furnish no more than one solitary barque with a crew of six. It was shortly after this date that the original church of 'Our Lady and St. Nicholas' was erected. Were the building, as it existed for upwards of 400 years, still intact, or nearly so, Liverpool would possess no memorial of the past more attractive. But in the first place, in 1774, the body was taken down and rebuilt. Then, in 1815, the same was done with the tower, the architect wisely superseding the primitive spire with the beautiful lantern by which St. Nicholas' is now recognised even from the opposite side of the water. Of the original ecclesiastical establishment all that remains is the graveyard, once embellished with trees, and in particular with a 'great Thorne,' in summer white and fragrant, which the tasteless and ruthless old rector of the time was formally and most justly impeached for destroying 'without leave or license.' Wilful and needless slaying of ornamental trees, such as no money can buy or replace, and which have taken perhaps a century or more to grow, is always an act of ingratitude, if not of the nature of a crime, and never less excusable than when committed in consecrated ground. Grand old decorative trees do not belong to *us ;* it is we who belong to *them.* The dedication to St. Nicholas shows that the old Liverpool townsfolk were superstitious, if not pious. It is he who on the strength of the legend is found in Dibdin as 'the sweet little cherub'—

> . . . . 'that sits up aloft,
> And takes care of the life of poor Jack.'

Up to 1699, St. Nicholas was only the 'chappell of Leverpoole,' the parish in which the town lay being Walton.

In 1533, or shortly afterwards, temp. Henry VIII., John Leland visited Liverpool, which he describes as being 'a pavid Towne,' with a castle, and a 'Stone Howse,' the residence of the 'Erle of Derbe.' He adds, that there was a small custom-house, at which the dues were paid upon linen-yarn brought from Dublin and Belfast for transmission to Manchester.* A fortunate circumstance it has always been for Ireland that she possesses so near and ready a customer for her various produce as wealthy Liverpool. Fifty years later, Camden describes the town as 'neat and populous'—the former epithet needing translation ; and by the time of Cromwell the amount of shipping had nearly doubled. The Mersey is the natural westward channel for the commerce of the whole of the active district which has Manchester for its centre. By the end of the sixteenth century this district was becoming distinguished for its productive power. A large and constantly increasing supply of

manufactures adapted for export implied imports. The interests of Manchester and Liverpool were alike, as they have remained to the present day. Of no two places in the world can it be said with more truth, that they have 'lived and loved together, through many changing years ;' though it may be a question whether they have always 'wept each other's tears.' In addition to the impulse given to shippers by extended manufacturing, the captains who sailed upon the Irish Sea found in the Mersey their securest haven, the more so since the Dee was now silting up,—a misfortune for venerable and unique Chester which at last threw it, commercially, quite into the shade. The Lune was also destined to lose in favour, an event not without a certain kind of pathos, since cotton was imported into Lancaster long before it was brought to Liverpool. Conditions of all kinds being so happy, prosperity was assured. Liverpool had now only to be thankful, industrious, honest, and prudent.

Singular to say, in the year 1635 Liverpool was not thought worthy of a place in the map of England. In Selden's '*Mare Clausum, seu de Dominio Maris*,' a curious old Latin book contained in the Chetham Library (page 239), there is a map in which Preston, Wigan, Manchester, and Chester, are all set down, but, although the Mersey lies in readiness, there is no Liverpool !

The period of the Restoration was particularly eventful. The Great Plague of 1665 and the Great Fire of 1666 led to a large migration of Londoners into Lancashire, and especially to Liverpool, trade with the North American 'Plantations,' and with the sugar-producing islands of the Caribbean Sea, being now rapidly progressive. Contemporaneously there was a flocking thither of younger sons of country squires, who, anticipating the Duke of Argyll of to-day, saw that commerce is the best of tutors. From these descended some of the most eminent of the old Liverpool families. The increasing demand for sugar in England led, unfortunately, to sad self-contamination. Following the example of Bristol, Liverpool gave itself to the slave-trade, and for ninety-seven years, 1709 to 1806, the whole tone and tendency of the local sentiment were debased by it. The Roscoes, the Rathbones, and others among the high-minded, did their best to arouse their brother merchants to the iniquity of the traffic, and to counteract the moral damage to the community ; but mischief of such a character sinks deep, and the lapse of generations is required to efface it entirely. Mr. W. W. Briggs considers that the shadow is still perceptible.* Politely called the 'West India trade,' no doubt legitimate commerce was bound up with the shocking misdeed, but the

---

kernel was the same. It began with barter of the manufactures of Manchester, Sheffield, and Birmingham, for the negroes demanded, first, by the sugar-planters, and afterwards, in Virginia, for the tobacco-farms. Infamous fraud could not but follow; and a certain callousness, attributable in part to ignorance of the methods employed, was engendered even in those who had no interest in the results. When George the Third was but newly crowned, slaves of both sexes were at times openly sold by advertisement in Liverpool! Money was made fast by the trade in human beings, and many men accumulated great fortunes, memorials of which it would not be hard to find. All this, we may be thankful, is now done with for ever. To recall the story is painful but unavoidable, since no sketch of the history of Liverpool can be complete without reference to it. There is no need, however, to dwell

merchants, Germans particularly. These have brought (and every year sees new arrivals) the habits of thought, the special views, and the fruits of the widely diverse social and political training peculiar to the respective nationalities.

A very considerable number of the native English Liverpool merchants have resided, sometimes for a lengthened period, in foreign countries. Maintaining correspondence with those countries, having connexions, one with another, all over the world, they are kept alive to everything that has relation to commerce. They can tell us about the harvests in all parts of the world, the value of gold and silver, and the operation of legal enactments. Residence abroad supplies new and more liberal ideas, and enables men to judge more accurately. The result is that, although Liverpool, like other places, contains its full quota of the incurably ignorant and prejudiced,

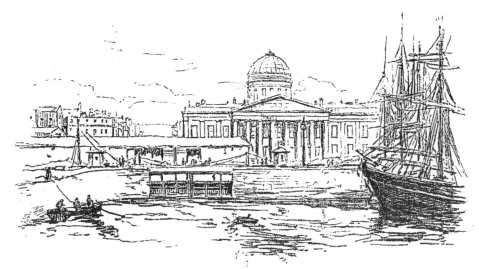

THE CUSTOM-HOUSE, LIVERPOOL.

further upon it. Escape always from the thought of crime as soon as possible. Every one, at all events, must acknowledge that, notwithstanding the outcry by the interested that the total ruin of Liverpool, with downfall of Church and State, would ensue upon abolition, the town has done better *without* the slave-trade.

The period of most astonishing expansion has been that which, as in Manchester, may be termed the strictly modern one. The best of the public buildings have been erected within the memory of living men. Most of the docks have been constructed since 1812. The first steamboat upon the Mersey turned its paddles in 1815. The first steam voyage to New York commemorates 1838. In Liverpool, it should not be forgotten, originated, directly afterwards, the great scheme which gave rise to the 'Peninsular and Oriental,' upon which followed, in turn, the Suez Railway, and then the Suez Canal. The current era has also witnessed an immense influx into Liverpool of well-informed American, Canadian, and continental

the spirit and the method of the mercantile community are in the aggregate vigorous, inviting, and enjoyable. The occupations of the better class of merchants, and their constant consociation with one another, require and develope not only business powers, but the courtesies which distinguish gentlemen. A stamp is given quite different from that which comes of life spent habitually among 'hands;'* the impression upon the mind of the visitor is that, whatever may be the case elsewhere, in Liverpool ability and good manners go hand in hand.

The description of business transacted in Liverpool is almost peculiar to the place. After the shipbuilders and the manufacturers of shipping adjuncts, chain-cables, &c., there are few men in the superior mercantile class who produce anything. Liverpool is a city of agents. Its function is not to make, but

---

* In Liverpool, strictly speaking, there are *no* 'hands,' no troops of workpeople, that is to say, young and old, male and female, equivalent as regard relation to employer, to the operatives of Oldham and Stalybridge.

to transfer. Nearly every bale or box of merchandise that enters the town is purely *en route*. Hence it comes that Liverpool gathers up coin even when times are 'bad.' Whether the owner of the merchandise eventually loses or gains, Liverpool has to be paid the expenses of the passing through. Much of the raw material that comes from abroad changes hands several times before the final despatch. In the daily reports of the cotton-market a certain quantity is always distinguished as bought 'upon speculation.' The adventurous do not wait for the actual arrival of this particular article. Like the Covent Garden wholesale men, who buy the produce of the Kentish cherry orchards while the trees are

pool. The owner of a 'works' must remain with his bricks and mortar; the Liverpool merchant, if he pleases, can weigh and depart. Though the day is marked by conjecture, it is natural to hope for good. Hence much of the sprightliness of the Liverpool character;—the perennial uncertainty underlying the equally well-marked disposition to 'eat, drink, and be merry, for to-morrow we die,' or, at all events, *may* die. This in turn seems to account for the high percentage of shops of the glittering class and that deal in luxuries. Making their money in the way they do, the Liverpool people care less to hoard it than to indulge in the spending. How open-handed they can be when called upon is declared by the

ST. GEORGE'S HALL, LIVERPOOL.

only in bloom, the Liverpool cotton-brokers deal in what they call 'futures.'

Another curious feature is the problematical character of every man's day. The owner of a cotton-mill or an iron-foundry proceeds, like a train upon the rails, according to a definite and pre-concerted plan. A Liverpool foreign merchant, when leaving home in the morning, is seldom able to forecast what will happen before night. Telegrams from distant countries are prone to bring news that changes the whole complexion of affairs. The limitless foreign connexions tend also to render his sympathies cosmopolitan rather than such as pertain to old-fashioned citizens pure and simple. Once a-day, at least, his thoughts and desires are in some far-away part of the globe. Broadly speaking, the merchants, like their ships in the river, are only at anchor in Liver-

sums lately raised for the new Bishopric and the University College. In proportion, they have *more* money than other people, the inhabitants of London alone excepted. The income-tax assessment has already been mentioned as nearly sixteen millions. The actual sum for the year ending April 5th, 1876, was 15,943,000*l.*, against Manchester, 13,907,000*l.*, Birmingham, 6,473,884*l.*, London, 50,808,000*l.* The superiority in comparison with Manchester may come partly, perhaps, of certain firms in the last-named place returning from the country towns or villages where their 'works' are situated. Liverpool is self-contained, Manchester is diffused.

Liverpool may well be proud of her public buildings. Opinions differ in regard to the large block which includes the Custom-house, commonly called 'Revenue Buildings'; but none dispute the claim of the sumptuous edifice known as St. George's Hall to represent the architecture of ancient Greece in the most remarkable and successful degree yet attained in England. The eastern façade is more than 400 feet in length ; at the southern extremity there is an octostyle Corinthian portico, the tympanum filled with ornament. Strange, considering the local wealth and the claim of a character for thoroughness and taste, that this magnificent structure should be allowed to remain unfinished, still wanting, as it does, the sculptures which formed an integral part of Mr. Elmes' carefully considered whole. Closely adjacent are the Free Library and the new Art Gallery, and, in Dale Street, the Public Offices, the Townhall, and the Exchange, which is arcaded. Among other meritorious buildings, either classical or in the Italian palazzo style, we find the Philharmonic Hall and the Athenæum. The Free Library is one of the best-frequented places in Liverpool. The number of readers exceeded, in the year ending at Michaelmas 1880, in regard to the population, that of every other large town in England where a Free Library exists. In Leeds, during that year, the number was 648,539 ; in Birmingham, 658,000 ; in Manchester, 985,079 ; in Liverpool, 1,163,795. In the Reference Department the excess was similar, the issues therefrom having been in Liverpool one-half ; in Birmingham, two-fifths ; in Manchester, one-fifth ; in Leeds, one-tenth. The Liverpool people seem apt to take advantage of their opportunities. When the Naturalists' Field Club starts for the country, the number is three or four times greater in proportion to the whole number of members than in other places where, with similar objects, clubs have been founded ;— whether as much work is accomplished when out, is undecided. They are warm supporters also of literary and scientific institutions, the number of which, as well as of societies devoted to music and the fine arts, is in Liverpool exceptionally high. At the 'Associated Soirée,' held on the 22nd December 1879, there were Presidents of no fewer than fifteen. Educational, charitable, and curative institutions exist in equal plenty. It was Liverpool that, in 1791, led the way in the foundation of Asylums for the Blind. The finest ecclesiastical establishment belongs to the Catholics, who in the diocese of Liverpool are no less powerful than in that of Salford. The new Art Gallery seems to introduce an agreeable prophecy. Liverpool has for more than 130 years striven unsuccessfully to give effect to the memorable project of 1769, when it sought to tread in the steps of the Royal Academy, founded a few months previously. There are now fair indications of rejuvenescence. If we mistake not, there is a quickening appreciation of the intrinsically pure and lovely, coupled with indifference to the qualities which catch and content the vulgar—mere bigness and showiness. Slender as the appreciation may be, still how much more precious than the bestowal of patronage, in ostentation of pocket, beginning there and ending there, which all true and noble art disdains.

Liverpool must not be quitted without a parting word upon a feature certainly by no means peculiar to it, but which to the observant is profoundly interesting and suggestive. This consists in the through movement of the emigrants, and the arrangements made for their departure. Our views and vignettes give some idea of what may be seen upon the river and on board the ships. But it is impossible to render in full the interesting spectacle presented by the strangers who come in the first instance from northern Europe. These arrive, by way of Hull, chiefly from Sweden and Denmark, and, to a small extent, from Russia and Germany —German emigrants to America usually going from their own ports, and by way of the English Channel. Truly astonishing are the piles of luggage on view at the railway stations during the few hours or days which elapse before they go on board. While waiting, they saunter about the town in parties of six or eight, full of wonder and curiosity, but still impressing every one with their honest countenances and inoffensive manners and behaviour. There are very few children among these foreigners, most of whom appear to be in the prime of life, an aged parent now and then accompanying son or daughter. In 1880 there left Liverpool, as emigrants, the prodigious number of 183,502, an increase on 1879 of 64,588. Analysis gave—English, 74,969 ; Scotch, 1811 ; Irish, 27,986 ; foreigners, 74,115.

III.

The Cotton District and the Manufacture of Cotton.

FIRST in the long list of Lancashire manufacturing towns, by reason of its magnitude and wealth, comes Manchester. By-and-by we shall speak of this great city in particular, For the present the name must be taken in the broader sense, equally its own, which carries with it the idea of an immense district. Lancashire, eastwards from Warrington, upwards as far as Preston, is dotted over with little Manchesters, and these, in turn, often possess satellites. The idea of Manchester, as a place of cotton factories, covers also a considerable portion of Cheshire, and extends even into Derbyshire and Yorkshire—Stockport, Hyde, Stalybridge, Dukinfield, Saddleworth, Glossop, essentially belong to it. To all these collateral towns Manchester stands in the relation of a Royal Exchange. It is the reservoir, at the same time, into which they pour their various produce. Manchester acquired this distinguished position partly by accident, mainly through its very easy access to Liverpool. At one time it had powerful rivals in Blackburn and Bolton. The former lost its chance through the frantic hostility of the lower orders towards machinery, inconsiderate men of property giving them countenance—excusably only under the law that mental delusions, like bodily ailments, are impartial in choice of victims. Bolton, on the other hand, though sensible, was too near to compete permanently. The old sale-rooms in Bolton, with their curious galleries and piazzas, now all gone, were, eighty years ago, a striking and singular feature of that famous and still remarkable hive of industry.

Most of these little Manchesters are places of comparatively new growth. A hundred years ago nearly all were insignificant villages or hamlets. Even the names of the greater portion were scarcely known beyond the boundaries of their respective parishes. How unimportant they were in earlier times is declared by the vast area of many of the latter, the parishes in Lancashire, as everywhere else, having been marked out according to the ability of the population to maintain a church and pastor. It is not in manufacturing Lancashire as in the old-fashioned rural counties,—Kent, Sussex, Hampshire, and appled Somerset,—where on every side one is allured by some beautiful memorial of the lang syne. 'Sweet Auburn, loveliest village of the plain,' is not here. Everything, where Cotton reigns, presents the newness of aspect of an Australian colony. The archæological scraps—such few as there may be—are usually submerged, unless hidden away among the fields, in the 'full sea' of recent building. Even in the graveyards, the places of all others which in their tombstones and inscriptions so tenderly 'make former times shake hands with latter,' the imagination has usually to turn away unfed. In place of yew-trees, old as York Minster, if there be anything in the way of green monument, it is a soiled shrub or two from the nearest nursery garden.

The situation of these towns is often pleasing enough : sometimes it is picturesque, and even romantic. Having begun in simple homesteads, pitched where comfort and safety seemed best assured, they are often found upon gentle eminences, the crests of which, like Oldham, they now overlap ; others, like Stalybridge, lie in deep hollows, or, like Blackburn, have gradually spread from the margin of a stream. Not a few of these primitive sites have their ancient character pleasingly commemorated in their names, as Haslingden, the 'place of hazel-nuts.' The eastern border of the county being characterised by lofty and rocky hills, the localities of the towns and villages are there often singularly favoured in regard to scenery. This also gives great interest to the approaches, as when, after leaving Todmorden, we move through the sinuous gorge that, bordered by Cliviger, 'place of rocks,' leads on to Burnley. The higher grounds are bleak and sterile, but the warmth and fertility of the valleys make amends. In any case there is never any lack of the beauty which comes of the impregnation of wild nature with the outcome of human intelligence. Manchester itself occupies part of a broad level, usually clay-floored, and with peat-mosses touching the frontiers. The world probably never contained a town that only thirty to a hundred years ago possessed so many ponds, many of them still in easy recollection, to say nothing of as many more within the compass of an hour's walk from the Exchange.

Rising under the influence of a builder so unambitious as the genius of factories and operatives' cottages, no wonder that a very few years ago the Lancashire cotton towns seemed to vie with one another which should best deserve the character of cold, hard, dreary, and utterly unprepossessing. The streets, excepting the principal artery (originally the road through the primitive village, as in the case of Newtcn Lane, Manchester), not being susceptible of material change, mostly remain as they were—narrow, irregular, and close-built. Happily, of late there has been improvement. Praiseworthy aspirations in regard to public buildings are not uncommon, and even in the meanest towns are at times undeniably successful. In the principal ones, Manchester, Bolton, Rochdale, and another or two, the old meagreness and unsightliness are daily becoming less marked, and a good deal that is really magnificent is in progress as well as completed. Unfortunately, the efforts of the architect fall only too soon under the relentless influence of the factory and the foundry. Manchester is, in this respect, an illustration of the whole group ; the noblest and most elegant buildings, sooner or later, get smoke - begrimed. Sombre as the Lancashire towns become under that influence, if there be collieries in the neighbourhood, as in the case of well-named 'coaly Wigan,' the dismal hue is intensified, and in dull and rainy weather grows still worse. On sunshiny days one is reminded of a sullen countenance constrained to smile against the will.

A 'Lancashire scene' has been said to resolve into 'bare hills and chimneys ;' and as regards the cotton districts the description is, upon the whole, not inaccurate. Chimneys predominate innumerably in the landscape, and from every summit there generally undulates a dark pennon—perhaps not pretty, but in any case a gladsome sight, since it means work, wages, food, for those below, and a fire upon

the hearth at home. Never mind the blackening of the marble statues ; the smoke denotes human happiness and content : when her chimneys are smokeless, working Lancashire is hungry and sad. Lancashire, it may be allowed here to remind the reader, is the only manufacturing district in England which depends entirely upon foreign countries for the supply of its raw material. The great distinction between England and other countries is that they send their natural produce away, usually as gathered together, England importing it, and working it up. How terribly the dependence in question was proved at the time of the Federal and Confederate war, all who were cognisant of the great Cotton Famine will remember. Next in order would come sugar and timber, a dearth of either of which would unquestionably be disastrous ; but not like want of cotton in Lancashire—the stranding of a whole community.

In the towns most of the chimneys belong to the factories—buildings of remarkable appearance. The very large ones are many storeys high, their broad and lofty fronts presenting tier upon tier of monotonous square windows. Decoration of an artistic kind seems to be studiously avoided, though there is often plenty of scope for inexpensive architectural effects that, to say the least, would be welcome. Seen by day, they are black ; after dark, when the innumerable windows are lighted up, the spectacle changes, and becomes unique. Were it desired to illuminate in honour of a prince, to render a factory more brilliant, from the interior, would be scarcely possible. Like all other great masses of masonry, the very large ones, though somewhat suggestive of prisons, if not grand, are impressive. In semi-rural localities, where less tarnished by smoke, especially when tolerably new, and not obscured by the contact of inferior buildings, they are certainly very fine objects. The material, it is scarcely needful to say, is red brick.

All the towns belonging to the Manchester family-circle present, more or less decidedly, the features mentioned. They differ from one another not in style, or habits, or physiognomy; the difference is simply that one makes calico, another muslins, and that they cover a less or greater extent of ground. Ancoats, the manufacturing portion of Manchester, supplies a fair index to the general character, wanting only the indications of superior taste and culture, as displayed in ornament, which render the villages, in turn, alone different in complexion, from the towns. The social, moral, and intellectual qualities of the various places form quite another subject of consideration. For the present it must wait; except with the remark that a Lancashire manufacturing town, however humble, is seldom without a lyceum, or some similar institution; and if wealthy, is prone to emulate cities. Witness the beautiful Art-exhibition held not long ago at Darwen!

The industrial history of the important Lancashire cotton-towns, although their modern development covers less than eighty years, dates from the beginning of the fourteenth century. As early as A.D. 1311, temp. Edward II., friezes were manufactured at Colne, but, as elsewhere in the country, they would seem to have been coarse and of little value. 'The English at that time,' says quaint old Fuller, 'knew no more what to do with their wool than the sheep that weare it, as to any artificial curious drapery.' The great bulk of the native produce of wool was transmitted to Flanders and the Rhenish provinces, where it was woven, England repurchasing the cloth. Edward III., under the inspiration of the incomparable Philippa, resolved that the manufacture should be kept at home. Parties of the Flemish weavers were easily induced to come over, the more so because wretchedly treated in their own country. Manchester, Bolton, Rochdale, and Warrington, were tenanted almost immediately, and a new character was at once given to the textile productions, both of the district and the island in general. Furness Abbey was then in its glory; its fertile pastures

supplied the wants of these industrious people: they seem, however, not to have cared to push their establishments so far, keeping in the south and east of the county, over which they gradually spread, carrying wherever they went, the 'merry music of the loom.' The same period witnessed the original use of coal,—except in so far as employed by the

Warrington. Dec 1880

Romans,—again, it is believed, through the sagacity of Philippa; the two great sources of Lancashire prosperity being thus, in their rise, contemporaneous. The numerous little rivers and waterfalls of East Lancashire contributed to the success of the new adventurers. Fulling-mills and dye-works were erected on the margins. The particular spots are now only conjectural; mementoes of these ancient works are nevertheless preserved in the springing up occasionally, to the present day, on the lower Lancashire river-banks, of plants botanically alien to the county. These are specially the Fullers' teasel, *Dipsacus Fullonum*, and the Dyers' weed, *Reseda Luteola*, both of which were regularly used in them, the refuse, with seeds, cast into the stream, being carried many miles down, and deposited where the plants now renew themselves. This ancient woollen manufacture endured for quite 300 years. Cotton then became a competitor, and gradually superseded it; Rochdale, and a few other places, alone vindicating to the present day the old traditions.

The Flemings also introduced the national *sabots*, from which have descended the wooden clogs heard in operative Lancashire wherever pavement allows of the clatter, only that while the *sabots* were wholly wooden, with a lining of lambskin, the Lancashire clogs have leathern tops.

In the writings of the period before us, and in others long afterwards, the Flemings' woollens are, by a curious prophecy, called 'cottonnes,' a circumstance which has led to much misapprehension as to the date of the original use in England of cotton *ipsissima*. In 1551-2, temp. Edward VI., an 'Acte' passed for the making of 'woollen clothe' prescribes the length and breadth of 'all and everie cottonnes called Manchester, Lancashire, and Cheshire cottonnes.' Leland, in the following reign, mentions in similar phrase, that 'divers villagers in the moores about Bolton do make cottons.' Genuine cotton fabrics manufactured abroad, were known in England, no doubt, though the raw material had not been seen. Chaucer habits his Knight in 'fustian,' a word which points to Spain as the probable source. The truth as regards the 'cottonnes' would seem to be that certain woollens were made so as to resemble cotton, and called by the same name, just as to-day certain calicoes are sold as 'imitation Irish.'

The employment of cotton for manufacturing in England is mentioned first in 1641, when it was accustomed to be brought to London from Cyprus and Smyrna. The word 'cotton' itself, we need hardly say, is of Oriental origin, taking one back to India, the old-world birthplace of the plant. Used there, as the clothing material, from time immemorial, it is singular that the movement westward should have been so slow. The people who introduced it, practically, to Europe, were the Moors, who in the tenth century cultivated cotton in old Granada, simultaneously with rice, the sugar-cane, and the orange-tree, all brought by themselves from Asia. In those days Moslems and Christians declined to be friendly, and thus, although the looms were never still, the superabundance of the manufacture went exclusively to Africa and the Levant. The cotton-plant being indigenous also to Mexico and the West Indies, when commerce arose with the latter, Cyprus and Smyrna no longer had the monopoly. Precise dates, however, are wanting till the first years of the

eighteenth century, when the United States and the Mersey of to-day had their prototype in Barbadoes and the Lune, already mentioned as having been a cotton port long anterior to Liverpool. Lancaster city is not accessible by ships. The cotton was landed either at Glasson, or upon the curious *lingula* which juts into the Irish Sea where the estuary disappears, and hither the country people used to come to wonder at it.* The first advertisement of a sale of cotton in Liverpool appeared, Mr. Picton says, in November 1758, but thirty years after that date Lancaster was still the principal Lancashire seat of import. One of the most distinguished of the 'Lancashire worthies,' old Mr. John Blackburne, of Orford Mount, near Warrington, an enthusiastic gardener, cultivated the cotton-plant to so great an extent that he was able to provide his wife with a muslin dress, the material derived wholly from the greenhouse he loved so fondly, and which was worn by Mrs. Blackburne in or about 1790. Strange, that except occasionally, in an engine-room, we scarcely ever see the cotton-plant in the county it has filled with riches—the very place where one would expect to find it cherished. How well would it occupy a few inches of the space so generally devoted to the pomps and vanities of mere colour-worship! Apart from the associations, it is beautiful; the leaves, though greatly diversified, resemble those of the grape-vine; the flowers are like single yellow roses.

The Lancashire cotton towns owe their existence essentially to the magic touch of modern mechanical art. During all the long procession of centuries that had elapsed since the time of the 'white-armed' daughter of Alcinous, her maidens, and their spinning-wheels, and of the swarthy weavers of ancient Egypt, the primæval modes of manufacture had been followed almost implicitly. The work of the Flemings themselves was little in advance of that of the Hebrews under Solomon. In comparison with that long period, the time covered by the change induced by machinery was but a moment, and the growth of the weaving communities, compared with that of previous times, like a lightning-flash. The movement commenced about 1760. Up till long after the time of Elizabeth, the staple manufacture of Lancashire, as we have seen, was woollen. Flax, in the sixteenth century, began to be imported largely, both from Ireland and the Continent, and when cotton at last arrived, the two materials were combined. Flax was used for the 'warp' or longitudinal threads, which in weaving require to be stronger than the 'woof,' while

---

* *Vide* the 'Autobiography of Wm. Stout,' the old Quaker, grocer, ironmonger, and general merchant of Lancaster. He mentions receiving cotton from Barbadoes in 1701, and onwards to 1725, when the price advanced 'from 10*d.* to near 2*s.* 1*d.* the lb.' Printed in 1851, under superintendence of John Harland, *vide* pp. 56, 62, 63.

cotton was employed only for the latter—technically the 'weft.'

Fabrics composed wholly of cotton do not appear to have been made in Lancashire before the time of George II., Bolton leading the way with cotton velvets about 1756. The cotton weft was spun by the people in their own cottages, chiefly by the women of the family, though as the century advanced, so greatly did the demand increase that, in one way or another, work was found not only for every adult, but for every child. Thus began 'infant labour,' afterwards so much abused. The employment of children over thirteen years of age in the modern factory is quite a different thing. Placed under legal restrictions, it is a blessing alike to themselves and to their parents, since if not there, the children now earning their bread would be idling, and probably in mischief. Those, it has been well said, who have to live by labour, should early be trained to labour. It is easy to be sentimental, but juvenile starvation and juvenile vagrancy are less good than juvenile wages, food and shelter. Diligent as they were, the spinsters could not produce weft fast enough for the weavers. Sitting at their looms, which

THE DINNER HOUR.

were also in the cottages, thoughtful men pondered the possibilities of quicker methods. Presently the dream took shape, and from the successive inventions of Whyatt, Kay, Highs, and Hargreaves, emerged the famous 'spinning-jenny,' * a machine which did as much work in the same time as a dozen pair of hands. Abreast of it came the warping-mill, the carding-engine, the drawing-frame, and the roving-frame, the latter particularly opportune, since the difficulty had

always been to disentangle the fibres of the cotton prior to twisting, and to lay them exactly parallel. Arkwright now came on the scene. He himself never invented anything ; but he had marvellous powers of combination, such as enabled him to assimilate all that was good in the ideas of other men, and to give them unity and new vitality. The result was machinery that gave exquisite evenness and attenuation to the 'rovings ;' and a patent being granted, July 15, 1769, Arkwright is very properly regarded as the founder of the modern modes of manufacture.

Arkwright possessed, in addition, a thoroughly feminine capacity for good management and perseverance, with that most excellent adjunct, the art of obtaining ascendancy over capitalists. Among the immediate results were the disuse of linen warps, the new frames enabling cotton warp to be made strong enough, and the concentration of all the early processes, spinning included, in special buildings, with employment of horse or water-power. The weaving, however, long remained with the cottagers, and even at the present day, the hand-loom may be found at work, though not upon calicos. There are articles, such as certain kinds of counterpanes, which, in Bolton and elsewhere, are, for various reasons, woven in the ancient way. The Lancashire cotton manufacture, strictly so called, is thus very little more than a century old. No further back than in 1774, fabrics made wholly of cotton were declared by statute to have been 'lately introduced,' and a 'lawful and laudable manufacture.'

The following year, 1775, saw the perfecting of Crompton's celebrated 'mule,' which produced, at less expense, a much finer and softer yarn even than Arkwright's. It was specially suitable for muslins ; and from this date, most assuredly, should be reckoned the elevation of the manufacture to its highest platform. Like the jenny, it was much

---

* That the spinning-jenny was so named after a wife or daughter of one of the inventors is fiction. The original wheel was the 'jenny,' a term corresponding with others well known in Lancashire, the 'peggy' and the 'dolly,' and the new contrivance became the '*spinning*-jenny.'

used, at first, in private houses, but a nobler application was close at hand—a new revolution—the superseding of hand, and horse, and water power, all at
one moment, by Steam. Had the former remained
the only artificial sources of help—even supposing
rivers and brooks not subject to negation by drought,
the cotton manufacture must needs have been confined within narrow limits, and the greatest conceivable supply of the raw material would not have
altered the case. Steam, which, like Lord Chatham,
'tramples upon impossibilities,' at once gave absolute
freedom ; and manufacturing, in the space of thirty
years, eclipsed its history during 3000. The 'mule'
was now transferred to the mill, and the factory
system became complete. Power-looms were first
employed in Manchester in 1806. Stockport followed,
and by degrees they became general, improvements
going on up till as late as 1830, when the crowning
triumph of cotton machinery was patented as the
'self-acting mule.' The pride of Lancashire, it must
be remembered, consists, after all, not in the delicacy
and the beauty of its cottons, for in these respects
India has not yet been out-run ; but in the rapidity, the cheapness, and the boundless poten-
tialities of the manufacture, which enable it to meet,
if called upon, the requirements of every nation in
the world. While any human creature remains imperfectly clad, Lancashire still has its work to do.
To be entrusted with this great business is a privilege,
and in the honourable execution consists its true and
essential glory. 'Over-production,' while any are
naked, is a phrase without meaning. That which
wants correcting is deficient absorption.

Reviewing the whole matter, the specially interesting point—rendered so through inciting to profoundest reflection—is that those poor and unlettered
men, Hargreaves, Arkwright, Crompton, and the
others, were the instruments, under Providence (for
such things do not happen fortuitously), by which
the world became possessed of an entirely new industrial power, fraught with infinite capacities for
promoting human welfare; and which, in its application, introduced quite new styles of thinking and
reasoning, and gave new bias to the policy of a great
nation. They had no prescience of what would come
of their efforts. In no part of the transformation was
there any precedent or example; it had neither
lineage nor inheritance ; it was anticipated in mo-
mentousness only by the inventions of Caxton and
Gioia ; * and if in our own day the electric telegraph
and the telephone reveal natural laws scarcely distinguishable from those of miracle, it may still be
questioned if these latter discoveries surpass in intrinsic value the three or four that gave life to the
modern cotton manufacture.

_____

* Inventor of the mariners' compass.

The interior of a great cotton factory, when at
work, presents a spectacle altogether unimaginable.
The vast area of the rooms, or 'flats,' filled in every
part with machinery, admits of no comparison with
anything else in England, being found in the factory
alone. A thousand great iron frames, exquisitely
composite, and kept fastidiously clean, some by self-
acting dusters, are in simultaneous movement, the
arms of some rising and falling, while parts of others
march in and out, and to and fro, giving perfect
illustrations of order, reciprocal adaptation, and
interdependence, and seeming not only alive, but
conscious. Nothing is more striking, perhaps, than
to watch the shuttles as they dart alternately right
and left, every movement meaning an added thread
to the beautiful offspring. The poets are supposed by
some to concern themselves only with fiction. They
are poets only when they deal with Truth, though
presented in the garb of fable ; and assuredly, for a
poet's theme, there is nothing to excel a skilfully
conducted human manufacture. Darwin, it will be
remembered, describes the whole series of processes
in connexion with cotton as observed by him in
Arkwright's original factory upon the Derwent.

A common practice is to have the looms in a
'shed' upon the surface of the ground. To be as
near the earth as possible is a desire no less with the
spinner, who like the weaver, finds the lower atmo-
spheric conditions much more favourable to his work
than the upper. In any case, where the power-looms
are, long lines of slender pillars support the roof,
presenting an unbroken, and almost endless, perspective ; and between the machinery and the ceiling,
connected with the horizontal shafts which revolve just
below it, are innumerable strong brown leather straps,
that quiver as they run their courses. According to
the department we may be in, either threads, or coils
of cotton, whiter than pearl, and of infinite number,
give occupation to those thousand obedient and tireless slaves—not of the ring or the lamp, but of the
mighty engine that invisibly is governing the whole ;
and in attendance are men and women, boys and
girls, again beyond the counting. Their occupations
are in no degree laborious: all the heavy work is
done by the steam-engine ; muscular power is not
wanted so much as delicacy and readiness of hand
and finger. Hence, in the factory and the cotton-
mill, there is opportunity for those who are too weak
for other vocations :—machinery, in all cases, has the
merit of at once increasing the workman's wages, and
lessening his fatigue. The precision in the working
of the machinery enforces upon those who attend to
it a corresponding regularity of action. There is no
re-twisting or re-weaving ; everything, if done at all,
must be done properly and at the proper moment.
Apart from its being a place wherein to earn, credit-
ably, the daily bread, if there be anything in the

world which conduces pre-eminently to the acquisition of habits such as lie at the foundation of good morals—order, care, cleanliness, punctuality, industry, early rising,—assuredly it is the wholesome discipline of the well-ordered Cotton Factory. Whatever may befall *outside*, there is nothing deleterious *inside;* the personal intercourse of the people employed is itself reduced to a minimum ; if they corrupt one another,

particular, are not unhappy is shown by their preference of the cotton-mill to domestic service. Their health is as good as that of any other class of operatives ; and though they have to keep upon their feet, it is not for so long a time as young women in city shops. Of course, there is a shadowy side to life identified with the factory. The hands do not live in Elysium, any more than the agricultural labourer

IN A COTTON FACTORY.

it is as people not in factories do. In the rooms and 'sheds' devoted to weaving, the rattle of the machinery forbids even conversation, except when the voice is adjusted to it. In the quieter parts, the girls show their contentedness, not unfrequently, by singing. 'How often,' says the living type of the true Lancashire poet, most genial of his race—Edwin Waugh,—'how often have I heard some fine psalm-tune streaming in chorus from female voices, when passing cotton-mills at work, and mingling with the spoom of thousands of spindles.' That the girls, in

does in Arcadia. The masters, as everywhere else, are both good and bad ; in the aggregate they are no worse than their fellows in other places, and to expect them to be better would be premature. In case of grievance or abuse, there is an 'Inspector' to apply to for remedy. The wages are as good as those earned by any other large class of English workpeople ; and if the towns in which so many thousands abide are unlovely, the Lancashire cotton-operatives at all events know little or nothing of the vice and filth of metropolitan St. Giles'.

IV.

Manchester.

THE writer of the entertaining article in the 'Cornhill' for February 1880, upon 'The Origin of London,' shows that had the choice of the best site for a capital to be made *now,* and for the first time, the selection would naturally fall upon south-east Lancashire, and on the particular spot covered by modern Manchester. Geographically, as the author points out, it is the centre of the three kingdoms; and its advantageousness in regard to commerce, all things considered, is paramount. These facts alone suffice to give interest to the locality; and that the town itself should have acquired the importance now possessed, in some respects almost metropolitan, looks not so much like accident or good fortune as the fulfilment of a law of Nature. The locality in question is by no means picturesque or even pretty. The ground, as said before, is, on the Cheshire side, and westwards, nearly level, the country being here bordered by the Mersey, a river, as Pennant long ago observed, utterly devoid, along its course, of the charms usually identified with fairly broad and winding streams. At Northen there are some pleasant shaded pathways, with willows and poplars like those upon which *Œnone* was carved; but the bank, if raised, is artificial, with a view to protecting the adjacent fields from inundation in time of floods, such as occur not infrequently—the Mersey being formed, in the beginning, by the confluence of several minor streams, which gather their waters from the moors and the Derbyshire hills.

At a few miles' distance in other directions, or receding from the Mersey, the ground becomes slightly elevated, and in parts agreeably broken, as at Prestwich, and near Heywood, where there are innumerable little dells and ravines, ferny and filled with trees. These are a pleasant change after the flatness on the Cheshire side, but are too far away to be called Manchester. To the Mersey Manchester makes no claim:—three other rivers are distinctly its own—the Irwell, which divides the town from Salford, with its tributaries, the Medlock and the Irk; and of these, though the colour is inexpressible, it is proud, since no three rivers in the world do harder work. All three pass their earlier life in valleys which in the bygones must have been delightful, and in some parts romantic. Traditions exist to this day of the times when in their upper reaches they were 'silver-eddied.' For a long distance before entering, and all the way while passing through, they have now for many years been converted into scavengers; the trout, once so plentiful, are extinct; there are water-rats instead. This, perhaps, is inevitable in a district which, though once green and tranquil, has been transformed into an empire of workshops.

The Manchester rivers do not stand alone in their illustration of what can be accomplished by the defiling energy of 'Works.' In the strictly manufacturing parts of South Lancashire it would be difficult to find a single watercourse of steady volume that any longer 'makes music with the enamelled stones.' Julia,* to-day, would be impelled less to charming similes than to epitaphs; no sylvan glade, however hidden, if there be water in it, has escaped the visitation of the tormentors. Are we, then, to murmur?—to feel as if robbed? By no means. Nothing can be regretful that is inseparable from the conditions of the industry and the prosperity of a great nation. A couple of hours' railway journey enables any one to listen to the 'liquid lapse' of streams clear and bright as Cherith. Everything lovely has its place of safety somewhere. However doleful the destiny of the South Lancashire streams, a thousand others that can never be sullied await us at a little distance.

Little can be said in praise of the Manchester climate, and that little, it must be confessed, however reluctantly, is only negative. The physicians are not more prosperous than elsewhere, and the work of the Registrar-general is no heavier. On the other hand, the peach and the apricot cannot ripen, and there is an almost total absence of the cheerful evergreens one is accustomed to see in the southern counties,—the ilex, to wit, the bay, the arbutus, and the laurustinus. In the flourishing of these consists the true test of geniality of climate; rhododendrons and gay flower-gardens, both of which Manchester possesses in plenty, certify nothing. Not that the climate is positively cold, though as a rule, damp and rainy.

---

* 'Two Gentlemen of Verona,' II., 7.

Snow is often seen in the Midlands, when in Manchester there is none. The special feature, again negative, is deficiency of bright, warm, encouraging sunshine. Brilliant days come at times, and sultry ones ; but often for weeks together, even in summer, so misty is the atmosphere, that where the sun should be in view, except for an hour or two, there is only a luminous patch.

The history of Manchester dates, the authorities tell us, from the time of the 'ancient Britons.' There is no need to go so far back. The genuine beginnings of our English cities and large towns coincide with the establishment of the Roman power. They may have been preceded, in many instances, by entrenched and perhaps rudely ramparted clusters of huts, but it is only upon civilisation that a 'town' arises. Laying claim, quite legitimately, to be one of the eight primitive Lancashire towns founded by Agricola, A.D. 79, its veritable age, to be exact, is 1802 years, or nearly the same as that of Warrington, where the invaders, who came from Chester, found the river fordable, as declared in the existing name of the Cheshire suburb, and where they fixed their original Lancashire stronghold. What is thought to have happened in Manchester during their stay may be read in Whitaker. The only traces remaining of their ancient presence are some fragments of the ' road ' which led northwards, over the present Kersal Moor, and which are commemorated in the names of certain houses at Higher Broughton. The fact in the local history which connects the living present with the past, is that the De Traffords of Trafford Hall possess lands held by their ancestor in the time of Canute. How it came to pass that they were not displaced by some Norman baron, an ingenious novelist may be able perhaps to tell. Private policy, secret betrothals, doubtless lay in the heart of as many adjustments of the eleventh century, as behind many enigmas of the nineteenth. The Traffords reside close to ' Throstlenest,' a name occurring frequently in Lancashire, where the spirit of poetry has always been vigorous, and never more marked than in appellations having reference to the simple beauty of unmolested nature. At Moston there is also Throstle-glen, one of the haunts, half a century ago, of Samuel Bamford. At the time spoken of the county was divided into 'tithe-shires.' The ' Hundred of Salford ' was called ' Salford-shire,' and in this last was included Manchester ; so that whatever dignity may accrue therefrom belongs properly to the town across the river, which was the first, moreover, to be constituted a free borough, receiving its charter in the time of Henry III., who died in 1272, whereas the original Manchester charter was not granted till 1301. To all practical intents and purposes, the two places now constitute a social and commercial unity. Similar occupations are pursued in both, and the intercourse is as constant as that of the people who dwell on the opposite sides of the Thames.

The really important date in the history of Manchester is that of the arrival of the Flemish weavers, in the reign of Edward III. Though referable in the first instance, as above mentioned, to the action of the king and the far-seeing Philippa, their coming to Manchester seems to have been specially promoted by the feudal ruler of the time—De la Warre, heir of the De Grelleys, and predecessor of De Lacy— men all of great distinction in old Manchester records. Leading his retainers to the field of battle, De la Warre literally, when all was over, turned the spear into the pruning-hook, bringing home with him some of these industrious people, and with their help converting soldiers into useful artisans. A wooden church had been erected, at a very early period, upon the sandstone cliff by the river, where the outlook was pleasant on the meadows and the arriving Irk. By 1422, so much had the town increased, it sufficed no longer, and then was built the noble and beautiful ' cathedral ' of to-day, the body of which is thus now nearly 460 years old.[*]

Up till 1656, the windows of this fine church, in conformity with the delightful principles of all first-class Plantagenet and Tudor ecclesiastical architecture, were coloured and pictorial ;—the design being that they should represent to the congregation assembled inside some grand or touching Scripture incident, making palpable to the eye what the ear might be slow to apprehend. In the year mentioned they were broken to pieces by the Republicans, one of the reasons, perhaps, why the statue of Cromwell—the dark and gloomy figure in the street close by—has been so placed as for the ill-used building to be behind it. While the church was in its full beauty, the town was visited by Leland.

' Manchestre,' he tells us, was at that period (temp. Henry VIII.), ' the fairest, best-builded, quikkest, and most populous Tounne of Lancastreshire ' (v. 78). Whatever the precise comparative meaning of ' fairest and best-builded,' there can be no doubt that in Leland's time, and for a long subsequent period, Manchester was rich in pretty houses of the Elizabethan type, including many old halls occupied by families of note. The greater number of these would be ' magpie,' or wood and plaster fronted, in black and white, the patterns, though simple, often very elegant, as indicated in relics which have only lately disappeared ; and in the glorious old country halls of the same period, still perfect, which we shall come to by-and-by. The

---

[*] The original tower remained till 1864, when, being considered insecure, it was taken down, and the existing *facsimile* erected in its place.

style of the inferior kind is shown in an old tavern, the 'Seven Stars,' in Withy Grove.

At the commencement of the Civil Wars, Manchester was important enough to be a scene of heavy contest. The sympathies of the town, as a whole, were with the Parliament; not in antagonism to royalty, but because of the suspicion that Charles secretly befriended Popery. It was the same belief which estranged Bolton,—a place never in heart disloyal, so long as the ruler does his own part in faithfulness and honour. Standing in the Cathedral graveyard, it is hard to imagine that the original of the bridge now called the 'Victoria' was once the scene of a deadly struggle, troops filling the graveyard itself. Here, however, it was that the severest assault was made by the Royalists, unsuccessfully, as were all the other attacks, though Manchester never possessed a castle, nor even regularly constructed fortifications.

The town was then 'a mile in length,' and the streets were '*open and clean*.' Words change their meaning with lapse of time, and the visitor who in 1650 thus describes them, may have been given a little to overpraise; but if Manchester deserved such epithets, alas for the condition of the streets elsewhere! As the town increased in size, the complexion may also, very possibly, have deteriorated. The fact remains, that after the lapse of another 150 years, say in 1800, it was inexpressibly mean and common, continuing so, in a very considerable degree, up to a period quite recent. People who know Manchester only as it looks to-day, can form no conception of the beggarly appearance of most of the central part no further back than during the reign of George IV., Her Majesty's uncle. Several years after he came to the throne, where Market Street now is, there was only a miserable one-horse lane, with a foot-path of less than twenty-four inches. Narrow

'entries' led to adjacent 'courts.' Railed steps led down to cellars, which were used as front parlours. The shops were dark and low-browed; of ornament there was not a scrap. Mosley Street, King Street, and one or two others, comparatively modern, presented, no doubt, a very decided contrast. Still, it was without the slightest injustice, that so late as in or about 1845, the late Mr. Cobden described Manchester as the shabbiest city in Europe for its wealth. That the town needed some improvement is indicated rather suggestively by the fact, that between 1832 and 1861 the authorities paved, drained, and flagged the footways of no fewer than 1578 streets, measuring upwards of sixty miles in length. Many of them, certainly, were new, but the great mass of the gracious work was retrospective. These matters are worth recalling, since it is only by comparison with the past that modern Manchester can be appreciated.

MANCHESTER CATHEDRAL.

Shortly after the Restoration there was a considerable influx, as into Liverpool, from the surrounding country; and by 1710 again had the population so much increased that a second church became necessary, and St. Anne's was erected, cornfields giving place to the 'Square.' St. Anne's being the 'new' church, the existing one was thenceforwards distinguished as the 'old.'* Commerce shortly afterwards received important stimulus by the Irwell being made navigable to its point of confluence with the Mersey, and by the erection of the original Exchange. In 1757 Warrington, the first town in Lancashire to publish a newspaper, was imitated in the famous old 'Manchester Mercury.' Then came the splendid inventions above described, upon which quickly arose the modern cotton

---

* St. Anne's was so named in compliment to the queen then on the throne. 'St. Ann's,' like 'Market-*Street* Lane,' came of carelessness or something worse.

manufacture. In 1771 a Bank and Insurance Office were found necessary, and in less than a year afterwards the renowned 'Jones Loyds' had its beginning. Social and intellectual movements were accelerated by the now fast developing Manchester trade. Liverpool had founded a Subscription Library in 1758: Manchester followed suit in 1765. In 1781 a Literary and Philosophical Society was set on foot, and in 1792 Assembly Rooms were built.

New streets were now laid out—to-day, so vast has been the subsequent growth, embedded in the heart of the town—the names often taken from those of the metropolis, as Cannon Street, Pall Mall, Cheapside, and Spring Gardens, and at a little later period Bond Street and Piccadilly, previously called 'Lever's Row.' Factories sprang up in not a few of the principal thoroughfares : perhaps it would be more correct to say that the building of factories often led to the formation of new streets. The kind of variety they conferred on the frontages is declared to the present day in Oxford Road. Similar buildings, though not so large, existed till very lately where now not a vestige of them remains. The 'Manchester and Salford Bank' occupies the site of a once famous silk-mill.

ST. ANNE'S SQUARE, MANCHESTER.

Gathering round them the inferior class of the population—the class unable to move into pleasanter neighbourhoods when the town is relished no longer—it is easy to understand how in most parts of Manchester that are fifty years old, splendour and poverty are never far asunder. In London, Bath, Leicester, it is possible to escape from the sight of rags and squalor: in Manchester they are within a bow-shot of everything upon which the town most prides itself. The circumstance referred to may be accounted for, perhaps, in part, by the extreme density of the population, which exceeds that of all other English manufacturing towns, and is surpassed only in Liverpool. Manchester, it may be added, has no 'court-end.' When the rich took flight they dispersed themselves in all directions. They might well depart. The reputation of the Manchester atmosphere in respect of vapours, not translucent, and of 'smuts,' that like the rain in Shelley are 'falling for ever,' is only too well deserved ; and despite of legal enactments, it is to be feared, inalienable.

Architecturally, modern Manchester is distinguished by the two magnificent buildings erected, quite recently, in the Gothic style. Classical models were followed up till about 1860, as in the original Town Hall (1822–25)—now the City Free Library ; the Royal Institution, the Concert Hall (1825–30), and the Corn Exchange—one of the happiest efforts of a man of real ability, the late Mr. Richard Lane, whose work, however, constantly reminds one of Stuart's book upon ancient Athens. The very gracefully designed Tudor buildings at Old Trafford, well known as the Asylums for the Blind and the Deaf and Dumb, were erected in 1838. After Mr. Lane, the town was fortunate in possessing Mr. Walters, since it was he who introduced artistic details into warehouse fronts, previously to his time bald and vacant as the face of a cotton-mill. Very interesting examples of the *primitive* Manchester warehouse style are extant in Peel Street and thereabouts. Manchester is now employed in rebuilding itself, to a considerable extent, under the inspiration received originally from Mr. Walters, and here and there very elegantly. Would that his impress could have been seen upon the whole of the newly-contrived ! We should then have been spared the not uncommon spectacle of the grotesque, to say nothing of the grimaces of the last year or two. The whole of the improvement in Manchester street architecture has been effected since 1840. Four-fifths of all the meritorious public buildings, the modern banks, and nearly all the ecclesiastical architecture that deserves the name, may be referred to the same period.

The two fine new Gothic structures are the Assize Courts and the new Town hall, both designed by Mr. Waterhouse. The former were completed in 1866, but not used till July 1868, three months after which time the first stone was laid of the superb pile in Albert Square. The gilt ball at the apex of the tower, 286 feet high, was fixed January 4th, 1876. The dimensions of this splendid structure may be imagined from the number of separate apartments (314), mostly spacious, and approached, as far as possible, by corridors, which are as well proportioned as elaborate in finish. The cost up to September 15th, 1877, when much remained to be done, including nearly the whole of the internal decoration, was 751,532*l*. In designing the coloured windows Mr. Waterhouse is said to have had the assistance of a lady. Without pressing for the secret, it is undeniable that the tints are blended with a sense of delicate harmony purely feminine. Some people prefer the Assize Courts—a glorious building, peculiarly distinguished for its calmness. Structures of such character cannot possibly correspond. Perhaps it may be allowed to say that the Assize Courts seem to present in greater perfection the unity of feeling indispensable to all great works of art, however varied and fanciful the details. Due regard being paid to the intrinsic fitness of things and their moral significance, which in Art, when aspiring to the perfect, should always be a prime consideration, it may be inquired, after all, whether Gothic is the legitimate style for municipal offices. We cannot here discuss the point. Liverpool would have to be heard upon the other side. Better, in any case, to have a Gothic Town hall than to see churches and chapels copy the temples devoted a couple of thousand years ago to the deities of pagan Greece and Rome. It is not pleasant on a Sunday forenoon to be reminded of Venus, Apollo, and Diana. The new Owens College buildings, Oxford Road, are early fourteenth century Gothic, and when complete will present one of the finest groups of the kind in England. The architect (Mr. Waterhouse), it has been well said, has here as elsewhere, 'not fettered himself with ancient traditions, but endeavoured to make his learning a basis rather than a limit of thought.' The fine Corinthian portico of the new Exchange throws into curious and very unexpected contrast the remarkable tower at the corner nearest Victoria Street. Many of the new Gothic churches have been ornamented with lofty and very well proportioned spires. One of the most chaste and harmonious, as well as spacious, ecclesiastical interiors in the north of England, awaits the visitor to the comparatively new Catholic 'Church of the Holy Name,' a few steps beyond the Owens College.

Manchester is much less of a manufacturing town at present, in proportion to its extent, and the entire breadth of its business life, than when the cotton trade was young. Now, as described in the preceding chapter, the towns and villages outside are all devoted to spinning and weaving. While Liverpool is one great wharf, the middle of Manchester is one great warehouse, a reservoir for the production of the whole district. The trade falls under two principal heads—the Home and the Export. In either case the produce of the looms, wherever situate, is bought just as it flows from them—rough, or, technically, 'in the grey.' It is then put into the hands of bleachers, dyers, or printers, according to requirement, and afterwards handed to auxiliaries called 'makers-up.' Very interesting is it to observe, in going through a great warehouse, not only how vast is the quantity waiting transfer, but how differently the various fabrics have to be folded and ornamented, so as to meet the taste of the nations and foreign countries they are intended for. Some prefer the absolutely plain; others like little pictures; some want bright colours, and embellishment with gold and silver. The uniformity of the general business of Manchester allowed of agreement, in November 1843, to shut all doors upon Saturdays at one o'clock. The warehouse half-holiday movement soon became universal, and now, by four or five p.m. on Saturdays large portions of the middle of the town are as quiet as upon Sundays.

The composition of the Manchester community is extremely miscellaneous. A steady influx of newcomers from all parts of Great Britain—Scotland very particularly—has been in progress for eighty or ninety years, and seems likely to continue. Not very long ago the suburb called Greenheys was regarded as a German colony. Many Levantine Greeks have also settled in Manchester, and of Jews the estimated number in September 1879 was ten thousand. Notwithstanding the influence which these new-comers have almost necessarily, though undesignedly, brought to bear upon the general spirit of the town, the original Lancashire character is still prominent, though greatly modified, both for the better and the worse. Primitive Lancashire is now confined perhaps to Rossendale, where, after all, it would be felt that Manchester is the better place to live in. The people were distinguished of old by industry and intense frugality, the women in particular being noted for their thrift. They were enterprising, vigilant, shrewd, and possessed of marvellous aptitude for business: they had judgment, and the capacity for minute and sleepless care which is quite as needful as courage to success in life, and which to many a man has been better capital to start with than a well-filled purse. Hence the countless instances in South Lancashire of men who, additionally fortunate in being born at the favourable moment, though at first earning wages of perhaps fifteen shillings a-week as porters or mill-hands, rose by degrees to opulence, and in many cases laid the foundations of families now in the front rank of local importance. Considering the general history, it is easy to understand why carriage-heraldry, except of the purchaseable kind, is scanty, and not difficult to account for the pervading local shyness as to pedigrees and genealogies. Curiously in contrast, one of the very rare instances of an untitled family having supporters to the heraldic shield is found in Ashton-under-Lyne, Mr. Coulthart, the banker, being entitled to them by virtue of descent from one of the

affectations, or less given to assumption of qualities they did not possess. If sometimes startled by their impetuosities, we can generally trust to their candour and whole-heartedness, especially when disposed to be friendly, the more so since they are little inclined to pay compliments, and not at all to flatter.

That men of small beginnings, and who have had little or no real education, are apt, on becoming rich, to be irritable, jealous, and overbearing, is true, perhaps, everywhere : in Lancashire it has been

DEANSGATE, MANCHESTER.

ancient Scottish kings. To a Lancashire magnate of the old school it was sufficient that he was *himself*. The disposition is still locally vigorous, and truly many of the living prove that to be so, when honourable, is a man's best recommendation. None of the excellent attributes possessed by, for instance, the original Peels and Ainsworths have disappeared, though it cannot be denied that in other cases there has been inheritance of the selfish habits, contracted ideas, and coarsely-moulded character, so often met with in men who have risen from the ranks. Given to saying and doing the things natural to them, no people were ever more devoid than the genuine Lancashire men, as they are still, of frigid

observed, with satisfaction, that the exceptions are more numerous than the rule. Whatever the stint and privations in the morning of life, these, it has again been observed, have seldom led to miserly habits when old. Most of the modern Lancashire wealthy (or their fathers, at all events, before them) began with a trifle. Hence the legitimate pride they take in their commercial belongings—a genuine Lancashire man would rather you praised his mill or warehouse than his mansion. So far from becoming miserly, no one in the world deteriorates less. Most Lancashire capitalists are well aware that it is no credit to a man of wealth to be in arrears with the public, and when money is wanted for some noble purpose are quick in response. This, however, represents them but imperfectly. Of a thousand it might be said with as much truth as of the late Sir Benjamin Heywood, the eminent Manchester banker, ' He dared to trust God with his charities, and without a witness, and *risk the consequences.*' So much for the Lancashire heart; though on many of its excellent attributes, wanting space, we have not touched. The prime characteristic of the *head* seems to consist, not in the preponderance of any particular faculty, but in the good working order of the faculties in general; so that the whole can be brought to bear at once upon whatever is taken in hand.*

The Lancashire man has plenty of faults and weaknesses. His energy is by no means of that admirable kind which is distinguished by never degenerating into restlessness; neither in disputes is he prone to courtly forbearance. Sincerity, whether in friend or foe, he admires, nevertheless; whence the exceptional toleration in Lancashire of all sorts of individual opinions. Possessed of good, old-fashioned common-sense, when educated and reflective he is seldom astray in his estimate of the essentially worthy and true; so that, however novel occasionally his action, we may be pretty sure that underneath it there is some definite principle of equity. Manchester put forth the original programme of the 'free and open church' system; and from one of the suburbs came the first cry for the enfranchisement of women. Lancashire, if nothing else, is frank, cordial, sagacious, and given to the sterling humanities of life. These always revolve upon Freedom, whence, yet again in illustration of the Lancashire heart, the establishment of the Society (original in idea, if not unique) for the Preservation of Ancient Foot-paths.† The large infusion of the German element has been immensely beneficial, not only in relation to commerce, but to the general culture of the town. It is owing in no slight degree to the presence of the educated Germans that the Manchester 'shippers,' in their better portion, now resemble the corresponding class in Liverpool. The change for the better, since the time when Coleridge met with his odd reception, is quite as marked, no doubt, among the leaders of the Home commerce, in whose ranks are plenty of peers of the Liverpool 'gentlemen.' Records of the past are never

without their interest. During the siege, the command of the defence was in the hands of Col. Rosworm, a celebrated German engineer, who, when all was over, considered himself ill-used, and published a pamphlet complaining of the town's injustice, enumerating the opportunities he had had of betraying it to the Royalists, and of dividing the inhabitants against themselves. 'But then,' he adds, 'I should have been a Manchester man, for never let an unthankful one, or a promise-breaker, bear another name!' On the title-page of 'The Pole Booke for Manchester, May 22nd, 1690,' an old list of the inhabitants, printed by the Chetham Society, the aforetime owner has written, 'Generation of vipers!'

Manchester is now, like Liverpool, if not a school of refinement, one of the principal seats of English culture. It possesses not fewer than ten or twelve fine libraries, including the branches of the Free or City Library, established under Mr. Ewart's Act, which last are available on Sundays, and are freely used by the class of people the opening was designed to benefit. The staff of assistants at the City Library and its branches consists very largely of young women. There is another first-class Free Library in Salford, with, in the same building, a fine Free Gallery of Paintings, and an admirably planned and thoroughly useful Museum, superintended by Mr. Plant. The 'Athenæum' provides its members with 60,000 newspapers per annum, and, in addition, 9500 weekly, and 500 monthly and quarterly magazines. Societies devoted to science, literature, and the Fine Arts, exist, as in Liverpool, in plenty. The exhibitions of paintings at the Royal Institution have always been delightful, and never better than during the last two or three years, when on Sunday afternoons they have been thrown open to the public *gratis*. The Institution has now been handed over to the city authorities, and before long will be the seat of a long-wanted Permanent Art-gallery. The 'School of Design,' founded in October 1838, now called the 'School of Art,' and having for its head-master the distinguished flower-painter, Mr. Wm. Jabez Mückley, has just provided itself with a handsome new building in Grosvenor Square, the pupils numbering 377. There is also a Society expressly of 'Women Painters,' the works of many of whom have earned honourable places. In addition to its learned societies, Manchester stands alone, perhaps, among English cities, in having at least seven or eight set on foot purely with a view to rational enjoyment in the fields, the observation of Nature in its most pleasing and suggestive forms, and the obtaining accurate knowledge of its details— the birds, the trees, and the wild-flowers. The oldest of these is the 'Field-Naturalists and Archæologists,' founded in 1860. The members of the youngest go by the name of the 'Grasshoppers.' Flower-shows, again, are a great feature in Manchester; some held in

---

* For delineations of local and personal character in full we look to the novelists. After supreme ' Scarsdale,' and the well-known tales by Mrs. Gaskell and Mrs. Banks, may be mentioned, as instructive in regard to Lancashire ways and manners, ' Coultour's Factory,' by Miss Emily Rodwell, and the first portion of Mr. Hirst's ' Hiram Greg.' Lord Beaconsfield's admirable portrait of Millbank, the Lancashire manufacturer, given in ' Coningsby,' in 1844, had for its original the late Mr. Edmund Ashworth, of Turton, whose mills had been visited by the author, then Mr. Disraeli, the previous year.

† Founded in 1826. See the interesting particulars in Mr. Prentice's ' Historical Sketches and Personal Recollections,' pp. 289-295. 1851.

the Town hall, others in the Botanical Gardens. In 1880 there were no fewer than nine, and as many more were provided in the immediately surrounding district. In August 1881, the greatest and richest Horticultural Exhibition of which there is record was held at Old Trafford, in the gardens, lasting five days, and with award in prizes of upwards of 2000*l*. It was laid out within a few yards of the ground occupied in 1857 by the celebrated Fine Art Treasures Exhibition, the only one of the kind ever attempted in England, and no less brilliant to the visitor than creditable to the promoters. No single spot of earth has ever been devoted to illustrations so exquisite of the most beautiful forms of living nature, and of the artistic talent of man.

Music is cultivated in Manchester with a zest quite proportionate to its value. The original 'Gentlemen's Concert Club' was founded as far back as the year of alarm, 1745. The local love of glees and madrigals preserves the best traditions of the Saxon 'glee-men.' On March 10th, 1881, the veteran Charles Hallé, who quite recently had been earning new and glorious laurels at Prague, Vienna, and Pesth, led the *five hundredth* of his great concerts in the Free-trade Hall. 'Our town,' remarked the 'Guardian,' 'in its next day's report of the proceedings, 'is at present the city of music, *par excellence*, in England. . . . The outside world knows three things of Manchester— that it is a city of cotton, a city of economic ideas, and a city of music. Cobden was, perhaps, the first who made all the world see that Manchester had a turn for the things of the mind as well as for the production of calico and the making of money. Similarly, Mr. Hallé has made it evident to all the world that there is here a public which can appreciate the best art expressed in the best way.' It is but fair to the sister city to add that the first musical festival in the north of England was held in Liverpool in 1784, and that the erection of St. George's Hall had its germ in the local musical tastes and desire for their full expression.

A good deal might be said in regard to the religious and ecclesiastical history of Manchester, a curious fact in connexion with which is, that between 1798 and 1820, though the population had augmented by 80,000, nothing was done on their behalf by the Episcopate. The Wesleyan body dates from May 7, 1747, when its founder preached at Salford Cross, a little apartment in a house on the banks of the Irwell, where there were hand-looms, being insufficient to accommodate the congregation assembled to hear him. The literary history of Manchester is also well worthy of extended treatment; and, above all, that of local thought and private spirit, the underlying current which has rendered the last sixty years a period of steady and exemplary advance. To some it may seem a mere coincidence, a part only of the general progress of the country; but advance, whether local or national, implies impetus received; and assuredly far more than simple coincidence is involved in the great reality that the growth of the town in all goodly respects, subsequently to the uprise of the cotton trade, has been exactly contemporaneous with the life and influence of the newspaper just quoted — the 'Manchester Guardian'—the first number of which was published May 5, 1821.

TOWN HALL, MANCHESTER. *By T. Riley*

V.

Miscellaneous Industrial Occupations.

LANCASHIRE is not only the principal seat of the English cotton manufacture. Over and above the processes which are auxiliary to it, and complete it, many are carried on of a nature altogether independent, and upon a scale so vast as again to give this busy county the pre-eminence. The mind is arrested not more by the variety than by the magnitude of Lancashire work. Contemplating the inexpressible activity, all directed to a common end, one cannot but recall the famous description of the building of Carthage, with the simile which makes it vivid for all ages. Like all other manifold work, it presents also its amusing phases. In Manchester there are professional 'knockers-up'—men whose business it is to tap at up-stair windows with a long wand, when the time comes to arouse the sleeper from his pillow.

The industrial occupations specially identified with the cotton trade are Bleaching, Dyeing, and Calico-printing. Bleaching, the plainest and simplest, was effected, originally, by exposure of the cloth to the open air and solar light. Spread over the meadows and pastures, as long as summer lasted, the country, wherever a 'whiter' or 'whitster' pursued his calling, was more wintry-looking in July than often at Christmas. The process itself was tedious, requiring incessant attention, as well as being liable to serious hindrance, and involving much loss to the merchant through the usually long delay. Above all, it conduced to the moral damage of the community, since the bleaching crofts were of necessity accessible, and furnished to the ill-disposed an incentive to the crime which figures so lamentably in their history. That changes, and events, both good and evil, are prone to come in clusters, is a very ancient matter of observation. At the very moment when the ingenious machinery produced by Hargreaves, Arkwright, and Crompton, was developing its powers, a complete revolution took place in regard to bleaching. Scheele discovered that vegetable colours give way to chlorine. Berthollet and Dr. Henry (the latter residing in Manchester) followed up the German discovery, and showed the way to the practical application. By 1774 the bleaching process had been shortened by one-half; the meadows

and pastures were released; the summer sunshine fell once more upon verdure,

'Diffugere nives, redeunt jam gramina campis;'

and by about 1790 the art became what we have it to-day, one purely for indoors. The new method was first practised, upon a large scale, in the neighbourhood of Bolton, which place has preserved its original reputation, though long since rivalled in every part of the cotton-manufacturing district, and often in more distant spots, an abundance of pure water being indispensable, and outweighing, in its value, the advantages of proximity to town. Many successive steps have to be taken before perfect whiteness can be secured, these demanding the utmost care and the strictest order of procedure. Finally, unless destined for the dye-house or the print-works, the cloth is stiffened with starch made from wheaten flour, the consumption of which article is very large also in the factories, where it is employed to give tenacity to the yarn, re-acting, beneficially, upon the agricultural interest;—then, in order to give it the beautiful smoothness and gloss which remind one of the petals of the snowdrop, it is pressed between huge rollers, which play against one another, under the influence of powerful engines. It is then said to have been 'cylindered,' or, corruptly, 'calendered.' Bleaching, it will appear from this, is a process which but slightly taxes human strength. Very interesting is it to note how, in the presence of chemistry and steam, the old word 'manufacture' has in modern times changed its meaning. To-day the office of human fingers is less to 'make' than to guide the forces of nature, delegating all the harder work to inanimate wood and iron. The time ordinarily allowed for bleaching is one or two days, though, if needful, the entire process can be greatly accelerated. The cost is about a halfpenny per yard.

Dyeing is carried on in Lancashire quite as extensively as bleaching. Here, again, the exactest chemical knowledge is wanted; the managers are usually men well versed in science: nothing can be left for an instant to good fortune. A visit to an important dye-works always awakens the liveliest sentiments of admiration, and were it not for the relentless

GLASS-BLOWING.   By G. P. Jacomb Hood

fouling of the streams which receive the refuse, few scenes of industry would live longer in pleasant memory. For although dye-works exist in towns, and their suburbs, they are more frequently established out in the country, where there are babbling brooks and 'shallow falls,' with a view to obtaining a plentiful and steady supply of clean water. Factories also are sometimes found amid the fields, occupying quite isolated positions, the object being similar—the command of some definite local advantage. When at the foot of a hill, it is interesting to observe that the chimney is placed halfway up the slope, a preliminary underground passage inducing a more powerful draught.

It is in the neighbourhood of these rural establishments that the hurt done by manufacturing to the pristine beauty of the country becomes conspicuous. Near the towns the results are simply dirt, withered hedges, and a general withdrawal of meadow adornment. In the country we perceive how the picturesque becomes affected. Railways are not more cruel. Cotton, with all its kindliness, reverses the celestial process which makes the wilderness blossom as the rose. There are differences in degree—the upper portion of the Irwell valley, near Summerseat, is, in a measure, exceptional; but we must never expect to find a spot wholly devoid of illustrations of blight and mischief. Against the destruction of natural beauty, when works and factories assume the sway, of course must be set not only the employment of the industrious, but the enormous rise in the value of the land; since rise of such character is a sign of advancing civilisation, which in due time will more than compensate the damage. In the manufacturing parts of Lancashire, land available for farming purposes commands ten times the rental of a century ago. Mr. Henry Ashworth's paper on the increase in the value of Lancashire property, published in 1841, showed that since 1692 the rise in Bolton had been six hundredfold.

The highest place in the trio of beautiful arts now before us is held, undeniably, by Calico-printing, since it not only 'paints' the woven fabric 'with delight,' but in its power to multiply and vary the cheerful pictures, is practically inexhaustible; thus representing, and in the most charming manner, the outcome of the sweet facility of the Seasons. Next to the diversities of living flowers, assuredly come the devices of the pattern-designer who discreetly goes to nature for his inspiration. Much of his work must of necessity be conventionalized, and some of it cannot be other than arbitrary and artificial; but there is no reason why, in its steadiest practice, strictly natural forms and colours should not always be regarded as truest and best. The tendency is daily more and more in this direction, so that

calico-printing may justly anticipate a future even more distinguished than its present and its past. The 'past,' if we press for the birthday, is an ancient one indeed. Not to mention the chintzes of India, in the days of Calidasa, Pliny shows us very plainly that printing by means of mordants was practised in Egypt in the first century of the Christian era. When introduced into western Europe, is not known;—for our present sketch it is enough that in England it began about A.D. 1700, coming, like many other excellent things, of the short-sighted efforts of Selfishness, which, fortunately for mankind, always, under the Divine government, invites the retaliations of Generosity. In the year mentioned, 1700, with a view to favouring the manufacturers of woollen and silk, the importation of prints from India was forbidden. Experiments were at once made with a view to production of similar work at home. This was soon discovered to be practicable, and preparations were made for printing upon a large scale, and at a moderate cost, when a new hindrance arose—say rather that the old malignant one, jealous opposition, reappeared. For a time this was successful, but at last the privilege to print in England was conceded, burdened, however, with the condition that the Metropolis and the immediate vicinity should alone possess the right—a circumstance which recalls to mind the original law as to Joint-Stock Banks. The monopoly wrought its own destruction, for there was one county at least, a despised but courageous one in the north, which was not likely to remain a passive spectator. Contemporaneously with the new bleaching-process above described, contemporaneously also with the employment of the new cotton machinery, calico-printing obtained the provincial footing which from that time forwards has never ceased to strengthen, and which now renders Lancashire the most important district in the world in regard alike to the immensity of production, and the inexpressible beauty of the workmanship. It is not too much to say, with an eminent author, that the calico-printing works of Lancashire are entitled to count with the most distinguished English seats of useful science, and the most interesting scenes of the exercise of tasteful invention. The earliest enterprise was at Bamber Bridge, near Preston, in 1760. Blackburn followed, and under the influence of the supreme abilities of the Peels, remained for many years the uncontested centre. Print-works are now met with in every little recess where there is supply of water, doubtless the first thing looked for when they were founded. The natural current sufficed at first; but it soon became customary to construct home or private reservoirs, and upon these the dependence is now essentially placed. No county in England needs so much water as Lancashire, and certainly there is not one that presents so many little bits of water-surface artificially prepared. It is pleasant to observe that the reservoirs belonging to 'works,' when belonging to a man of taste, have often been rendered extremely pretty by the introduction of water-lilies, flowers not only of unrivalled queen-liness among aquatics, but distinguished among our native vegetation by the elegant languor always associated with the idea of the Oriental—the water-lilies' birthright—for, as a race, they are much more Asiatic than European, and by happy coincidence the most appropriate that could be placed there, the water-lily being the emblem not more of the Nile than of the Ganges.

The multiplicity of the printing processes, and their complexity, call for many distinct buildings. Hence, when large, and isolated away in the country, as very generally happens, a print-works has quite the look of a rising village. There is a laboratory, with library, for the managing chemist; a suite of apartments for the designers; and a house and fruitful garden for the resident partner; with, in addition, not uncommonly, a school-room for the children. When the designers have completed their sketches, the engraver's work begins—a business in itself, and carried on almost exclusively in town, and especially in Manchester. Originally, the pattern was cut upon a block of wood, usually sycamore, the success of the transfer to the cloth depending chiefly upon the dexterity of the workman. In 1785 this very primitive mode was superseded by 'cylinder-printing,' the pattern being engraved upon copper rollers, as many as there are colours; and though 'block-printing' shares the unquenchable vitality of hand-loom weaving, the roller may now be considered universal. The employment of copper supplies another very interesting illustration of the resort made to this metal in almost every kind of high decorative art, and prepares us to understand the fitness of the ancient mythological use, and why associated with the goddess of love and beauty.

These great undertakings—the bleaching, the dyeing, and the printing of the calico—demand immense supplies of the chemicals and other agents by means of which the various objects are attained. Hence, in Lancashire, the unrivalled number and extent of the manufacturing chemical works; and, especially in Manchester, the business, never heard of in many English counties, but there locally distinguished as the 'Drysalter's.' The drysalter sees to the importation from foreign countries of the indigo, the madder, and other dye-stuffs in daily request; he deals also in the manifold kinds of gum constantly asked for, supplying himself partly from abroad, *via* Liverpool, partly from the local works which prepare it artificially. A well-known sight in Manchester is that of a cartload of logs of some curious tropical dye-wood, rudely hewn by the axe, and still retaining, in

the cavities of the bark, little relics of the mosses and lichens of their native forest.

The chemical works are located principally in the extreme south-west, especially near Widnes, a place which at once betrays itself to the passing traveller in the almost suffocating atmosphere, and the total extinction of the beauty of trees and hedges, spectres and gaunt skeletons alone remaining where once was verdure. Here we find, in its utmost vigour, the manufacture of 'soda-ash' (an impure carbonate), and of chloride of lime, both for the use of bleachers; also, prepared from the first-named, 'caustic soda,' for the soap-boilers of Liverpool and Warrington; and chlorate of potash, peculiarly for the dyers. Nitric acid, also, is made in immense quantity, the basis being Chilian saltpetre, though for their materials for the soda-products the manufacturers have no need to go further than Cheshire, the supply of salt being drawn entirely from the Northwich mines. The discharge of stifling vapours was much worse before the passing of the Alkali Act than at present; and, curiously enough, though by no means without a parallel, involved positive loss to the manufacturer, who now manages to detain a considerable amount of good residuum previously wasted. The Act permits a limited quantity of noxious matter to go up the chimney; the stream is tested every day to see that the right is not abused: how terrible is the action even of that little the surrounding fields are themselves not slow to testify; everything, even in summer, looks dirty, lean, and dejected. Sulphuric acid is likewise manufactured on a great scale, especially at Newton-le-Willows, the basis (except when required to be very pure, when sulphur is employed) being iron pyrites imported from Spain. Hundreds of thousands of tons are prepared every year. There is probably not a single manufacturing process carried on in England in which chemical agency is involved which does not call for this powerful agent. Hence, in the consumption of sulphuric acid, we have always a capital index to the state of trade, so far as regards appeal to the activity of the producing classes.

In the extent of its manufacture of all the substances above mentioned, Lancashire is far ahead of every competitor in the world; Germany comes next, and then probably France.

Carbolic acid is of peculiarly Lancashire origin, having been originally introduced, commercially, by the late Dr. Crace Calvert. Supplies are in daily request for the production of colour: the employment for antiseptic purposes is larger yet; the export is also very considerable. Other immensely important chemicals prepared in South Lancashire, and on a scale almost incredible—Manchester helping the Widnes corner—are sulphate of soda and sulphate of copper, the last-named being now in unlimited demand, not only by the dyers and calico-printers, but for the batteries used in electric telegraphy. In the presence of all this marvellous work, how quaintly reads the history of the Lancashire chemistry of 500 years ago. It had then not emerged from alchemy, which, forbidden by Henry IV., and legalised by Henry VI., had already been warmly encouraged by the credulous Edward III., and had no devouter adherents than the Asshetons and the Traffords, who in their loyalty undertook to supply the King with silver and gold to the extent of his needs—so soon as the 'philosopher's stone' should be discovered! Before we laugh at their misdirected zeal, it may be well to inquire whether the world has suffered more from scornful and premature rejection, or from honest and simple enthusiasm, such as in playing with alchemy brought to life the germs of the profoundest and most variously useful of the sciences.

Though Lancashire tries no longer to transmute the baser metals into the precious ones by means of alchemy, it succeeds by the honester and less circuitous route of industry. Lead is obtained, though not in any large quantity, at Anglezark, near Rivington Pike; and iron, in the excellent form of hæmatite, plentifully in the Ulverston and Furness district. The smelting is carried on chiefly at Barrow, where the business will, no doubt, continue to prosper, though hæmatite, of late years, has somewhat lost its ancient supremacy, methods having been discovered by which ores hitherto deemed inferior are practically changed to good and useful ones.

IN THE WIRE WORKS.

In any case the triumphs of Lancashire will continue to be shown, as heretofore, in her foundries and engine-works, the latter innumerable. Whitworth, Fairbairn, Nasmyth, are names too well known to need more than citation. Nasmyth's steam-hammer in itself is unique. Irresistible when it smites with a will, a giant in power and emphasis, it can assume, when it pleases, the lightsome manners of a fairy. Let a lady place her hand upon the anvil, the mighty creature just gives it a kiss, gently, courteously, and retires. It is rather a misfortune for the stupendous products of the foundry and engine-works, that, except in the case of the locomotive, as soon as completed, they are hidden away for evermore, embedded where completely lost to view, and thought of as little as the human heart. Happily in the streets of Manchester there is frequent reminder, in the shape of some leviathan, drawn slowly by a team of eight, ten, twelve, or even fourteen magnificent horses. Bradford,

one of the suburbs of Manchester, supplies the world with the visible factor of its nervous system—those mysterious-looking threads which now everywhere show against the sky, and literally allow of intercourse between 'Indus and the Pole.' At the Messrs. Johnson's works there are manufactured every week from 280 to 300 tons of telegraph-wire. It hardly needs to say that they outstrip all other makers—works that cover ten or twelve acres of ground, and give employment to 600 men, are not likely to be second to any of their own kind. In addition to their manufacture of telegraph-wire, the Messrs. Johnson prepare the whole of what is wanted for the wire-rope bridges now common in America. Large quantities of wire are produced also at Warrington; here, however, of kinds adapted more particularly for domestic use. In connexion with metal it is worthy also of note that Lancashire is the principal seat of the manufacture of the famous safes which, defying thieves and fire, challenge even the earthquake. They are made in Liverpool by Milner & Co., and near Bolton by the Chatwoods.

Lancashire was long distinguished for its manufacture of Silk, though it never acquired the importance held by Macclesfield. In Europe this beautiful art came to the front as one of the results of the later Crusades—enterprises which, though productive of untold suffering, awoke the mind of all the civilised parts of the Continent from its slumber of ages, enlarging the sphere of popular thought, reviving the taste for elegant practices forgotten since the fall of the Western Empire, and extending commerce and knowledge in general. To Lancashire men the history is thus one of special interest. Italy led the way in the manufacture; Spain and France soon followed, the latter acquiring distinction, and at the close of the sixteenth century the English Channel was crossed. Tyranny, as in the case of calico-printing, was the prime cause, the original Spitalfields weavers having been part of the crowd of Protestants who at that period were constrained, like the unhappy and forlorn in more modern times, to seek the refuge always afforded in our sea-girt isle.* James the First was so strongly impressed

---

* The late greatly respected Mr. E. R. Le Mare, who came to Manchester in 1829, and was long distinguished among the local silk-merchants, belonged, by descent, to one of these identical old Huguenot families. Died at Clevedon, Feb. 4th, 1881, aged 84.

with the importance of the manufacture, that, hoping to promote it at home, he procured many thousands of young mulberry-trees, some of which, or their immediate descendants, are still to be found, venerable but not exhausted, in the grounds and gardens of old country-houses. The Civil Wars gave a heavy check to further progress. Little more was done till 1718, when a silk-mill, worked by a water-wheel, was built at Derby. This, in time, had to close its doors awhile, through the refusal of the King of Sardinia to permit

weaving was further congenial to these men in being more cleanly and less laborious than the former work, requiring more care and vigilance, and rather more skill, thus exactly suiting a race of worshippers of the polyanthus, the carnation, and the auricula. The last-named, locally called the 'basier,' a corruption of 'bear's ear,' is the subject of a charming little poem, by one of the old Swinton weavers, preserved intact, reprinted in Wilkinson's 'Lancashire Ballads,' and peculiarly valuable in the light it throws upon the

MAKING COKE.

the exportation of the raw material, always so difficult to procure in quantity. At last there was recovery; the manufacture crept into Cheshire, and at the commencement of the present century into Lancashire, taking root especially in the ancient villages of Middleton and Eccles, and gradually spreading to the adjacent hamlets.

The arrival was opportune, and helped to break the fall of the hand-loom cotton weavers, many of whom could not endure the loss of freedom imposed by the rules of the factory, and whose latent love of beauty, as disclosed in their taste for floriculture, was called forth in a new and agreeable manner. Silk-

temperament of a simple and worthy race, now almost extinct. We may be allowed to quote two of the verses:—

'Come and listen awhile unto what we shall say
Concerning the season, the month we call May;
For the flowers they are springing, the birds they do sing,
And the basiers are sweet in the morning of May.

When the trees are in bloom, and the meadows are green,
The sweet-smelling cowslips are plain to be seen;
The sweet ties of nature we plainly do say,
For the basiers are sweet in the morning of May!'

The silk-weavers about Middleton were renowned also for their zest in entomology, and truly wonderful

Smelting. Dec/80

Old market place Wigan.

were their cabinets of Lepidoptera, reminding one of the ancient fame of the Spitalfields weavers in the same science—one in which extreme delicacy of touch is indispensable, while in the lovely wings of their embroidered favourites they had a kind of reflex of their own delicious art. Unfortunately, when all was prosperous, there came a change. Ever since 1860, the year of the new, and still current, silk-treaties with France, whereby its original command of the

trade was restored, the manufacture of silk in Lancashire, and everywhere else in England, has been steadily and hopelessly declining; and at the present day, compared with half a century ago, the production is less than a tenth of what it was. Bad for the masters, it is the men after all who have suffered most in proportion, hand-loom weaving having almost wholly disappeared. When there is a choice between power-loom and hand-loom, and work enough only for one of them, and perhaps not half enough, the preference naturally goes to the power-loom, since this represents invested capital, whereas the hand-loom weaver, however sorry the employer may be for him, has merely to be told that he is not wanted. In the disappearance of the hand-loom silk-weavers there is something which it is impossible to regard without regret. One looks in vain for the peculiar simplicities of their character and their pastimes. Possibly we have better things to look at, but certainly none that are so peaceful as was the devotedness to the velvetpetaled basier. The Lancashire silk-trade, such as remains, gathers chiefly about Leigh. Middleton, once so famous for its 'broad silks'—those adapted for ladies' dresses,—now spends its time chiefly in the preparation of 'trimmings;' and wherever carried on, the manufacture is almost wholly of the kind called 'mixed,' or cotton and silk combined, this being more in demand, because lower in price, though not wearing so well.

From silk, that befits empresses, to hemp, the material of sack-cloth, the way is long. But it must not be overlooked, in regard to the textile manufactures of Lancashire, that each extreme is familiar. Warrington, in the bygones, prepared more than half the entire quantity of sail-cloth required for the navy. It was a ship laden with hemp from the Baltic for use in Lancashire, which, touching at the Isle of Skye, brought the first news of the arrival there of Prince Charles Edward.

Lancashire produces one-sixth of all the paper made in England. In other words, there are in this county about fifty of the nearly 300 English paper-mills, including the very largest of them—Messrs. Wrigley & Sons', near Bury. The first to be established was Crompton's, at Farnworth, near Bolton, which dates from 1676, or exactly 88 years after the building of the famous Kentish one referred to by Shakspeare,* which itself followed, by just a century, the primæval one at Stevenage. Every description of paper, except that required for Bank-notes, is made in Lancashire. The mills themselves, like the dyeworks, haunt the river-sides, though they no longer draw their supplies of water from the stream. Paper-works cannot possibly prosper if there be iron in the water they use, or decomposed vegetable matter. Hence, in Lancashire it is now customary to sink wells of considerable depth, and in any case to provide for elaborate filtration. No spectacle in its way is more wonderful than that of a paper-machine at its work. There is no limit to the length of the piece it is able to produce continuously, save that which is imposed by its own restricted dimensions. A roll could be made, as it is, of three or four miles in length, the cylinder gradually gathering up the pulp, till it can hold no more. Very interesting also is it to observe the variety of material now employed. Esparto, or 'Spanish grass,' is brought to Liverpool (as to Cardiff and Newcastle) in exchange for coal, and wood-pulp from Norway and Sweden, *via* Hull.

At Darwen, long celebrated for its paper of kinds in general, we find the largest and most important production in England, of the ornamental descriptions, which to-day take the place of the distemper

painting of ancient Egypt, so beautifully illustrated also at Herculaneum and Pompeii. The manufacture was originally very similar to block calico-printing, and continued so until about 1839, when Messrs. C. and J. G. Potter of Darwen introduced 'rollers,' with the additional novelty of the pattern being cut in relief; and this is now almost universal, the Messrs. Potter having progeny, as it were, all over the country, though they themselves still produce at least one-half of all the wall-paper consumed. They have customers in every part of the civilised world, and adapt their work to the diverse and often fantastic tastes of all in turn, directed not uncommonly, as in the case of the Hindoos and the Japanese, by native designs, which they are required to follow implicitly.

To go further into the story of modern Lancashire manufacturing is not possible, since there is scarcely a British industry which in this county is without example, and to treat of the whole, even briefly, would require thrice the space already occupied. Among the foremost scenes of admirable labour to be described would be the famous plate-glass works at St. Helens; and the Manchester india-rubber works, the original, now fifty-seven years old, still carried on under the familiar name of Charles Macintosh and Co. The first were established in Glasgow; London, and then Manchester, were the next following centres, beginning with simple waterproof, but now producing articles of every conceivable variety. Thread, tape, pins, carpenters' tools, nails, screws, terra-cotta, bottles, aniline, soap, brass and pewter work, are also Lancashire staples. Gunpowder is manufactured near the foot of Windermere; and at Prescot and thereabouts, the people employ themselves, as they have done now for nearly three centuries, in manufacturing the delicate 'works' and 'movements' required for watches. Not without significance either, in regard to the general capabilities of the county, is the preparation, at Newton, by Messrs. McCorquodale, of the whole of the requirements of the Government, both for home use and in India, in the way of stationery and account-books. For the Government alone they manufacture forty millions of envelopes every year. They also execute the enormous amount of printing demanded by the L. & N. W. Railway Company. The establishment of the great ship-building works at Barrow, the village near Furness Abbey just now mentioned, has of late acquired prominence so marked that it needs no more than a reference. The magnificent Atlantic Inman steamer, the 'City of Rome,' a ship with a gross tonnage of 8400, and to be propelled by, upon the lowest estimate, 8500 indicated horse power, was launched here in June, 1881. All has come into existence since about 1860, when the population of this out-of-the-way Lancashire village was under 4000, though now 47,000, a growth without parallel except in the

---

* Sir John Spielman's, at Dartford.— *Vide* 2nd Henry VI., Act 4, Scene 7.

United States. In the 'City of Rome' Lancashire has produced the largest vessel afloat after the 'Great Eastern.'

Omitting a considerable number of minor activities, there is, in addition to the above, the vast sphere of industry, part of the very life of working Lancashire, though not a manufacture, indicated by the little word Coal. In their value and importance the Lancashire collieries vie with the cotton-mills, declaring once again how close and constant is the dependence of the prosperity of a great manufacturing district upon its geology. Coal-fields, lying

branches running out in various directions from the principal mass. What the exact thickness may be of course is not known, but, according to Mr. Dickenson, it may be estimated at 6450 feet. Some of the deepest pits in the country have been sunk in it, as at the Rosebridge Colliery, near Wigan, where the depth already reached is nearly 2500 feet, and the Ashton Moss Pit, near Ashton-under-Lyne, which goes still lower—it is said to 2700 feet—in which case this last will be the deepest in England. The direction of the dip is described by the colliers in a very pretty way. They say it is towards 'the rising sun,' or 'the setting

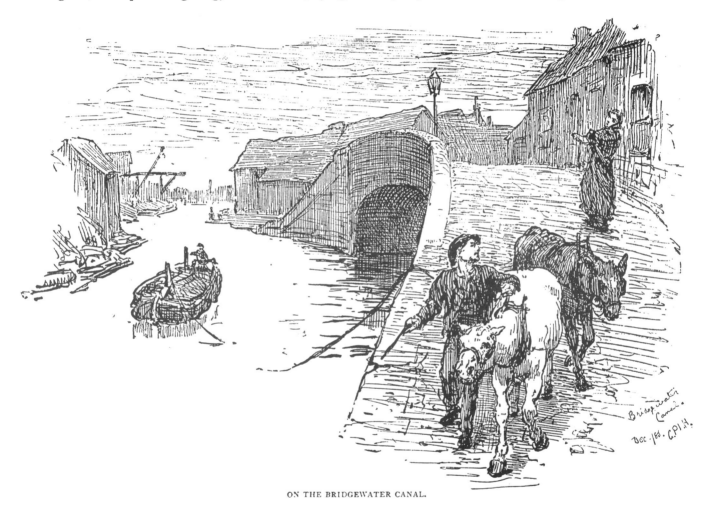

ON THE BRIDGEWATER CANAL.

below the surface, leave the soil above them free for the purposes of the farmer and the builder ; in other words, for the raising of human food, and the development of useful constructive arts. Where there is plenty of coal, double the number of people can exist ;—the enormous population of Lancashire, south of the Ribble, has unquestionably come as much of its coal-fields as of the invention of the spinning-jenny. The prevailing rock in this portion of Lancashire is the well-known new red sandstone, the same as that which overlies all our other best English coal deposits. Concurrently with it, and with the mill-stone grit, the measures which have brought so much wealth to the county, extend from Pendleton, two miles from Manchester, to Colne, in the north-east, and to St. Helen's, in the west, many vast

sun,' the different points included between these opposites being similarly expressed by 'dipping towards nine-o'clock sun,' 'twelve-o'clock sun,' and so on. The sun is thus their compass, though few men see less of it during their hours of labour. The neighbourhood of a colliery is generally well declared. Independently of the apparatus over the opening of the pit, there is no mistaking the significance of the row of neat cottages, all fashioned on the same architectural model, a few stray ones here and there, a trim little front garden seldom wanting, with, close by, a few shops, a school-house, a chapel, both very plain, and the proprietor's or agent's residence, somewhat ornate, and garnished with evergreen shrubs, ready always for the washing of a kindly shower. In many places, as at Wigan, Atherton, Tyldesley, and

St. Helen's, women, both single and married, work at the collieries, but only above ground, or at the bank. They are prohibited by statute from descending the pit, and their names and ages are all exactly registered. Up to the waist they are dressed like men; above the knees, instead of a coat, they have a peculiarly-fashioned tunic, a compromise between gown and jacket, by which they may be distinguished from afar; a limp bonnet, tied under the chin, protects the head, but never conceals the earrings and plaited hair. Many of these women are plainly equal to their masculine colleagues in physical power, yet they earn only two-thirds of the wages given to men. The decorum of their behaviour while at work is unimpeachable; on Sundays they do their best to dress like ladies.

Nothing does more to sustain and encourage the industry of a working population than a steady system of transit, and a well-timed delivery, alike of the natural products of the ground and of the articles manufactured. Hence the early development in Lancashire of the idea of the Canal, and, sixty years afterwards, of that of the Railway. The history of the famous Bridgewater Canal is one of the most interesting connected with the county enterprise, the more so since all other canals were imitations of it. Many, however, are not aware that the celebrated peer under whose dictation it was constructed—Francis Egerton, the third and last Duke of Bridgewater—was led to devote himself, for solace sake, to engineering, through a disappointment in love. That women should take refuge in works of charity when troubled or bereaved,

and, when wealthy, found hospitals and build orphanages, is very natural, and has plenty of exemplification; but for a man to turn, when similarly circumstanced, to science, is phenomenal, and the records of the latter would probably be searched in vain for a parallel case. Several versions of the story are afloat; whichever may be the true one, it is beyond a doubt that one of the greatest industrial achievements ever witnessed in England had for its prime cause the caprice or the temper of the widowed Duchess of Hamilton—to whom a second coronet was offered— she who in her early days was the celebrated belle, Elizabeth Gunning. There is a waterway of this description in Lancashire more remarkable in some respects even than the Duke's canal—that one called the Leeds and Liverpool, the Lancashire portion of which curls round from the great sea-port, by way of Ormskirk, Southport, Wigan, Chorley, Burnley, and Colne, where the Yorkshire boundary is crossed. Near the towns, and especially in the south-west and south-east, these useful highways are dreary and uninteresting; but in rural districts, such as they must needs traverse, often for lengths of many miles, the borders sometimes acquired an unlooked-for picturesqueness, and are prettily dressed with wild flowers, as exemplified, very pleasingly, in the vicinity of the Whittle Springs. In any case they never fail in possession of the rude charms of the gliding boat, the slow-paced horse, and artless guide. The Lancashire railway system, it may be remarked, extends to within a trifle of six hundred miles.

ON THE BRIDGEWATER CANAL.   *By G. P. Jacomb Hood*

VI.

Peculiarities of Character, Dialect, and Pastimes.

THE primitive Lancashire character — industrious, frugal, sanguine, persevering, inflexible in determination—has already been sketched in brief. Some additional features, observable more particularly among the operatives and away in the country, deserve notice, the more so since it is in a people's average temperament that the key is usually found to their pursuits in play-time—after the songs, the most interesting chapter in a local history. The sum total of the private morals of working Lancashire probably does not differ, *pro ratâ*, from that which would be disclosed by a census of any other county. So with the manners and customs, for although in Lancashire the suavity of the South is soon missed, and though there is little touching of the hat or saying of ' Sir,' the absence of a courteous spirit is more apparent than real, and in any case is amply compensated by a thoroughness of kindly sentiment which more polished communities do not always share. The ' factory-folk,' the colliers, and others, are usually considered turbulent and given to outrages. They are not so by nature. Though often rough, self-willed, and obstinate, the working population as a whole is too thoroughly Saxon for the riotousness one looks for while in the presence of the Celt. Social conflicts, when they arise, are set on foot by mischief-makers and noisy idlers whose personal interest it is to promote antagonisms. Save for these veritable ' disturbers of the peace' the probability is that there would be few or none of the 'strikes' and 'turn-outs' which bring so much misery to the unfortunate women and children who have no say in the matter. The people who ' strike' are in the mass more to be pitied than held chargeable with love of disorder, for, as a rule, they have been cruelly misled into the notion that it is the master's interest to pay as little as possible for their labour, the truth being that for his own sake he pays them the utmost the business will justify, so that they shall be strong enough, healthy enough, cheerful and good-tempered enough, to work with a will, thus augmenting his personal profits. Every master of common-sense understands the principle, and *does* so pay. It may be useful to remind the reader that the profits made by a Lancashire ' cotton-lord' differ

totally in their composition from the payment received for his work by an artist, a physician, or a barrister. The cotton-manufacturer's profits consist of an infinite number of particles, an atom per head on the work of 500, and often 1000 assistants. To the outside and afar-off public, who hear of contentions over pennies, the sum seems nothing, and the man who refuses the penny a sordid fellow. But to the employer it very soon means hundreds of pounds, and represents perhaps half a year's income.

In Lancashire, whatever may be the case elsewhere, the people who 'strike' are deceived in no slight measure, through their own honesty and sincerity of purpose. One of the original characteristics of the county is to be fair and unsuspecting ; no people in the world have a stronger dislike of deceit ; one of the reasons why a genuine Lancashire man can usually be trusted is, that he is so little inclined to overstate or misrepresent. The very circumstance that wins our esteem thus renders him vulnerable. Disposed to be honest themselves, the operatives fall so much more readily a prey to unscrupulous agitators. It is amusing, at the same time, to note how soon, when he detects an impostor, a Lancashire man will put him out of countenance ; and how quick he is, in excellent balance, to perceive the meritorious, either in person or subject, and, perceiving, to appreciate.

A remarkable instance of the promotion of strikes by mischief-makers occurred at the commencement of the spring of 1881, when the colliers stood out for six weeks, at a loss to themselves of no less than 250,000*l.* in wages, such as otherwise they would have earned. The Chairman of the London and North-Western Railway Company explained it at the Shareholders' Meeting on July 24th, pointing out at the same time the immense collateral harm inflicted :—

' They might remember that at the beginning of the year there was a settlement made with the colliers of Lancashire and their employers with regard to a mutual insurance fund against accident; but a Member of Parliament went down, and persuaded these poor, unhappy people that they had better not accept it, but take care of themselves. He also persuaded them to make a strike, the result of which was disaster to everyone. Prices did not go up, and unless prices went up wages could not; and the men afterwards suffered great distress. From this cause they estimated that the Company had lost traffic to the amount of about 100,000*l.*'

Another result was the permanent loss of an important market to the local colliery proprietors. Many thousands of tons of Lancashire steam-coal were previously being sent weekly to Birkenhead; but during the stoppage of the Wigan collieries the coal-masters of North and South Wales obtained possession of the market, and the quantity now sent to Birkenhead is confined to only a few hundreds of tons. The general question as to strikes, and of the kind of grievances that may sometimes be not unreasonably complained of, is, no doubt, a very large and complex one. But whatever may be the case elsewhere, it is impossible for the 'strikers' to deny that, in the aggregate, and in the long run, the tendency of the masters' doings is to create and diffuse social happiness among the employed. It is the master's interest that his people should be not only strong and healthy, and good workmen, but good *men.* Comfortable homes are prepared for their families. Schools were provided by innumerable Lancashire masters long before they were required to do so by law. Many an employer is noted for the pains he takes, and the money he spends, with a view to the operatives' enjoyments.

During the continuance of these ill-advised 'strikes,' and when the depression of trade—quite as distasteful to the master as to the man—involves 'short time'— four or five days' work in the week, or even less, instead of six, another capital feature of the Lancashire character comes to the front. No people in the world are capable of profounder fortitude. Patience under suffering never fails. Though pinched by hunger, such is the manly and womanly pride of the Lancashire operatives, that they care less about privations than to be constrained to surrender any portion, however trifling, of their independence. That the large-hearted and the intelligent among mankind are always the last to complain in the hour of trial, no one needs telling. People of this character are probably more numerous everywhere than may be thought, for the simple reason that they are the least likely to be heard of; but it is worth putting on paper that no better illustrations are to be found than exist in plenty in working Lancashire. It is delightful also to note the singular kindness of the Lancashire operatives one to another in time of distress. Not upon 'Trades' Union' principles, but upon the broad and unselfish basis of strong, natural, human sympathy, familiar to the friendly visitor; and which, when elevated, as it often is, by religion, and warmed and expanded by personal affection, becomes so beautiful that in its presence all shortcomings are forgotten. These good qualities are

unfolded very specially on the occurrence of a terrible accident, such as a coal-pit explosion. In the yearning to be foremost in help to rescue; in the gentleness, the deference to authority, the obedience to discipline, the resignation then exhibited—this last coming not of indifference, but of calmness—a capacity is plainly shown for the highest conceivable moral development.

The Dialect.—The Lancashire dialect, as said above, is of two-fold interest. It forms not only a striking characteristic of the people, but presents material of the highest value to the scientific student of the English language. To the ears of strangers who know nothing about it, the sound is often uncouth and barbarous. That it is far from being so is proved by the use long made of this dialect for lyric poetry and for tales both racy and pathetic. We are indebted to Mr. George Milner for a masterly exposition of its singular fitness for song and ballad;* the titles of the stories hold a conspicuous place in Mr. Axon's list of no fewer than 279 publications illustrative of the general subject of the Lancashire dialect;† the literature of which, he justly remarks in the Introduction, is richer than that of the popular speech of any other English county. This is so much the more noteworthy since with the famous manufacturing epoch of 1785, everything belonging to primitive Lancashire began to experience change and decay. In a certain sense it may be said that the dialect has not only survived unhurt, but has risen, during the last thirty or forty years, to a position worthy of the native talent; and that the latter, in days to come, will have no better commemoration than the metrical literature will abundantly afford. Two particulars at once arrest attention. No English dialect more abounds in curious and interesting archaisms; and certainly not one is so little tainted with expressions of the nature of slang.‡

Rochdale occupies the centre of the most celebrated Lancashire-dialect region. As ordinarily employed, the phrase denotes indeed the rural speech of the manufacturing districts. Beyond the Ribble, and more particularly beyond the Lune, there is unmistakable variation, and in Furness there is an echo of Cumberland. In the former we have first the old-accustomed permutations of the vowels. Then come elisions of consonants, transpositions, and condensations of entire syllables, whereby words are often most singularly transformed. Ancient idioms attract us next; and lastly, there are the fascinating

---

* 'On the Lancashire Dialect considered as a vehicle for Poetry.' Manchester Literary Club Papers, vol. i., p. 20. 1875.

† *Ibid.* Appendix to the vol. for 1876.

‡ The modern slang of great towns is of course quite a different thing from the ancient dialect of a rural population. Affected mis-spellings, as of 'kuntry' for country, are also to be distinguished *in toto* from the phonetic representation of sounds purely dialectical.

old words, unknown to current dictionaries, which five centuries ago were an integral part of the English vernacular. The vowel permutations are illustrated in the universal 'wayter,' 'feyther,' 'reet,' 'oi,' 'aw,' 'neaw,' used instead of water, father, right, I, now. 'Owt' stands for aught, 'nowt' for naught. Elisions and contractions appear in a thousand such forms as 'dunnoyo' for 'do you not,' 'welly' for 'well-nigh.' 'You' constantly varies to thee and thou, whence the common 'artu' for 'art thou,' 'wilto-hameh' for 'wilt thou have me.' A final *g* is seldom heard; there is also a characteristic rejection of the guttural in such words as scratched, pronounced 'scrat.' The transpositions are as usual, though it is only perhaps in Lancashire that gaily painted butterflies are 'brids,' and that the little field-flowers elsewhere called birds' eye are 'brid een.'

The old grammatical forms and the archaic words refer the careful listener, if not to the Anglo-Saxon of King Alfred, at all events to the 'Canterbury Tales;' —they take us pleasantly to Chaucer, and Chaucer in turn, introduces us, agreeably, to Lancashire, where 'she' is always 'hoo,' through abiding in the primitive 'he, heo, hit;' and where the verbs still end in *n*,— 'we, ye, they loven,' as in the Prologue,

'For he had geten him yet no benefice.'

Very interesting is it, also, when the ear catches the antiquated *his* and *it* where now we say *its*. Often supposed to be in harmony with the poetical usage of 'his' in personifications, the Lancashire *his* corresponds in truth with the Shaksperean one, being the simple genitive of the old English *hit*, as in 'Midsummer Night's Dream,' ii. 1 :—

'There is a willow grows aslant the brook,
That shows *his* hoar leaves in the glassy stream.'

So with the obsolete possessive, *it*. When a Lancashire woman says, 'Come to it mammy!' how plain the reminder of the lines in 'King John:'—

'Do, child, go to *it* grandam, child;
Give grandam kingdom, and *it* grandam will
Give it a plum, a cherry, and a fig;
There's a good grandam.'

Archaic words are illustrated in many a familiar phrase. A Lancashire girl, in quest of something, 'speers' for it (A. S. *spirian*, to inquire). If alarmed, she 'dithers;' if comely and well conducted, she behaves herself 'farrantly;' if delicately sensitive, she is 'nesh :'

'It seemeth for love his herte is tendre and neshe.'

Words of the Elizabethan age also occur, as when the poor 'clem' for want of food. 'Hard is the choice,' says Ben Jonson, 'when the valiant must eat their arms or clem.' Very many others, which, though not obsolete in polite society, are seldom

heard, help to give flavour to this delightful old dialect. To embrace is in Lancashire to 'clip;' to move house is to 'flit;' when the rain descends heavily, 'it teems;' rather is expressed by 'lief' or 'liefer,' as in 'Troilus and Cresseide :'

'Yet had I levre unwist for sorrow die.'

Pastimes and Recreations.—The pastimes and recreations of the Lancashire people fall, as elsewhere, under two distinct heads; those which arise upon the Poetic sentiment, the love of purity, order, and beauty, and those which come of simple desire to be entertained. Where Poesy has a stronghold, we have never long to wait for the 'touches of sweet harmony ;'—hence a characteristic of working Lancashire, immemorial as to date, is devotedness to Music. In all Europe it would be difficult to find a province where the 'first and finest of the fine arts' is better understood, or more reverently practised. High-class sacred music—German music in particular—fills many a retired cottage, in leisure hours, with solace and joy; and very generally, in villages, as well as in the large towns, there are clubs and societies instituted purely for its promotion. 'On the wild hills, where whin and heather grow, it is not uncommon to meet working-men, with their musical instruments, on their way to take part in some village oratorio many miles distant . . . . Up in the forest of Rossendale, between Derply Moor and the wild hill called Swinshaw, there is a little lone valley, a green cup in the mountains, called Dean. The inhabitants of this valley are so notable for their love of music that they are known all through the neighbouring country as "Th' Deign layrocks."'[*] In many of the large country manufacturing establishments—the Printworks, for instance—the operatives have regularly organized 'bands'—the employers giving encouragement—the value of which, in regard to moral culture, is shown in the members being usually the trusted men.

The same primitive inclination towards the poetic would seem to underlie the boundless Lancashire love of flowers and gardens. Not that the passion is universal. The chief seat, as of the intrinsically best of the dialect, is the south-eastern part of the county: the portion abutting on Yorkshire is unfavourably cold, and though in the north there are fine examples of individual enthusiasm, there is little illustration of confederated work. Societies strong and skilful enough to hold beautiful exhibitions are dotted all over the congenial parts of the cotton district. They attend as diligently to the economic as to the decorative; one never knows whether most to admire the onions, the beans, and the celery, or

---

[*] *i.e.* The larks, or singing-birds, of Dean. Edwin Waugh, 'Sketches,' p. 199.

the splendid asters, dahlias, and phloxes :—in many parts there is ancient renown also for gooseberries. After the manner of the wise in other matters, the operative Lancashire gardeners, as they cannot grow the things they might prefer, give their whole hearts to liking those they have at command. Their rivalry and ambition in regard to gooseberries is unique. While the fruit is ripening upon the bushes, it is sacrilege for a stranger to approach within a distance of many yards. On cold and hurtful nights, the owner sits up to watch it, like a nurse with an invalid, supplying or removing defence according to the conditions, and on the show day the excitement compares in its innocent measure with that of Epsom. The exhibitors gather round a table : the chairman sits with scales and weights before him, calling in turn for the heaviest red, the heaviest yellow, and so on, every eye watching the balance, the end of all being a bright new kettle for the wife at home.

Many of the operative gardeners are assiduous cultivators of 'alpines,' the vegetable *bijouterie* of the Highland mountains ; others are enamoured of ferns, and these last are usually possessed of good old-fashioned botanical knowledge. At the great Old Trafford Horticultural Exhibition, in August, 1881, the premier prize for the best collection of hardy ferns—a hundred or more—was awarded to the Tildesleys, father and son, working colliers of the village of Worsley.*

The beginning of this very assiduous cultivation— say, in particular, of the 'basier,' the polyanthus, and the carnation—would seem to date from the time of Elizabeth, thus from the time of Shakspeare, when other immigrations of the Flemish weavers took place. 'As things of home,' Mr. Horner told his audience in his spring lecture at South Kensington,† 'too dear to leave behind them, these refugees brought with them their favourite flowers, the tulip and the auricula.' These early growers would doubtless for a time be shyly looked upon as aliens. Nothing is known definitely of the work of the ensuing century, but there is certain proof that by 1725 Lancashire had already become distinguished for its 'florists' flowers,' the cultivation lying almost entirely in the hands of the artisans, who have never for an instant slackened, though to-day the activity is often expressed in new directions.

It is owing, without doubt, to the example of the operative Lancashire gardeners of the last century and a half, that floriculture at the present moment holds equal place with classical music among the enjoyments also of the wealthy ; especially those whose early family ties were favourable to observation of the early methods. More greenhouses, hothouses, and conservatories ; more collections of valuable orchids, and other plants of special beauty and lustre, exist in South Lancashire, and especially in the immediate neighbourhood of Manchester, than in any other district away from the metropolis. Orchid culture was practised here, as in Macclesfield and Birmingham, long before what orchids are was even a question in many parts. The name of one of the noblest species yet discovered, the *Cattleya Mossiæ,* commemorates a Liverpool merchant, the late Mr. John Moss, one of the first to grow these matchless flowers ; while in that of the *Anguloa Clowesii* we are reminded of the beautiful collection formed at Higher Broughton, and which, after the decease of the possessor, went to Kew. A very remarkable and encouraging fact is that orchids, the queenliest and most fragrant of indoor flowers, can, like auriculas, with skilful management be brought to the highest possible state of perfection in an atmosphere in which many plants can barely exist—the smoky and soot-laden one of Manchester. The proof is supplied by Dr. R. F. Ainsworth, of Cliff Point, to whom flower-show honours are as familiar as to Benjamin Simonite of Sheffield, that astonishing old florist whose auriculas are grown where the idea of a garden seems absurd.

These very practical proofs of the life and soundness of the poetic sentiment in working Lancashire prepare us for a county feature in its way quite as interesting and remarkable—the wide-spread and very deep-seated local taste for myth, legend, and superstition, which, in truth, is the same sentiment uncultured and gone astray. Faith in 'folk-lore' is by no means to be confounded with inane credulity. The folk-lore of a civilised nation is the *débris* of the grand old spirit-worship—vague, but exquisitely picturesque, and figuratively significant, which, in the popular religion of the pre-Christian world, filled every sweet and romantic scene with invisible beings— Dryads, who loved the woodland ; Naïads, that sported in the stream and waterfall ; Oreads, who sat and sang where now we gather their own fragrant *Oreopteris,** and which assigned maidens even to the sea, the Nereids never yet lost. 'Nothing,' it has been well said, 'that has at any time had a meaning for mankind ever absolutely dies.' How much of the primæval faith shall survive with any particular race or people—to what extent it shall be transformed—depends upon their own culture, spiritual insight, and ideas of the omnipresence of the Almighty, of which the fancies as to the nymphs, &c. declared a dim recognition : it is affected, also, very materially by the physical character and complexion of their country. This has

---

* An account of the Tildesleys' fernery is given in the 'Gardeners' Chronicle' for Sept. 18, 1880. See, also, 'Lancashire Gardens,' in the same periodical for Oct. 2, 1880.
† April, 1881.

---

* *Lastrea Oreopteris,* the 'sweet mountain-fern,' abundant in south-east Lancashire.

been illustrated in the most beautiful manner, as regards the eastern borders of Lancashire, by the accomplished author of 'Scarsdale,'* already named ; the influence of the daily spectacle of the wild moor ; the evening walk homewards through the shadowy and silent ravine, the sweet mysteries of the green and ferny clough, with its rushing stream, all telling powerfully upon the imagination of a simple-hearted race, whose tendency was already towards the supernatural. The local fairy tales having now been pretty well collected and classified,† it remains only to recognise their immense ethnographical value, since there is probably not a single legend or superstition afloat in Lancashire that, like an ancient coin, does not refer the curious student to distant lands and long-past ages. Lancashire, we must remember, has been successively inhabited, or occupied, more or less, by a Celtic people—the Romans, Danes, and Anglo-Saxons —all of whom have left their foot-prints. No one can reside a year in Lancashire without hearing of its 'boggarts'—familiar, in another form, in the Devonshire 'pixies,' and in the 'merry wanderer of the night,' Titania's 'sweet Puck.' Absurd to the logician, the tales and the terrors connected with the boggarts carry with them, like all other fables, a profound interior truth—the truth for which, as Carlyle says, 'reason will always inquire, while half-reason stands indifferent and mocking.' The nucleus of the boggart idea is, that 'the power of the human mind, exercised with firmness and consistency, triumphs over all obstacles, and reduces even spirits to its will ;' while, contrariwise, 'the weak and undetermined are plagued and domineered over by the very same imps whom the resolute can direct and control.' So with the superstitions as to omens. When, in spring, the anglers start for a day's enjoyment, they look anxiously for 'pynots,' or magpies, *one* being unlucky, while *two* portend good fortune. The simple fact, so the ornithologists tell us, is that, in cold and ungenial weather, prejudicial to sport with the rod, one of every pair of birds always stays in the nest, whereas in fine weather, good for angling, they both come out. Illustrations of this nature might be multiplied a hundred-fold, and to unabating advantage. Time is never ill spent upon interpretation of the mythic. The effort, at all events, is a kindly one that seeks

'To unbind the charms that round slight fables lie,
    And show that truth is truest Poësy.'

The dialect itself is full of metaphor, images of great beauty and antiquity not infrequently turning up. Light and sound are reciprocally representative. From the earliest ages the idea of music has always

accompanied that of sunrise. Though to-day the heavens declare the glory of God silently, in the beginning 'the morning stars sang together.' In Lancashire old Homer's 'rosy-fingered morn' is the 'skryke' or cry 'of day.'

Though much that is deplorably brutal occurs among the lowest Lancashire classes, the character of the popular pastimes is in general free from stain : and the amusements themselves are often eminently interesting, since there is always an archæology in rustic sports. This, in truth, now constitutes the chief attraction of the older ones. The social influences of the railway system have told no less upon the village-green than on the streets of cities ; any picture that may now be drawn must needs owe its best colours to the retrospective. Contemplating what remains of them, it is pleasant, however, to note the intense vitality of customs and ceremonials having their root in feelings of reverence ; such, for example, as the famous annual Rush-bearing, still current in many parts, and not unknown even in the streets of modern Manchester. That in the olden time, prior to the introduction of carpets, the practice was to strew floors and indoor pavements with green rushes every one knows. Among the charges brought against Cardinal Wolsey was his extravagance in too frequent spreading of clean ones. Employed also in churches and cathedrals, on the anniversary of the feast of the saint to whom the building was dedicated, they were renewed with special solemnity. In an age when processions full of pomp and splendour were greatly delighted in, no wonder that the renewal became an excuse for a showy pageant ; and thus, although to-day we have only the rush-cart, the morris-dancers, the drums and trumpets, and the flags —the past, in association, lives over again. Small events and great ones are seldom far asunder. In the magnificent 'Rush-bearing' got up for the delectation of James I. when at Hoghton Tower, Sunday, August 17, 1617, lay one of the secret causes of the Stuart downfall. Sports on the Sabbath-day had been forbidden by his predecessor. James, admitting as argument that the cause of the reformed religion had suffered by the prohibition, gave his 'good people of Lancashire' leave to resume them. The Puritans took offence ; the wound was deepened by Charles ; and when the time of trial came it was remembered.

'Pace-egging' (a corruption of Pasche or Pasque-egging) is another immemorial Lancashire custom, observed, as the term indicates, at Easter, the egg taking its place as an emblem of the Resurrection. Perverted and degraded, though in the beginning decorous, if not pious, the original house-to-house visitation has long had engrafted upon it a kind of rude drama, supposed to represent the combat of St. George and the Dragon,—the victory of good

---

* The late Sir James Phillips Kay-Shuttleworth, Bart.
† 'Lancashire Folk-lore.' By John Harland and T. T. Wilkinson. 1867.

over evil, of life over death. So with 'Simnel-Sunday,' a term derived from the Anglo-Saxon *symblian*, to banquet, or *symbel*, a feast, a 'simnel' being literally 'banquet-bread.'* This corresponds with the Midlent-Sunday of other counties, but, particularly in Bury, is a time of particular festivity.

The annual village 'wakes,' observed everywhere in Lancashire, and equivalent to the local Rush-bearings, partake, it is to be feared, of the general destiny of such things. Happily the railway system has brought with it an inestimable choice of pleasure for the rational. The emphatically staple enjoyment of the working Lancashire population to-day consists in the Whitsun-week trip to some distant place of loveliness or wonder. In Lancashire it is not nearly or so much, Whitsun-Monday or Whitsun-Tuesday, as the whole of the four following days. In the south-eastern part, Manchester particularly, business almost disappears; and very delightful is it then to observe how many little parties of the toiling thrifty are away to North Wales, Scotland, Ireland,

* In the Anglo-Saxon version of the Old Testament, there are many examples of derivative words. In Exod. xxiii. 15, 16, feasting-time is *symbel-tid*; xxii. 5, a feast-day is *symbel-dæg*. In Ps. lxxxi. 3, we have *symelnys*, a feast-day.

and even France. So, to a certain extent, with the 'hands.' The Factory system always implies *masses*. The people work in masses, and suffer in masses, and rejoice in masses. In Whitsun-week, fifty miles, a hundred miles, away, we find in a score of places, five hundred, perhaps a thousand. Manchester does wisely in holding its principal Flower-show during this great annual holiday, drawing, upon an average, some 50,000 visitors. The example is a good one, since with the growing disposition of the English people to enjoy their holidays, it behoves all those who have the management of places of healthy pleasure to supply the most humanising that may be possible, and thus mitigate the influence of the hurtful ones. The staple games of muscular Lancashire are bowls and cricket. A history of Manchester would be incomplete without plenty of lively chat about the former; and in regard to the latter it is no vaunt to add that while the chief cricketing in England lies in the hands of only nine out of its forty counties, the premiership last year was claimed as fairly by Lancashire as by its great rival on the banks of the Trent. Nottinghamshire, moreover, retained its position without facing half the difficulties that befell Lancashire.

VII.

The Inland Scenery south of Lancaster.

SCENERY more diversified than that of Lancashire, taking the Duddon as its northern boundary, does not exist in any other English county. For the present we shall keep to the portion south of the Lune, deferring the Lake District to the next chapter, to which may also be left the little that has nearly level. Nothing must be expected where it borders upon the Mersey, above the estuary. To quote the precise terms employed by Pennant, 'The Mersey is by no means a pleasing water.' The country bordering upon it, he might have added, appeals very slenderly to the imagination ; and most assuredly,

BLACKSTONE EDGE.

to be said concerning the shore south of that river. The eastern parts have charms quite as decided as those of the north, though of a character totally different. Every acknowledged element of the picturesque may be discovered there, sometimes in abundance. The only portion of the county entirely devoid of landscape beauty is that which is traversed by the Liverpool and Southport Railway, not unjustly described as the dullest in the kingdom. The best that can be said of this dreary district is, that at intervals it is relieved by the cheerful hues of cultivation. From Liverpool, northwards to the banks of the Ribble, excepting at some distance from the sea, and eastwards to Manchester, the ground is

since the old topographer passed along, Nature has made no change for the better as regards the river, while man has done his best to efface every attraction it may once have owned. But we have not to go very far from the modern Tyre in order to find hills and the picturesque. Newborough and the vicinity present a remarkable contrast to the plains beneath. Here the country begins to grow really beautiful, and thenceforward it constantly improves. Some of the slopes are treeless, and smooth as a lawn ; others are broken by deep and wooded glades, with streamlets bound for the Douglas (an affluent of the Ribble), one of the loveliest dells of the kind in South Lancashire occurring near Gathurst. On the summits, at Ashurst particularly, a sweet and pleasant air always 'invites our gentle senses.' Here, too, we get our first lesson in what may be truly said, once for all, of Lancashire, —that wherever the ground is sufficiently bold and elevated, we are sure not only of fine air and an extensive prospect, but a glorious one. At Ashurst, while Liverpool is not too far for the clear discerning of its towers and spires, in the south are plainly distinguished the innumerable Delamere pines, rising in dark masses, like islands out of the sea; and far away, beyond the Dee, we may perceive the soft swell of the hills of North Wales, Moel Famma never failing. This celebrated eminence, almost as well known in South Lancashire as in Denbighshire, may

maximum altitude of nearly 1900 feet. Were a survey possible from overhead, the scene would be that of a great tempest-ruffled ocean, the waves suddenly made solid.

Very much of this vast hill-surface consists of desolate, heathery, unsheltered moorland. The amount of unreclaimed land still existing in Lancashire, and which must needs remain for ever as it is, constitutes, in truth, one of the striking characteristics of the county. Not merely in the portion now specially under notice are there cold and savage wastes such as laugh the plough to scorn. The 'fells' of the more northern districts present enormous breadths of similar character, incapable of supporting more than the

THE LAKE AT LITTLEBOROUGH.

be descried even at Eccles, four or five miles, or thereabouts, from the Manchester Exchange.

Eastwards of the great arterial line of railway which, running from Manchester to Lancaster, through Bolton and Preston, almost exactly bisects the county, the scenery, if not everywhere fine and imposing, is at all events rich in the eloquent features which come of wild and interminable surges of broad and massive hill, often rocky, with heights of fantastic form, the irregularities giving token, in their turn, of deep chasms and clefts, that subdivide into pretty lateral glens and moist hollows, crowded with ferns. The larger glens constitute the 'cloughs' so famous in local legend, and the names of which recur so frequently in Lancashire literature. As Yorkshire is approached, the long succession of beautiful uplands increases in volume, rising, at last, in parts, to a

poorest aboriginal vegetation, affording only the scantiest pasturage for a few scattered mountain-sheep, thus leaving the farmer without a chance. In itself, the fact, of course, is in no degree remarkable, since there are plenty of hopeless acres elsewhere. The singular circumstance is the association of so much barrenness with the stupendous industries of the busiest people in the world. It is but in keeping, after all, with the general idea of old England,—

'This precious gem, set in the silver sea,'—

the pride of which consists in the constant blending of the most diverse elements. If we have grim and hungry solitudes, bleak and sterile wildernesses, not very far off, be sure there is graceful counterpoise in placid vale and fruitful mead. Lancashire may not supply it. Let every county do its own particular part. The soil and climate, though good for potatoes, are unfriendly to the cerealia. There is no need, either, to be so precise; the set-off is never far beyond the borders.

A few miles beyond Bolton the hills begin to rise with dignity. Here we find far-famed and far-seen Riven, or, as it is now usually called, Rivington Pike, conspicuous, like Ashurst, through ascending almost

case of the classic mound at Samos which Callimachus connects so elegantly with the name of the lady Parthenia. There are spots, however, where the mamelon disappears. From all parts of the summit the prospect is delightful. Under our feet, unrolled like a carpet, is a smooth and verdant flat, which stretches unbrokenly to the sea-margin, twenty miles distant, declared, nevertheless, by a soft, sweet gleam

WATERFALL IN CLIVIGER.

immediately out of the plain. 'Pike' is in Lancashire, and in parts of the country closely adjacent, the equivalent of Peak, the highest point of a hilly neighbourhood, though by no means implying an exactly conical or pyramidal figure, and very generally no more than considerable elevation, as in the case of the 'Peak of Derbyshire.' Rivington Well deserves its name, the summit presenting, from many points of view one of those beautiful, evenly and gently rounded eminences which the ancient Greeks were accustomed to call τιτθοι and μαστοι, as in the

of silver or molten gold, according to the position of the sun in the heavens. The estuary of the Ribble, if the tide be in, renews that lovely shining; and in the remote distance, if the atmosphere be fairly clear, fifty or sixty miles away, the grand mountains that cast their shadows into Coniston. Working Lancashire, though it has lakes of its own, has made others! From the summit of Rivington we now look down upon half-a-dozen immense reservoirs—the stronghold of the Liverpool water-works—grouped, yet not unpleasantly near together, and so charmingly located that to believe them the work of man is scarcely possible. Fed by the inflow of several little streams, and no pains taken to enforce straight margins, except when necessary, these ample waters exemplify in the best manner how art and science are able at times to recompense nature,

> Leaving that beautiful which always was,
> And making that which was not.'

After heavy and continuous rain, the overflow gives rise to grand waterfalls. Up in the glen called Deanwood there is also a natural and nearly permanent cascade.*

The eastern slopes of the Rivington range descend into the spacious and remarkable valley which, beginning just outside Manchester, extends nearly to Agricola's Ribchester, and in the Roman times was a soldiers' thoroughfare. In this valley lie Darwen, Blackburn, and Turton, near which last-named place, at Entwistle, there is another magnificent reservoir, a mile in length, for local service. The hills, both right and left, again supply prospects of great extent, and are especially attractive through containing many fine recesses, sometimes as round as amphitheatres. Features of much the same kind pertain to the nearly parallel valley in which Summerseat nestles, with the pleasurable additions that come of care to preserve and to compensate in case of injury. By this route we may proceed, for variety, to Whalley, the Mecca of the local archæologist; thence on to Clitheroe, and to the foot of Pendle. Whalley is overlooked by the terminating point of the Altham range, usually called Nab or Nab's Hill, but properly Whalley Nab —though this is the name, also, of a neighbouring hamlet, 'nab' being a form of the Scandinavian *nibbé* or *nibba*, a promontory—as in Nab-scar, near Rydal, and Nab-crag, in Patterdale. To ascend it is pastime enough for a summer's evening. Inconsiderable in comparison with some of its neighbours, this favoured eminence gives testimony once again to the advantages conferred by situation and surroundings, when the rival claims consist in mere bulk and altitude. Lord Byron might have intended it in the immortal lines :—

> ' Green and of mild declivity, the last,
> As 'twere the cape of a long ridge of such,
> Save that there was no sea to lave its base,
> But a most living landscape.'

Westwards, from the summit, the eye ranges, as at Rivington, over a broad champaign, the loveliest of the district, the turrets of princely Stonyhurst rising amid a green throng of oaks and beeches. In the north it rests upon the flanks of distant Longridge, the nearer scene delightfully accentuated by the

ruined keep of the ancient castle of the Norman De Lacys. On the right towers Pendle itself, most massive of English mountains, its ' broad bare back' literally ' upheaved into the sky ;' and completing the harmonious picture—since no landscape is perfect without water—below runs the babbling Calder. Whalley Nab has been planted very liberally with trees. How easy it is for good taste to confer embellishment !

Pendle, the most distinguished and prominent feature in the physical geography of Mid-Lancashire, is not, like mountains in general, broken by vast defiles, but fashioned after the manner of the Dundry range in Somersetshire, presenting itself as a huge and almost uniform green mound, several miles in length, and with a nearly level sky-line. Dundry, however, is much less steep. The highest point is at the upper or north-east extremity, stated by the Ordnance Survey to be 1850 feet above the sea. The superficial extent is estimated at 15,000 statute acres, or about 25 square miles, including the great gorge upon the southern side called Ogden Clough—a broad, deep, and mysterious-looking hollow, which contributes not a little to the fine effect of this gigantic hill as seen from the Yorkshire side.

The slope which looks upon Yorkshire marks the boundary of the famous ' forest of Pendle,' a territory of nearly 25,000 acres—not to be understood as now or at any former period, covered with great and aged trees, but simply as a tract which, when the property was first apportioned, lay *ad foras*, or outside the lands deemed valuable for domestic purposes, and which was left undisputed to the wild animals of the country. Immense breadths of land of this description existed in England in early times, and in no part was the proportion larger than in Lancashire, where many of the ancient ' forests' still retain their primitive appellation, and are peculiarly interesting in the marked survival among the inhabitants of the language, manners, and customs of their ancestors. Generally speaking, these ancient ' forests' are distinguished also by dearth of primitive architecture and of rude primæval fences, the forest laws having forbidden all artificial hindrances to the chase, which in the refuges thus afforded to ' deer,' both large and small, had its most ample and enjoyable scope.

From the summit of Pendle, all that is seen from Whalley Nab, now diminutive, is renewed on a scale of the utmost grandeur. The glistening waters of the Irish Sea in the far west ; in the north the mountains of Westmoreland ; proximately the smiling valleys of the Ribble, the Hodder, and the Calder ; and, turning to the east, the land as far towards the German Ocean as the powers of the eye can reach. When the atmosphere is in its highest state of transparency the glorious view includes the towers of York Minster. Well might the old historian of Whalley commend the prospect from mighty Pendle as one upon which

---

* The surface of these great reservoirs, when they are full, is 500 acres. They were first used for the supply of Liverpool in January, 1857.

'the eye, the memory, and the imagination, rest with equal delight.' To the same author we owe the showing that the common Lancashire term Pendle-*hill* is incorrect, seeing that the sense of 'hill' is already conveyed, as in Penmanmawr and Penyghent.

All these grand peaks and soaring masses belong essentially to the great family group reached another time by going from Manchester to Littleborough. Littleborough lies at the base of that once-again-majestic mountain range called Blackstone Edge, so lofty (1553 feet), and, when climbed, so impressive in all its circumstances, that we seem to be pacing the walls of an empire. All the topmost part is moorland.

atmosphere is free from mist, the prospect—now an old story—is once again magnificent, and, as at Rivington, made perfect by water. Nowhere, perhaps, in England has so much landscape beauty been provided artificially, and *undesignedly*, by the construction of great reservoirs, as in the country of twenty miles radius around Manchester. The beautiful sheets of water at Lymm and Taxal belong respectively to Cheshire and Derbyshire. Independently of those at Rivington, Lancashire excels both in the romantic lake under Blackstone Edge, well known to every pleasure-seeker as 'Hollingworth.' The measurement round the margin is at least two

IN THE BURNLEY VALLEY.

Below, or upon the sides, there is abundance of the picturesque; precipitous crags and rocky knolls, receding dells and ravines, occurring frequently. Many of the dells in summer bear witness to the descent in winter of furious torrents, the broad bed of the now tiny streamlet that falls from ledge to ledge, being strewed with stones and boulders, evidently washed down from the higher channel by the vehement water, heedlessly tossed about, and then abandoned. The desolate complexion of these winter-torrent gullies (in Lancashire phrase, 'water-gaits') in its way is unique, though often charmingly redeemed by innumerable green fern-plumes on the borders. The naturalist's enjoyment is further promoted by the occurrence, not infrequently, of calamites and other fossils. The ascent to the crest of Blackstone Edge is by no means arduous. Attaining it, provided the

miles; hills almost completely encircle it, and as seen from the Edge, near Robin Hood's crags, so utterly is it detached from all that pertains to towns and cities as to recall the remotest wilds beyond the Tweed. Hollingworth Lake was constructed about eighty years ago, with a view to steady maintenance of the Rochdale Canal. Among the hills upon the opposite or north-western side of the valley, Brown Wardle, often named in story, is conspicuous; and adorning the lofty general outline may be seen—best, perhaps, from near 'Middleton Junction'—another beautiful mamelon.

Looking westwards from the Robin Hood pinnacles, the prospect includes the valleys of the Roch and the Spodden, the last-named stream in parts wild and wilful. At Healey, its walls of rock appear to have been riven at different times. Here, struggling through a lengthened and tortuous cleft, and forming more than one lively cascade before losing itself in the dingle below, so plainly does the water seem to have forced a passage, asserting mastery over all impediments, that in the vernacular this spot is called the 'Thrutch.' The first phrase heard in a Lancashire crowd is, 'Where are you thrutching?' and to a Lancashire man such metaphors come naturally. The perennial attrition of the broken and impending rocks causes many of them to terminate in sharp ridges, and in one part has given birth to the 'Fairies' Chapel.' The streams spoken of have their beginning in the lofty grounds which intervene between Rochdale and Cliviger, and amid which occur the grand summits called Hades Hill and Thieveley Pike. The last named, in the bygones, served the important use of a station for beacon-fires, signalling on the one hand to Pendle, on the other to Buckton Castle. The prospect from the top, 1474 feet above the sea, is inexpressibly noble, comprehending, to the north, almost the whole of Craven, with Ingleborough, and the wilds of Trawden Forest. The nearer portions of the Lake District mountains, now familiar, are discernible, and on sunny evenings, when the river is full, once more the bright-faced estuary of the Ribble. The view reaches also to North Wales and Derbyshire, the extremities of this great map being at least sixty miles asunder.

Cliviger, after all, is the locality which most astonishes and delights the visitor to this part of Lancashire. Soon after quitting Rochdale, the railway passes through the great 'Summit Tunnel,' and so into the Todmorden Valley, there, very soon, passing the frontier formed by the Calder,* and entering Yorkshire. The valley is noted for its fine scenery, new combinations of the most varied elements, rude but not inhospitable, rising on each side in quick succession. Turning to the left, up the Burnley Valley, we enter Cliviger proper, a district having a circuit of nearly twenty miles, and presenting an endless variety of the most romantic and commanding features possible to mingled rock and pastured slope, constantly lifted to mountain-height, the charm of the huge grey bluffs of projecting gritstone augmented in many parts by abundance of trees, the predominant forms the graceful ones of larch, birch, and mountain-ash. The trees are now very nearly a century old, having been planted during the fifteen years ending with 1799, yet, to appearance, still in the prime of their calm existence. A very striking characteristic of this admired

valley is the frequent apparent closing-in of the passage by protruding crags, which, nevertheless, soon give way to peculiarly beautiful and verdant curves. Cliviger, in every part, is more or less marked by such crags and sweeping curves, so that we incessantly come upon vast green bowls or hemispherical cavities, the bases of which change at times into circular plateaux, at midsummer decked with carpets of the prettiest wild-flowers of the province,—

'In emerald tufts, flowers purple, blue, and white,
Like sapphire, pearl, and rich embroidery.'

For introduction to these pretty bits it is needful, of course, to leave the main thoroughfares, and take one of the innumerable by-paths which lead away to the lonely and impressive silence of the moors, which, though desolate, and sometimes bleak, have a profoundly delightful influence upon the mind. Their interest is heightened by the parts which are vivid green with bog-moss, being the birth-place of important streams. No slight matter is it to stand at any time where rivers are cradled. Here the flow of water is at once both east and westwards—a phenomenon seen several times in the English Apennine, and always curiously fascinating. The Ribble and the Wharfe begin this way; so do the Lune and the Swale; playmates in childhood, then parting for ever. Similarly, in Cliviger Dean, the two Calders issue from the same fragment of watery waste, destined immediately for opposite courses. Hard by, in a stream called Erewell, at the foot of Derply Hill, on the verge of Rossendale, may be seen the birthplace of the Manchester Irwell.

The promise given at Newborough in regard to the scenery of East Lancashire is thus perfectly fulfilled. The wild and imposing character of the hills does not terminate either with Cliviger, being renewed, after passing Pendle, in long succession all the way to the borders of Westmoreland. Ward Stone, eight or nine miles south-east of Lancaster, part of the Littledale Fells, has an altitude exceeding even that of Pendle.

The most inviting portions of the Lancashire River scenery come of streams not really its own—the Lune, approaching from Westmoreland, by way of Kirkby Lonsdale, to which place it gives name; and the Ribble, descending from the high moorlands of Craven, first passing Ingleborough, then Settle and Bolton Abbey. The only two important streams which actually rise within the confines of the county are the Irwell and the Wyre. Lancashire is rich in home-born *minor* streams, a circumstance said to be recognised in the ancient British name of the district —literally, according to Whitaker, 'the well-watered.'*

* This, of course, is not the Calder seen at Whalley, there being three rivers in Lancashire of the name—the West Calder, the East, and a little stream which enters the Wyre near Garstang. The West Calder enters the Ribble; the eastern, after a course of forty miles, joins the Aire in the neighbourhood of Wakefield.

* It may not be amiss here to mention the names, in exact order, of the Lancashire rivers, giving first those which enter the sea, the affluents and their tributaries coming afterwards :—

Many of these, the affluents in particular, lend themselves freely and gracefully to the production of the picturesque, as in the case of the Darwen, which, after gliding beneath Hoghton Tower, joins the Ribble at Walton ; and in that of the Wenning, which at Hornby forsakes its sheltering trees to strengthen the Lune. The Irwell itself, though incurably sullied, presents, just above Manchester, some remarkably pretty reaches. Tributaries — the little primitive streamlets which swell the affluents— since they begin, almost always, among the mountains, are at all times, all over the world, wherever they run, pure and voiceful, therefore lovely. Still, as regards

proud and wealthy Ribchester was in existence, fifteen centuries ago, there is reason to believe that the Ribble, for many miles above Preston, was considerably broader and deeper than at present, or, at all events, that the tide came very much further up than it does to-day. It did so as late as the time of Leland. The change, as regards the bed of the river, would thus be exactly the reverse of the helpful one to which we owe the modern Liverpool harbour. England does not contain scenery of its kind more grateful than that of the Ribble, from Ribchester upwards. The river winds ; in parts it is impetuous. Whether rapid or calm, it is the life of a peaceful

THE RIBBLE AT CLITHEROE.

claims to high distinction, the river-scenery of Lancashire is that, as we have said, which pertains to its welcome guests, the Ribble and the Lune. When

(1.) The Mersey, formed of the union of the non-Lancashire Tame, Etherowe, and Goyt. Affluents and tributaries—the Irwell, the Roche, the Spodden, the Medlock, the Irk. (2.) The Alt. (3.) The Ribble. Affluents and tributaries—the Douglas, the Golforden, the Darwen,* the West Calder, the Lostock, the Yarrow, the Brun. (4.) The Wyre, which receives the third of the Calders, the Brock, and several others. (5.) The Lune, or Loyne. Affluents and tributaries—the Wenning, the Conder, the Greeta, the Leck, the Hindburn. Then, north of Lancaster, the Keer, the Bela, the Kent, the Winster, the Leven (from Windermere), the Crake (from Coniston - water), and the Duddon.

* The river immortalised by Milton, alluding to the conflict of August 17, 1648 :—

‘And Darwen stream with blood of Scots imbrued.’

dale, from which the hills retire in the gentlest way imaginable, presenting, as they go, green, smooth faces, fit for pasture ; then in the sweetest of quick variety — delightful wooded banks and shaded recesses, followed by more green lawns, then woods again, the last seeming to lean against the sky. When the outline drops sufficiently, in the distance, according to the point of observation, rises proud old Pendle, or Penyghent, or Wharnside. Near Mitton, where Yorkshire darts so curiously into Lancashire, the channel is somewhat shallow. Here, after a busy and romantic course of its own, the Hodder surrenders its waters, thus in good time to take part in the wonderful whirl at Salesbury, a little lower down, an eddy of nearly twenty yards in depth, and locally known as ‘Sale-wheel.’ If a haven ever existed at the mouth of the Ribble, it has now disappeared. The sands at the bar continually shift with high tides, so that navigation is hazardous, and vessels of light draught can alone attempt the passage.

The very interesting portion of the scenery on the banks of the Lune, so far as concerns Lancashire, lies just above Lancaster itself. Nearly all the elements of perfect landscape intermingle in this part of the valley. If either side of the stream possesses an advantage, perhaps it will belong to the road along the southern border, or that which proceeds by way of Melling and Caton to Hornby, distant from Lancaster about nine miles. The river winds so waywardly that in many parts it seems a string of lakelets. Masses of woodland creep down to the edge, and whichever way the eye is turned, green hills form pictures that leave nothing to be desired.

The Roman Road.—The portion of Roman Road above referred to (page 3) as crossing Blackstone Edge presents, like all similar remains in our island, one of the most conclusive as well as interesting memorials we possess of the thorough conquest of the country by the Cæsars. Labour and skill, such as were so plainly devoted to the construction of these wonderful ways, would be expended only by conquerors determined on full and permanent possession, such as the Romans maintained for three hundred and seventy years. The Blackstone Edge road has in addition the peculiar interest which attaches to features not found anywhere else in England. The roads in question were designed not more to facilitate the movements of the troops than for the easier transport of merchandise and provisions, a purpose which this one seems to indicate perfectly. In the 'Lancashire' of to-day there were several roads of the principal class, these serving to connect Warrington, Manchester, Ribchester, and Lancaster, from which last there was continuation to Carlisle; and to furnish ready access to modern 'Yorkshire,' thus to Ickley—the Olicana of Ptolemy—and York, the famous city which saw the death of Severus and the birth of Constantine. Manchester and Ribchester were the two most important strongholds in Western Brigantia, standing on the direct great western line from the south to the north. There were also many branch or vicinal roads leading to minor stations; those, for instance, represented to-day by Wigan, Colne, Burnley, Kirkham, Urswick, Walton-le-Dale, and Overborough. The lines of most of these roads have been accurately determined, the chief of them having been usually straight as an arrow, carried forward with undeviating precision regardless of all

obstacles. They were formed generally, in Lancashire, of huge boulder stones, probably got from neighbouring watercourses, or of fragments of rock embedded in gravel, and varied in width from four yards to perhaps fourteen. The stones have in most places disappeared—made use of, no doubt, by after-comers for building purposes; as exemplified on Blackstone Edge itself, where the materials of which the wall near the road has been constructed point only too plainly to their source. Complete remains, continuous for any considerable distance, are found only upon elevated and unfrequented moorlands; where also the substance of the road appears to have been more rigid. The Blackstone Edge road, one of this kind, ascends the hill at a point about two miles beyond Littleborough—an ancient Roman station, here consisting of a strip of pavement exactly sixteen feet wide. It is composed of square blocks of mill-stone-grit, obtained upon the spot, laid with consummate care, and presenting, wherever the dense growth of whortleberry and other coarse herbage has been cleared away; a surface so fresh and even, that for seventeen centuries to have elapsed since its construction seems incredible. The great and unique feature of the road consists in the middle being formed of blocks considerably larger than those used at the sides—harder, and altogether of better quality, laid end to end, and having a continuous longitudinal groove evidently the work of the chisel. This groove, or 'trough,' evidently extended down the entire roadway, where steep, beginning at the top of the hill. Nothing like it is found anywhere else in England, for the simple reason, it would appear, that no other British Roman road descends by so steep an incline. For it can hardly be doubted that Dr. March is correct in his conjecture, that it was intended to steady the passage of waggons or other vehicles when heavily laden; brakes adjusted to the wheels retarding their progress, as indicated by marks still distinguishable. In some parts there are indications also of lateral trenches cut for the downflow of water, the road itself being kept dry by a slight convexity of surface. Over the crest of the hill the descent is easy, and here the paving seems to have been discontinued. The Robin Hood rocks, close by, present remarkably fine examples of typical mill-stone-grit. Rising to the height of fifty feet and fantastically 'weathered,' on the summits, there are basin-like cavities, popularly attributed, like so many other things they had no hand in, to the Druids; but palpably referable to a far less mythical agency—the quiet action, during thousands of years, of the rain and the atmosphere.

VIII.

The Seashore and the Lake District.

THE coast of Lancashire has already been described as presenting, from the Mersey upwards as far as the estuary of the Kent, an almost unbroken surface of level sand. In several parts, as near Birkdale, the western sea-breeze, pursuing its work for ages, has heaped up the sand, atom by atom, into hills that have a romantic and attractive beauty all their own. But of overhanging rocks and crags there are no examples, except when at Heysham, in Morecambe Bay, the millstone grit, cropping out so as to form a little promontory, gives pleasing change. Almost immediately after entering this celebrated bay—although the vast expanse of sand remains unaltered—the mountains begin to draw nearer, and for the rest of the distance, up to the estuary of the Duddon, where Cumberland begins, the scenery close inshore is strikingly picturesque. The peculiar feature of the coast consists, perhaps, in its estuaries. No seaside county in England has its margin interrupted by so many as there are in Lancashire, every one of the rivers which leave it for the Irish Sea, excepting the insignificant Alt (six or eight miles north of Liverpool), widening immensely as the sands are approached. Embouchures more remarkable than those of the Ribble, the Wyre, the Lune, and the various minor streams which enter Morecambe Bay, are certainly not to be found, and there are none that through association awaken interest more curious.

When, accordingly, the visitor to any one of the Lancashire watering-places south of the Ribble desires scenery, he must be content with the spectacle of the sea itself, and the glimpses obtained in fair weather of the mountains of maritime North Wales. At Blackpool—or rather from a green bank behind the town, by some called 'Forest Hill'—it is possible, also, on clear evenings, to descry the lofty peaks of the Isle of Man, and occasionally even Cumberland Black Combe. At Fleetwood these quite compensate the dearth of inland beauty, and with every step northwards more glorious becomes the outlook. Not to mention the noble sea in front—an ocean when the tide is in—all the higher grounds of Cartmel and Furness are plainly in view. Upon these follow the majestic fells of Coniston, and a little

more to the east the dim blue cones which mark the near neighbourhood of the head of Windermere. Everything is renewed at Morecambe, and upon a scale still more commanding: the last reflection, as one turns homeward from that favoured spot, is that the supreme seaside scenery of old England pertains, after all, to the many-sided county of the cotton-mills.

The watering-places themselves are healthful, well conducted, and ambitious. None of them had substantial existence sixty or seventy years ago. Southport, the most important, and the most advanced in all that is honourable, is a daughter of the primitive neighbouring village of Churchtown,—*filia pulchrior*, very emphatically. Blackpool, in 1817, was only a rabbit-warren, rich, like Birkdale and Churchtown, until quite recently, in quick-eyed lizards. Fleetwood has grown up within easy recollection; Morecambe is a creation almost of yesterday. Unexcelled, in summer, for the visitor in search of health, in its cool, firm, and ample sands, and magnificent views across the water, Fleetwood bids fair to become important also commercially, the Wyre offering peculiar advantages as a port. Morecambe, though destitute of a deep channel, and unable to offer the security of a natural harbour, is making vigorous efforts in the same direction. Sir J. E. Smith, in his account of the evening-primrose in 'English Botany,' described the Lancashire coast as a sort of *ultima Thule*. To-day, at Southport, there is the finest Winter Garden out of London; and at a couple of miles distance, reached by tram-car, a Botanical Garden, including fernery and conservatories, that puts to shame many an ancient and wealthy city. A drawback to these South Lancashire watering-places, as mentioned before, is that the water, at low tide, recedes so far, and ordinarily is so reluctant to return. But is the tide everything? When out, there is the serene pleasure of silent stroll upon the vast expanse, the inspiring solitude beyond which there is only Sea. On these smooth and limitless sands there is plenty alike for repair of body, the imagination, and the solace of the naturalist. Shells may be gathered in plenty, and in different parts, of very various kinds. Solens, long and straight; pretty Mactras, crowded with semicircles; Tellinas, that seem scattered rose-petals, are abundant; and towards Fleetwood there are pearly Trochuses, dappled with lilac. A more delicious seaside walk for those who love the sound of the rolling surge, the sense of infinite tranquillity, total seclusion from every circumstance of town and city life, and the sight of old Ocean's playthings, may be sought the world over, and not found more readily than by pursuing the five or six miles between Fleetwood and Blackpool, one's face turned all the while to the poetic west. Wanting rocks, upon these quiet sands there are no native seaweeds, though fragments, torn from beaches far away, are stranded in plenty.

Peculiar interest attaches to the physical history of this part of the coast, the elevation of which was at some not very remotely distant period, almost without doubt, much higher. Mr. Joseph Dickinson, the well-known geologist, and Government Inspector of Mines, believes that in certain portions it has subsided through the solution of rock-salt in the strata below—the circumstance to which the formation of most, if not all, of the natural Cheshire meres is attributed. The existence of the rock-salt has been clearly proved by the sinking of a shaft and subsequent borings, near Preesal, a village about a mile and a half south-east of Fleetwood. The thickness of the deposit is similar to that met with in the salt districts of Cheshire, at Port Clarence, near the mouth of the Tees, and at Stoke Prior, Worcestershire. The subsidence of the shore at Blackpool is, on the northern side, very remarkable and distinct. Here the path to Rossall is pursued for some distance along the brow of an earthy, crumbling, seaward cliff, not very far from which, exposed at the lowest of low tides, there is a little insulated mound, upon which, according to well-sustained tradition, there once stood a cottage long since overwhelmed by envious Neptune.

The great rampart of sand-hills which stretches for so many leagues, and which has been calculated to have an area of twenty-two square miles, is thought by another distinguished geologist—Mr. T. Melland Reade—to have taken certainly not less than 2500 years to form, probably a much longer time. Some of the mounds, however, are palpably quite recent, inter-stratifications of cinders and matter thrown up from wrecks, being found near the base. A strong westerly wind brings up the sand vehemently, and very curious then becomes the spectacle of its travel, which is like thin waves of transparent smoke over the flat wet shore. The wind alternately heaps up the sand and disperses it, except where a firm hold has been obtained by the maram,* or 'star-grass,' which, running beneath the surface, binds and holds all together. A

very beautiful decoration of the smooth surface of the sloping sand-hills is constantly produced by the wind-whirling of the slender stalks half way round, and sometimes quite so, when there is room for free play. Elegant circles and semicircles are then grooved, smaller ones often inside, as perfect as if drawn with compasses. Another curious result of the steady blowing of the sea-breeze is that on the level of the shore there are innumerable little cones of sand, originating in shells, or fragments of shells, which arrest the drifting particles, and are, in truth, rudiments of sand-hills, such as form the barrier a little further in.

Further north the shore has little to offer in the way of curiosities, nor is there any agreeable bathing-ground; not even at Grange. Never mind. The further we advance towards the county frontier, the more wonderful become the sands, these spreading, at low water, like a Sahara, with the difference, that the breath of ocean, nowhere in the world sweeter, blows across them for ever and ever. On a moonlight night, when the tide is at the full, Morecambe Bay, surveyed from Kent's Bank, presents an aspect of inexpressible fascination, the rippled lustre being such as a shallow sea, gently moving, alone can yield.

'Splendet tremulo sub lumine pontus.'

Moving onwards, or towards Cumberland, we find that Lancashire is not without its island. This is Walney, off the estuary of the Duddon, closely abutting on the mainland of Furness—a very singular bank or strip of mingled sand, pebbles, and shingle, nearly ten miles in length, and half-a-mile broad where widest. Barren as it may seem from the description, the soil is in parts so fertile that capital crops of grain are reaped. There are people on it likewise, though the inhabitants are chiefly sea-gulls. Walney Island is the only known locality for that beautiful wild-flower the *Geranium Lancastriense*, a variety of the *sanguineum*, the petals, instead of blood-colour, as at Fleetwood, on St. Vincent's Rocks, and elsewhere, cream - white pencilled with rose. The seaward or western side of Walney Island is defended by a prodigious heap of pebbles, the mass of which is constantly augmenting, though left dry at low water. At the lower extremity there is a light-house, sixty-eight feet high, and adjacent to it there are one or two islets.

The portion of Lancashire to which Walney Island belongs, or that which, as it is locally said, lies 'north of the sands' (the sands specially intended being those of Morecambe Bay), agrees, in natural composition, with Westmoreland and Cumberland. It is distinguished by very elevated mountain-summits, greatly exceeding those found upon the confines of Yorkshire, and the lower slopes of which are, as a rule, no longer

---

* Maram, the popular name of the *Ammophila arenaria*, is probably the Danish *marhalm*, sea-haulm or straw, a term applied in Norway to the Zostera.

naked, but dressed with shrubs and various trees. Concealed among these noble mountains are many deep and romantic glens, while their feet are often bathed by lakes of loveliest outline and matchless purity. No feature is more striking than the exchange of the broad and bulky masses of such hills as Pendle for the rugged and jutting outlines characteristic of the older rocks, and particularly of the unstratified. Before commencing the exploration, it is well to contemplate the general structure of the country from some near vantage-ground, such as the newly-opened Public Park at Lancaster; or, better still, that unspeakably grand terrace upon the Westmoreland side of the Kent, called Stack-head, where the 'Fairy steps' give access to the plain and valley below, and which is reached most pleasantly by way of Milnthorpe, proceeding thence through Dallam Park, the village of Beetham, and the pine-wood—in itself worth all the journey. The view from the Stack-head terrace (profoundly interesting also, geologically) comprises all that is majestic and beautiful as regards the elements of the picturesque, and to the Lancashire man is peculiarly delightful, since, although he stands actually in Westmoreland, all the best part of it, Arnside Knot alone excepted, is within the borders of his own county.* Whether the most pleasing first impressions of the scenery of the Lake District are obtained in the way indicated; or by taking the alternative, very different route, by way of Fleetwood and Piel, is nevertheless an open question. The advantage of the Lancaster route consists in the early introduction it gives to the mountains themselves—to go *viâ* Fleetwood and Piel involves one of those sweet initiative little voyages —only thirteen miles—which harmonize so well with hopes and visions of new enjoyment, alluring the imagination no less delightfully than they gratify the senses.

The Lancaster route implies, in the first instance, quiet and unpretending Silverdale; then, after crossing the estuary of the Kent, leafy Grange—unrivalled upon the north-west coast, not only for salubrity, but for the exhaustless charms of the neighbouring country. Whatever the final intentions in visiting this part of England, a few days' delay at Grange will never be regretted: it is one of those singularly happy places which are distinguished by wild nature cordially shaking hands with civilization. Sallying forth from the village in an easterly direction, or up the winding and shady road which leads primarily to Lindal, we may, if we please, proceed almost direct to Windermere, distant about six miles. Turn, before this, up the green slope just beyond

the village on the left, the pretty summer-house called Ellerhow perched conspicuously on the highest hill in front, thus reaching Hampsfell, a summit so inspiring that even Pendle seems an undertone. Many beautiful views will have been enjoyed upon the way, land and sea contributing equally; all, at the top of Hampsfell, are renewed threefold, the verdure of innumerable trees in many shades adding the sweet decorum of graceful apparel, while in the valley below grey and secluded Cartmel talks of a remote historic past. Fully to realise the majestic beauty of the scene, there must be no hesitation in ascending to the Hóspice; where the 'herald voice' of 'good tidings' heard at Lindal is proved not to have uttered a single syllable in excess. Hampsfell may be reached also by a path through the Eggerslack woods, noted for the abundance of their hazelnuts, and entered almost immediately after emerging from Grange; and again by a third, somewhat circuitous, near the limestone crags called from their drapery, Yewbarrow.

Kent's Bank, a couple of miles beyond Grange, supplies hill scenery little inferior. The heights above Allithwaite command almost the whole of the fine outlook characteristic of the northern shore of Morecambe Bay. Kirkhead and Humphrey Head also give delightful prospects, especially when the tide is in: the man who loves solitude will find them lonely enough for hermitages; blackberries beyond measure grow on the slopes. Humphrey Head is specially remarkable, consisting of a limestone promontory, the sides, in part, nearly vertical; thus closely resembling the celebrated rock at the south-western extremity of Clevedon. Grange, Kent's Bank, Kirkhead, and Humphrey Head, constantly awaken recollections of the beautiful village on the shore of the Bristol Channel. The scenery corresponds, and in productions there is again a very interesting similarity, though Clevedon has a decided advantage in regard to diversity of species. Hampsfell and Allithwaite recur at intervals all the way to the borders of the Leven; thence, with infinite change, westward to the banks of the Duddon, and southward to the Furness Valley: not, indeed, until we reach Piel—the little cape where the boats arrive from Fleetwood—do these beautiful hills subside.

Piel, as said above, is preferable as a route to the Lake District, because of the preliminary half-hour upon the water, which is generally smooth and exhilarating. It offers the most interesting way of approach, also, to Duddon Bridge, where the coast of Lancashire ends—a place itself of many attractions. The river, it is scarcely necessary to say, is the Duddon immortalized by Wordsworth in a series of charming sonnets, one of which describes the 'liquid lapse serene' of this too-seldom visited stream

---

* 'Knot,' in the Lake District, properly denotes a rocky protuberance upon a hill. But it is often used, as in the present instance, for the hill in its entirety. Hard Knot, in Eskdale, and Farleton Knot, near Kendal, are parallel examples.

as it moves through Dunnerdale, after entering, near Newfield, through a rent in the rocky screen which adds so much to the romantic features of its early existence. The bridge gives ready approach to Black Combe, most gloomy and austere of the Cumberland mountains, but affording inexpressible compensation in the magnificence of the prospects, the height being little short of 2000 feet. Close by, in Lancashire, we find the ancient and celebrated village of Broughton, the lords of which, four or five centuries ago, gave their name to a well-known suburb of Manchester—so curious is the history of estates.

The railway, after touching at Broughton, leads right away to Coniston, then to the foot of the supreme 'Old Man,' the summit, 2649 feet above the level of the sea, so remarkable in its lines and angular curves, that, once exactly distinguished from the crowd of lower heights, like the head of Ingleborough, it is impossible to be mistaken. Towards the village it throws out a ridge, upon which the houses are chiefly placed. A deep valley intervenes, and then the mountain rises abruptly, the walls in some places nearly perpendicular, but in others disappearing, so that, if well selected, the path upwards is by no means arduous, or even difficult, though impeded here and there by rocks and stones. The toil of climbing is well repaid. From the brows of the old giant are seen mountains innumerable, lakes, rivers, woods, deep valleys, velvety meads, with, in addition, all the fascinating accessories of landscape when perfect, which come of its being impregnated with the outcome of human intelligence and human feeling, the love of gardens, and of refined and comfortable homes. Looking south, south-west, and south-east, there are changing views of Morecambe Bay, flooded with brightness; the estuaries of the Kent, the Leven, and the Duddon; the capes and promontories that break the sea margin; Walney Island, the shining Irish Sea, with the Isle of Man beyond, and the whole of the long line of coast which runs on to the portals of the Wyre, and more distant Ribble.

Over the mouth of the Leven, Lancaster Castle is distinguishable. Far away, in the same line, the lofty ranges of the Craven district come in view; and when the atmosphere is very clear, a dim blue mountain wave on the side where sunset will be indicates Snowdon. In other directions the views are somewhat circumscribed, Coniston being situated upon the frontiers rather than within the actual area of the hill country it so greatly enriches. The figure in general, of all that is seen, so far as the nature of the barriers will allow, is nevertheless majestic, and in itself worth all the labour of the ascent. The Old Man, it must be admitted, is prone to hide his ancient brows in mist and vapour: the

time for climbing must therefore be chosen carefully and deliberately; opportunity and desire are not infrequently far asunder.

The lake, called Coniston Water, extends to a length of about six miles. It is in no part quite a mile in breadth, but although so narrow never gives the slightest idea of restriction; thus agreeing with Windermere, to which, however, Coniston bears not the least resemblance in detail, differing rather in every particular, and decidedly surpassing it in respect of the wildness and purple sublimity of the surroundings. The immediate borders, by reason of the frequently recurring showers of rain, are refreshingly green all the year round; they allure, also, at every season, by the daintiness and the freedom with which the greater portion has been planted. Beyond the line to which the handiwork of man has been continued, or where the ground becomes steep and rocky, there are brown and heathy slopes, fissures and winding ravines that give the most delightful impressions imaginable of light and shade, the sunward parts often laced exquisitely with little white streamlet waterfalls, that in the distance seem not cascades, but streaks or veins of unmelted winter snow. The slopes, in turn, like the arches in a Gothic cathedral, lead the eye upwards to lovely outlines that often please so much the more because imperfectly translateable; for when the clouds hover round the summits of these glorious peaks, they change to mystery and fable, wooing the mind with the peculiar charm that always waits upon the margin of the undiscovered.

From what particular point the best views, either of the lake or of the adjacent mountains, are readily obtainable, must of necessity be very much a matter of taste. Perhaps it is discreetest to take, in the first instance, the view *up* the lake, or from Nibthwaite, where the waters contract, and become the beautiful little river Crake—the stream which, in conjunction with the Leven from Windermere, forms the estuary named after the latter.

Contemplated from Nibthwaite, the mountains in which the lake is bosomed are certainly less impressive than when viewed from some distance further up; but the mind is touched with a more agreeable idea of symmetry, and the water itself seems to acquire amplitude. None of the mountains are out of sight; the merit of this particular view consists jointly in their presence, and in the dignified composure with which they seem to stand somewhat aloof. The view *down* the lake,—that which is obtained by approaching Coniston *viâ* Hawkshead and Waterhead, is indescribably grand, the imposing forms of the adjacent mountains, those in particular of the Furness fells (the altitude of which is nearly or quite 2600 feet), being here realized perfectly, the more distant summits fading delicately, the nearer ones dark and solemn. To our own fancy, the most impressive idea alike of the water and its framework is obtained, after all, not from either extremity, but from the surface, resting upon one's oars, as nearly as possibly in the middle. Coniston Water contains two little islands or islets, the upper one named, after its abundant Scotch pines, 'Fir Island.' Many little streamlets contribute to its maintenance, the principal

portion of the margin is, nevertheless, in Lancashire, without leaving which county the beauty of the 'English Zurich' may be gathered perfectly.

The finest view of the lake, as a whole, is unquestionably obtained near Ambleside, on the road through the valley of Troutbeck, where it is visible for nearly the whole extent, the islands seeming clustered in the middle. Yet nothing can be lovelier,

NEAR THE COPPER MINES, CONISTON.

being Coniston Beck and Black Beck. No celebrated waterfall occurs very near. All the famous lake waterfalls bearing names belong either to Cumberland or Westmoreland.

Windermere, or more correctly, as in the well-known line,—

'Wooded Winandermere, the river-lake,'

is nearly twice the length of Coniston Water, but of very little more than the same average width. Superficially it belongs to Westmoreland; the greater

as regards detail, than the views obtained by ascending from Newby Bridge, the point at which the Leven issues. The scenery commences long before the lake is actually reached, the river having a fall, in the short space of four miles, of no less than 105 feet, consequently flowing with great rapidity, and supplying a suitable introduction to the charms above its source. Newby Bridge deserves every word of the praise so often bestowed upon it. Lofty and wood-mantled hills enclose the valley on every side, and whichever way we turn the impression is one of Eden-like retirement. The pine-crowned summit of Finsthwaite, reached by a wood-land path having its base near the river-side, commands a prospect of the most admirable variety, the lake extending in one direction, while on the other the eye ranges over Morecambe Bay. The water of Windermere is clear as crystal—so limpid that the bottom in the shallower parts shows quite plainly, the little fishes darting hither and thither over the pebbles. Taken in its entirety, Windermere is the deepest of the English lakes, excepting only Wast-water, the level of the surface being, in parts, up-wards of 240 feet above the bed. The maximum depth of Wastwater is 270 feet. Whether, on quitting Newby Bridge, the onward course be made by boat, or, more wisely, on foot or by carriage, along the road upon the eastern margin of the lake, the prevailing character of the scenery, for a considerable distance, will be found to consist in consummate softness and a delicacy of finish that it may be permitted to call artistic.

Not until we reach the neighbourhood of Storrs Hall (half way to Ambleside), where Lancashire ends, and Westmoreland begins, is there much that can be termed either wild or imposing. The scenery, so far, has been captivating, but never grand. Here, however, and of rarest hues, especially towards sunset, come in view the majestic Langdale Pikes, with mountains of every form, and Windermere

proves itself the veritable 'Gate Beautiful.' Every-where, upon the borders, oak and ash fling out their green boughs, seeking in quiet friendship those that spring from neighbours as earnest. Woodbine loves to mingle its fragrant coronals of pink, white, and amber with the foliage amid which the spirals 'gently entwist;' and at all seasons there is the deep rich lustre of the peerless 'ivy green.' The largest of the Windermere islands (in the Lake District, as in the Bristol Channel, called 'holms') has an area of thirty acres.

Esthwaite, the third and last of the trio of lakes claimed by North Lancashire, is a quiet, un-assuming water, so cheerful, withal, and so different in character from both Coniston and Windermere, that a day is well devoted to it. The length is not quite three miles; the width, at the broadest part, is about three furlongs; the best approach is by the ferry across Windermere, then ascending a mountain-path rich with trees, the lake presently appearing upon the left, silvery and unexpected, so suddenly does it come in view; while a rampart of noble though distant mountains gives completeness to the lovely scene. Esthwaite, like the Duddon, has been immortalized by Wordsworth, who received his education at Hawkshead, the little town at the northern extremity. The outlet is a pretty stream called the Cunsey, which carries the overflow into Windermere.

CONISTON. *By David Law*

IX.

The Ancient Castles and Monastic Buildings.

AT the period so memorable in history when Wiclif was giving his countrymen the first complete English Bible—this under the kindly wing of John o' Gaunt, who shielded the daring reformer in many a perilous hour—Lancashire possessed six or seven baronial castles ; and no fewer than ten, or rather more, of the religious houses distinguished by the general name of abbeys and priories. Every one of the castles, except John o' Gaunt's own, has disappeared ; or if relics exist, they are the merest fragments. Liverpool Castle, which held out for twenty-four days against Prince Rupert, was demolished more than 200 years ago. Rochdale, Bury, Standish, Penwortham, are not sure even of the exact spots their citadels occupied. A fate in some respects heavier has overtaken the monastic buildings, these having gone in every instance ; though the ruins of one or two are so beautiful architecturally, that in their silent and elegant pathos there is compensation for the ruthless overthrow : one is reconciled to the havoc by the exquisite ornaments they confer, as our English ruins do universally, on parts of the country already picturesque.

> ' I do love these ancient ruins!
> We never tread among them, but we set
> Our foot upon some reverend history.'

Lancaster Castle, the only survivor of the fortresses, stands upon the site of an extremely ancient stronghold ; though very little, somewhat singularly, is known about it, or indeed of the early history of the town. The latter would seem to have been the Bremetonacis of the Romans, traces of the fosse constructed by whom around the castle hill are still observable upon the northern side. On the establishment of the Saxon dynasty the Roman name was superseded by the current one ; the Saxon practice being to apply the term *caster*, in different shapes, to important former seats of the departed Roman power, in the front rank of which was unquestionably the aged city touched by the waters of the winding Lune. Omitting fractions, the name of Lancaster is thus just a thousand years old. The Saxons seem to have allowed the castle to fall into decay. The powerful Norman baron, Roger de Poictou (leader of the centre at the battle of Hastings)—who received from the Conqueror, as his reward, immense portions of Lancashire territory, from the Mersey northwards— gave it new life. He, it is believed, was the builder of the massive Lungess Tower, though some assign this part of the work to the time of William Rufus. In any case, the ancient glory of the place was restored not later than A.D. 1100.

After the disgrace of Roger de Poictou, who had stirred up sundry small insurrections, the possession was transferred to Stephen, Earl of Boulogne, inheritor of the crown, and from that time forwards, for at least two centuries, the history of Lancaster Castle becomes identified with that of the sovereigns of our island to a degree seldom equalled in the annals of any other away from London. King John, in 1206, held his court here for a time, receiving within the stately walls an embassy from France. Subsequent monarchs followed in his wake. During the reign, in particular, of Henry IV., festivities, in which a brilliant chivalry had no slight share, filled the courtyard with inexpressible animation. The magnificent gateway tower was not built till a later period, or the castle would probably not have suffered so severely as it did when the Scots, after defeating Edward II. at Bannockburn, pushed into Lancashire, slaying and marauding. The erection of this splendid tower, perhaps the finest of its kind in the country, is generally ascribed to John o' Gaunt (fourth son of Edward III.), who, as above mentioned, was created second Duke of Lancaster (June 13th, 1362) by virtue of his marriage to Blanche, daughter of the first Duke, previously Earl of Derby, and thus acquired a direct personal interest in the place. But certain portions of the interior—the inner flat-pointed archway, for instance, the passage with the vaulted roof, and a portion of the north-west corner—are apparently thirteenth-century work ; and although it is quite possible that the two superb semi-angular towers, and the front wall as high as the niche containing the statue, may have been built by this famous personage, the probabilities point rather toward Henry, Prince of Wales, eventually Henry V. Ten years after the death of John o' Gaunt, or in 1409, this prince was himself created Duke of Lancaster, and may reasonably be supposed to have commemorated the event in a manner at once substantial and agreeable to the citizens. The presumption is strongly supported by the heraldic shield, which could not possibly have been John o' Gaunt's, since the quartering for France consists of only three fleurs de lys. The original bearing of the French monarchy, as historians are well aware, was *azure*, semée de fleur de lys, *or*. Edward III. assumed these arms, with the title of King of France, in 1340. In 1364 the French reduced the number of fleurs de lys to the three we are so familiar with, and in due time England followed suit. But this was not until 1403, when John o' Gaunt had been in his grave nearly four years. The shield in question is thus plainly of a period too late for the husband of the Lady Blanche.

But whoever the builder, how glorious the features! how palatial the proportions! Defending the south-east corner of the castle, and overlooking the town, this superb gateway tower is not more admirably placed than exalted in design. The height, sixty-six feet, prepares us for the graceful termination of the lofty wings in octagonal turrets, and for the thickness of the walls, which is nearly, or quite, three yards: it is scarcely possible to imagine a more skilfully proportioned blending of strength, regal authority, and the charm of peacefulness. The statue of John o' Gaunt above the archway is modern, having been placed there only in 1822. But the past is soon recalled by the opening for the descent of the portcullis, though the ancient oaken doors have disappeared.

The entire area of Lancaster Castle measures 380 feet by 350, without reckoning the terrace outside the walls. The oldest portion—probably, as said above, Roger de Poictou's—is the lower part of the massive Lungess Tower, an impressive monument of the impregnable masonry of the time, 80 feet square, with walls 10 feet in thickness, and the original Norman windows intact. The upper portion was rebuilt temp. Queen Elizabeth, who specially commended Lancaster Castle to the faithful defenders of her kingdom against the Spaniards. The height is 70 feet; a turret at the south-west corner, popularly called John o' Gaunt's Chair, adding another ten to the elevation. Delightful views are obtained from the summit, as, indeed, from the terrace. The chapel, situated in the basement, 55 feet by 26, here, as elsewhere in the ancient English castles, tells of the piety as well as the dignity of their founders and owners. In this, at suitable times, the Sacraments would be administered, not alone to the inmates, but to the foresters, the shepherds, and other retainers of the baron or noble lady of the place; the chapel was no less an integral part of the establishment than the

well of spring water; the old English castle was not only a stronghold but a sanctuary. Unhappily, in contrast, but in equal harmony with the times, there are dungeons, in two storeys, below the level of the ground.

The Lancaster Castle of 1881 is, after all, by no means the Lancaster Castle of the Plantagenets. As seen from Morecambe and many another spot a few miles distant, the old fortress presents an appearance that, if not romantic, is strikingly picturesque:

'Distance lends enchantment to the view,'

and the church alongside adds graciously to the effect, seeming to unite with the antique outlines. But so much of the building has been altered and remodelled, in order to adapt it to its modern uses—those of law-courts and prison; the sharpness of the new architecture so sadly interferes with enjoyment of the blurred and wasted old; the fitness of things has been so violated, that the sentiment of the associations is with difficulty sustained, even in the consecrated inner space, once so gay with knights and pageantry. The castle was employed for the trial of criminals as early as 1324, but 1745 seems to be the date of its final surrender of royal pride. No sumptuous halls or storied corridors now exist in it. Contrariwise, everything is there that renders the building convenient for assizes; and it is pleasing to observe, that with all the medley of modern adaptations there has been preserved, as far as practicable, a uniformity of style—the ecclesiastical of temp. Henry VII.

Clitheroe Castle, so called, consists to-day of no more than the Keep and a portion of the outermost surrounding wall. The situation and general character of this remarkable ruin are almost peculiar. Half a mile south of the Ribble, on the great green plain which stretches westwards from the foot of Pendle, there suddenly rises a rugged limestone crag, like an island out of the sea. Whether it betokens an upheaval of the strata more or fewer millions of years ago, or whether it is a mass of harder material which withstood the powerful denuding currents known to have swept in primæval times across the country from east to west, the geologists must decide. Our present concern is with the fine old feudal relic perched on the summit, and which, like Lancaster Castle, belongs to the days of Roger de Poictou and his immediate successors, though a stronghold of some kind no doubt existed there long previously—a lofty and insulated rock in a country not rich in strong military positions, being too valuable to be neglected even by barbarians. The probability is, that although founded by Roger de Poictou, the chief builders were the De Lacys, those renowned Norman lords whose head-quarters were at Pontefract, and who could travel hither, fifty miles, without calling at any hostelrie not virtually their own. They came here periodically to receive tribute and to dispense justice. There was never any important residence upon the rock. The space is not sufficient for more than might be needed for urgent and temporary purposes; and although a gentleman's house now stands upon the slope, it occupies very little of the old foundation.

The inside measurement of the keep is twenty feet square; the walls are ten feet thick, and so slight has been the touch, so far, of the 'effacing fingers,' that they seem assured of another long seven centuries. The chapel was under the protection of the monks of Whalley Abbey. Not a vestige of it now remains; every stone, after the dismantling of the castle in 1649, having been carried away, as in so many other instances, and used in the building of cottages and walls. After

Nor will the tourist exploring Lancashire think the time lost that he may spend among the sea-beaten remains of the Peel of Fouldrey,—the cluster of historic towers which forms so conspicuous an object when proceeding by water to Piel Pier, *en route* for Furness Abbey and the Lakes. The castle owes its existence to the Furness abbots, who, alarmed by the terrible raid of the Scots in 1316, repeated in 1322, temp. Edward II., discreetly constructed a place for personal safety, and for deposit of their principal treasures. No site could have been found more trustworthy than the little island off the southern extreme of Walney. While artillery was unknown the castle must have been impregnable, for it was not only wave-girt but defended by artificial moats, and of substance so well knit that although masses of tumbled wall are now strewn upon

CLITHEROE CASTLE.

four generations, or in little more than a hundred years, the line of the De Lacys became extinct. Do we think often enough, and with commensurate thankfulness, of the immense service they and the other old Norman lords rendered our country during their lifetimes? The Normans, like the Romans, were scribes, architects, reclaimers of the waste, instruments of civilisation—all the most curious and interesting relics Old England possesses bear Norman impress. Contemplating their castles, few things more touch the mind than the presence, abreast of the venerable stones, of the shrubs and flowers of countries they never heard of. Here, for instance, sheltering at the knee of old Clitheroe Castle Keep, perchance in the identical spot where a plumed De Lacy once leaned, rejoicing in the sunshine, there is a vigorous young Nepalese cotoneaster. From whatever point Clitheroe may be approached, the castle keep salutes the eye long before we can possibly reach it; and no one who cares either for the past or for scenery will consider the visit unrewarded.

the beach, they refuse to disintegrate. These huge lumps are composed partly of pebbles, and of cement now hard as rock. The keep is still standing, with portions of the inner and outer defences. Traces of the chapel are also discoverable, indicating the period of the erection; but there is nothing anywhere in the shape of ornament. The charm of Fouldrey is now purely for the imagination. Hither came the little skiffs that brought such supplies to the abbey as its own broad lands could not contribute. Here was given the welcome to all distinguished visitors arriving by sea, and from Fouldrey sailed all those who went afar. To-day all is still. No voices are heard save those of the unmusical sea-fowl, and of the waves that toss up their foam,

'Where all-devouring Time
Sits on his throne of ruins hoar,
And winds and tempests sweep his various lyre.'

'Peel,' a term unknown in the south of England, was anciently, in the north, a common appellation for castellets built as refuges in times of unusual peril. They were often no more than single towers, square, with turrets at the angles, and having the door at a considerable distance above the ground. The word is variously spelt. Pele, pile, pylle, and two or three other forms, occur in old writers, the whole resolving, apparently, into a mediæval *pelum*, which would seem to be, in turn, the Latin *pila*, a mole or jetty, as in the fine simile in Virgil, where the Trojan falls pierced by a dart :—

'Qualis in Euboico Baiarum litore quondam
Saxea pila cadit,' &c.—*Æneid*, ix. 710-11.

Fouldrey itself is not assured of immortality, for there can be no doubt that much of the present sea in this part of Morecambe Bay covers, as at Norbreck, surface that aforetime was dry, and where fir-trees grew and hazel-nuts. Stagnant water had converted the ground into moss, even before the invasion of the sea ; for peat is found by digging deep enough into the sands, with roots of trees and trunks that lie with their heads eastwards. Walney, Fouldrey, and the adjacent islets, were themselves probably formed by ancient inrush of the water. The beach hereabouts, as said by Camden, certainly 'once lay out a great way westward into the ocean, which the sea ceased not to slash and mangle . . . . until it swallowed up the shore at some boisterous tide, and thereby made three huge bays.' Sand and pebbles still perseveringly accumulate in various parts. Relentless in its rejection of the soft and perishable, these are the things which old Ocean loves to amass.

The castle was dismantled by its own builders at the commencement of the fifteenth century, probably because too expensive to maintain. From that time forwards it has been slowly breaking up, though gaining perhaps in pictorial interest ; and seen, as it is, many miles across the water, never fails to excite the liveliest sentiments of curiosity. One of the abbots of Furness was probably the builder also of the curious old square tower still standing in the market-place of Dalton, and locally called the 'Castle.' The architecture is of the fourteenth century.

Furness Abbey, seven miles south-west of Ulverston, once the most extensive and beautiful of the English Cistercian houses—which held charters from twelve successive kings, and whose abbots had jurisdiction, not only ecclesiastical but civil, over the whole of the great peninsula formed by the Duddon, the Leven, Windermere, and the sea—still attests in the variety and the stateliness of the remains that the 'pomp and circumstance' of monastic authority must here have been played forth to the utmost limit. In its day, if not magnificent, the building must have been perfect in design and commodiousness. The outermost walls enclosed no less than sixty-five acres of ground, including the portion used as a garden. This great area was traversed by a clear and swiftly flowing stream, which still runs on its ancient way ; and the slopes of the sequestered glen chosen with so much sagacity as the site, were covered with trees. To-day their descendants mingle with the broken arches ; hither, too, comes the faithful blue campanula, which in its season decks every ledge and crumbling corbel, flowering, after its manner, luxuriantly—a reflex of the 'heavens' own tinct,' smiling, as Nature always does, upon the devastation she so loves to adorn. The contrast of the lively hues of the vegetation with the grey-red tint of the native sandstone employed by the builders, now softened and subdued by the touch of centuries, the painter alone can portray. When sunbeams glance through, falling on the shattered arcades with the peculiar tenderness which makes sunshine, when it creeps into such places, seem, like our own footsteps, conscious and reverent, the effects are lovely and animating beyond expression. Even when the skies are clouded, the long perspectives, the boldness with which the venerable walls rise out of the sod, the infinite diversity of the parts—to say nothing of the associations—render this old Lancashire ruin one of the most fascinating in the country.

Furness Abbey was founded in the year 1127, the twenty-sixth of Henry I., and sixty-first after the Norman Conquest. The original patron was the above-named Stephen, Earl of Boulogne, afterwards King of England, a crowned likeness of whom, with a corresponding one of his queen, Matilda, still exists upon the outer mouldings of the east window. The carving is very slightly abraded, probably through the sculptor's selection of a harder material than that of the edifice, which presents, in its worn condition, a strong contrast to the solid, though simple, masonry. The Furness monks were seated, in the first instance, on the Ribble, near Preston, coming from Normandy as early as 1124, and then as Benedictines. On removal to the retired and fertile 'Valley of Nightshade,' a choice consonant with their custom, they assumed the dress of the Cistercian Order, changing their grey habiliments for white ones, and from that day forwards (July 7th, 1127) they never ceased to grow steadily in wealth and power. The dedication of the Abbey, as usual with the Cistercians, was to Our Lady, the Virgin Mary. The building, however, was not completed for many years, transition work being abundant, and the lofty belfry tower at the extreme west, plainly not older than the early part of the fifteenth century, by which time the primitive objection with the Cistercians to aspiring towers had become lax, if not surrendered altogether. The oldest portions, in all likelihood, are the nave and transepts

LANCASTER.   *By David Law*

Furness Abbey. By R. Kent Thomas

of the conventual church, the whole of which was completed perhaps by the year 1200. Eight pillars upon each side, alternately clustered and circular, their bases still conspicuous above the turf, divided the nave from the aisles, the wall of the southern one still standing. Beneath the window of the north transept the original early Norman doorway (the principal entrance) is intact, a rich and delectable arch, retiring circle within circle. Upon the eastern side of the grand cloister quadrangle (338 feet by 102) there are five other noble and deeply-recessed round arches, the middle one leading into the vestibule of the Chapter-house—a very choice apartment, the fretted roof of

abbeys no doubt prepared the way for the advent of a better order of things; but it is not to be forgotten that the destruction of Furness Abbey brought at least a hundred years of decay and misery to its own domain.

Of Whalley Abbey, within a pleasant walk from Clitheroe, there is little now to be said; but few of the old monasteries have a more interesting history. The original establishment, as with Furness, was at a distance, the primitive seat of the monks to whose energy it owed its existence having been Stanlaw, a place at the confluence of the Gowy with the Mersey. In all Cheshire there is not a locality more

FURNESS ABBEY.

which, supported by six pillars, fell in only about a hundred years ago. The great east window, 47 feet in height, 23½ in width, and rising nearly from the ground, retains little of the original detail, but happily is still uninjured in regard to outline.

Scrutinising the various parts, the visitor will find very many other beautiful elements. With the space at our command it is impossible here even to mention them, or to do more than concentrate material for a volume into the simple remark that Furness Abbey remains one of the most striking mementos England possesses alike of the tasteful constructive art of the men who reared it and of the havoc wrought, when for four centuries it had been a centre of public usefulness, by the royal thirst, not for reformation, but for spoil. The overthrow of the

desolate, bleak, and lonely. It was selected, it would seem, in imitation of the ascetic fathers of the Order, who chose Citeaux—whence their name—because of the utter sterility. After a time the rule was prudently set aside, and in 1296, after 118 years of dismal endurance, the whole party migrated to the delightful spot under the shadow of Whalley Nab, where now we find the ruins of their famous home. The Abbey grounds, exceeding thirty-six acres in extent, were encircled, where not protected by the river, by a deep trench, crossed by two bridges, each with a strong and ornamental gatehouse tower, happily still in existence. The principal buildings appear to have been disposed in three quadrangles, but the merest scraps now remain, though amply sufficient to instruct the student of monastic architecture as to the position and uses of the various parts. Portions of massive walls, dilapidated archways, little courts and avenues, tell their own tale ; and in addition there are piles of sculptured stones, some with curiously wrought bosses bearing the sacred monogram 'M,' referring to the Virgin, to whom, as said above, all Cistercian monasteries were dedicated. The abbot's house did not share in the general demolition, but it has undergone so much modernizing that little can now be distinguished of the original structure. The abbot's oratory has been more fortunate, and is now dressed with ivy.

The severest damage to this once glorious building was not done, as commonly supposed, temp. Henry VIII., nor yet during the reign of his eldest daughter, when so great a panic seized the Protestant possessors of the abolished abbeys, and the mischief in general was so cruel. 'For now,' says quaint old Fuller (meaning temp. Mary), 'the edifices of abbeys, which were still entire, looked lovingly again on their ancient owners ; in prevention whereof, such as for the present possessed them, plucked out their eyes by levelling them to the ground, and shaving from them as much as they could of abbey characters.' Whatever the time of the chief destruction wrought at Furness, that of Whalley did not take place till the beginning of the reign of Charles II.

Third in order of rank and territorial possessions among the old Lancashire religious houses came Cokersand Abbey, founded in 1190 on a bit of seaside sandy wilderness about five miles south of Lancaster, near the estuary of the streamlet called the Coker. There is no reason to believe that the edifice was in any degree remarkable, in point either of extent or of architectural merit. Nothing now remains of it but the Chapter-house, an octagonal building thirty feet in diameter, the roof supported upon a solitary Anglo-Norman shaft, which leads up to the pointed arches of a groined ceiling. The oaken canopies of the stalls, when the building was dismantled, were removed, very properly, to the parish church of Lancaster.

Burscough Priory, two miles and a half north-east of Ormskirk, founded temp. Richard I., and for a long time the burial-place of the Stanleys, has suffered even more heavily than Cokersand Abbey. Nothing remains but a portion of the centre archway of the church. This, as shown by the head of a piscina, is half entombed in earth and rubbish many feet deep, grass supplying a new floor upon the surface. Burscough has interest, nevertheless, for the antiquary and the artist. The former, though not the latter, finds pleasure also in the extant morsel of the ancient priory of Cartmel—a solitary gateway, standing almost due west of the church, close to the little river Ea, and containing some of the original windows, the trefoil mouldings of which appear to indicate the early part of the fourteenth century. The foundation of the edifice, as a whole, is referred to the year 1188, the name then given being 'The Priory of the Blessed Mary of Kartmell.' The demolition took place very shortly after the fatal 1535, when the church, much older, was also doomed, but spared as being the parochial one. Contemplating old Cartmel, one scarcely thinks of Shakspeare, but it was to the 'William Mareshall, Earl of Pembroke,' in *King John*, that the priory owed its birth.

Of Conishead Priory, two miles south of Ulverston, there are but the scantiest relics remaining, and those are concealed by the splendid modern mansion which preserves the ancient name. The memory of good deeds has more vitality than the work of the mason. The monks of Conishead were entrusted with the safe conveyance of travellers across the treacherous sands at the outlet of the Leven ; the Priory was also a hospital for the sick and maimed. Upholland Priory, near Wigan, dates from 1319, though a chantry existed there at a period still earlier. One of the large lateral walls still exists, having a row of small windows, and covered with ivy. Some fragments of Penwortham Priory, near Preston, also remain ; and lastly, for the curious there is the never-finished building called Lydiate Abbey, four miles south-west of Ormskirk, the date of which appears to be temp. Henry VIII., when the zeal of the Catholic founders received a sudden check. The walls are covered with ivy, 'never sere,' and the aspect in general is picturesque ; so calmly and constantly always arises under Providence, out of the calamities of the past, agreeable nutriment for our highest pleasure in the present.

X.

The Old Churches and the Old Halls.

CHRISTIANITY in Lancashire—so far, at all events, as concerns the outward expression through the medium of places of worship—had a very early beginning, the period being that of Paulinus, one of the missionaries brought into England by Augustine. In 625, the kingdom of Northumbria, which included the northern portions of the modern county of Lancaster, had for its monarch the celebrated Edwin—he who espoused the Christian princess Edilberga, daughter of the king of Kent—the admirable and pious woman to whom the royal conversion was no doubt as largely owing as to the exhortations of the priest who found in her court welcome and protection. The story is told at length by Bede. There is no necessity to recapitulate it. The king was baptized, and Christianity became the state religion of the northern Angles. Paulinus nowhere in his great diocese—that of York—found listeners more willing than the ancestors of the people of East Lancashire ; and as nearly as possible twelve and a half centuries ago, the foundations were laid at Whalley of the mother church of the district so legitimately proud to-day of a memorial almost unique. Three curious stone crosses, much defaced by exposure to the weather, still exist in the graveyard. They are considered by antiquaries to have been erected in the time of Paulinus himself, and possibly by his direction ; similar crosses occurring near Burnley Church, and at Dewsbury and Ilkley in Yorkshire. The site is a few yards to the north of that one afterwards chosen for the abbey. The primitive Anglo-Saxon churches, it is scarcely requisite to say, were constructed chiefly, and often entirely, of wood.* Hence their extreme perishableness, especially in the humid climate of Lancashire ; hence also the long step to the next extant mementoes of ecclesiastical movement in this county, for these, with one solitary exception, pertain, like the old castles, to the early Norman times. The Saxon relic is one of the most interesting in the north of England ; and is peculiarly distinguished by the mournful circumstances of the story which envelopes it, though the particular inci-

dents are beyond discovery. At Heysham, as before mentioned, four miles from Lancaster, on the edge of Morecambe Bay, there is a little projecting rock, the only one thereabouts. Upon the summit formerly stood 'St. Patrick's Chapel,' destroyed ages ago, though the site is still traceable ; fragments of stonework used in the building of the diminutive Norman church just beneath, and others in the graveyard, adding their testimony. That, however, which attracts the visitor is the existence to this day, upon the bare and exposed surface of the rock, of half-a-dozen so-called 'coffins,' excavations in reality adapted to hold the remains of human beings of various stature—children as well as adults. They tell their own tale. Upon this perilous and deceitful coast, one dark and tempestuous night a thousand years ago, an entire family would seem to have lost their lives by shipwreck. The bodies were laid side by side in these only too significant cavities, the oratory or 'chapel' was built as a monument by their relatives, with, in addition, upon the highest point of the hill, a beacon or sort of rude lighthouse, with the maintenance of which the priest and his household were charged. On this lone and peaceful little North Lancashire promontory, where no sound is ever heard but that of the sea, the heart is touched well-nigh as deeply as by the busiest scenes of Liverpool commerce.

The church architecture of the Norman times has plenty of examples in Lancashire. It is well known also that many modern churches occupy old Norman and even Saxon sites, though not a vestige remains of the original structure. The remains in question usually consist, as elsewhere, of the massive pillars always employed by the Norman architects for the nave, or of the beautiful arch which it was their custom to place at the entrance of the choir. Fine examples of Norman pillars exist at Colne, Lancaster, Hawkshead, Cartmel, Whalley, and Rochdale ; the last-named, with the arches above, bringing to mind the choir of Canterbury Cathedral. At Clitheroe we find a noble chancel-arch ; and at the cheerful and pretty village of Melling, eleven miles north-west of Lancaster, a handsome Norman doorway, equalled perhaps in merit by another at Bispham, near Blackpool. Chorley parish church also declares itself of Norman origin, and at Blackburn are preserved various sculp-

---

* Thus in conformity with their general architectural practice, and as expressed in the Anglo-Saxon word for 'to build'—*getymbrian.*

tured stones plainly from Norman tools, and which belonged to the church now gone, as rebuilt or restored in the De Lacy times. The most ancient ecclesiastical building still entire in Lancashire is Stede, or Styd, Chapel, a mile and a half north of the site of Ribchester. The period of the erection would appear to be that of Stephen, thus corresponding with the foundation of Furness Abbey. The windows are narrow lancet; the doors, though rather pointed, are enriched with Norman ornaments; the floor is strewed with ancient gravestones. In this charming little place divine service is still, or was recently, held once a-month.

Whalley Church, as we have it to-day—a building commemorative in site of the introduction of the Christian faith into this part of England—dates apparently, in its oldest portion—the pillars in the north aisle—from the twelfth century. The choir is a little later, probably of about 1235, from which time forwards it is evident that constructive work was carried on for at least 200 years, so that Whalley, like York Minster, is an epitome of architectural progress. The sedilia and piscina recall, in the most interesting manner, times antecedent to the Reformation. But every portion of the church is crowded with antiquities, all of engaging character, many of them heraldic; the supreme ones are the stalls in the chancel, eighteen in number, transferred hither from the conventual church at the time of the spoliation. The luxuriant carving of the abbot's stall is in itself enough to repay an artist's journey; in the east window there is ornamentation quite in keeping. At the head of one of the compartments of the latter we have the Lancastrian rose; the flower being tinctured *gules,* and almost the only representation of it in the county :—

> 'Let him that is no coward, nor no flatterer,
> But dare maintain the party of the truth,
> Pluck a red rose from off this thorn with me.'
> *1st Henry VI.,* ii. 4.

The floral badge of the house of Lancaster, it may be well to say, is the purely heraldic rose, the outline being conventionalized, as is the case also with the white rose of York. When used as the emblem of England, and associated with the thistle and the shamrock, the queen of flowers is represented as an artist would draw it, or truthfully to nature, and with stalk, leaves, and buds, but still, as in the Lancastrian, of a soft crimson hue, 'rose-colour' emphatically.

The history of Cartmel Church reads like a romance. The original building was of earlier date than the Conquest, but changes subsequently made bring it very considerably forwards—up indeed to the time of Edward III. It was then that the beautiful windows of the south aisle of the chancel were inserted, and painted as usual in that glorious art-epoch, as shown by the few portions which remain.

Other portions of the coloured glass were probably brought from the adjacent priory when broken up by the unhallowed hands of Henry VIII., under whose rule the church was threatened with a similar fate, but spared, in answer to the cry of the parishioners, who were allowed to purchase it at an indulgent price, with the loss of the roof of the chancel. Thus laid open to the rain and snow, these were allowed to beat into it for eighty years, with results still plainly visible upon the woodwork. A partial restoration of the fabric was then effected, and within the current half century every part has been put in perfect order.

The ground-plan of this interesting old church is that of a Greek cross. The nave, 64 feet in length (Furness exceeding it by only a few inches), leads up through angular pillars, crowned with the plain abacus, to a choir of unusual proportionate magnitude; and here, in contrast to the pointed nave-arches, the form changes to round, and the faces are carved.

In one of the chapels to which the chancel-arches lead, there is some fine Perpendicular work. Similar windows occur in the transepts; and elsewhere there are beautiful examples of late Decorated. The old priory-stalls, twenty-six in number, are preserved here, as at Whalley.

Externally, Cartmel Church presents one of the most curious architectural objects existing in Lancashire, the tower being placed diagonally to the body of the edifice; a square crossways upon a square, as if turned from its first and proper position half-way round. What particular object was in view, or what was the motive for this singular deviation from the customary style of building, does not appear. We owe to it, however, four pillars of great beauty and strength, necessarily placed at the points of the intersection of the transepts.

The interior of the church is encrusted with fine monuments, many of them modern, but including a fair number that give pleasure to the antiquary. The most ancient belong to a tomb upon the north side of the altar, within a plain arch, and inscribed, upon an uninjured slab of grey marble, in Longobardic characters, *Hic jacet Frator Willemus de Walton, Prior de Cartmel.* Opposite this will be found a magnificent record of one of the celebrated old local family of Harrington—probably the Sir John who in 1305, when Edward I. was bound for Scotland, was summoned by that monarch to meet him at Carlisle. An effigy of the knight's lady lies abreast of that of the warrior; the arch above is of pleasing open work, covered with the grotesque figures in which the monks delighted.

Had exact annals been preserved of early church-building in Lancashire in the twelfth and thirteenth centuries, they would tell, most assuredly, of many important foundations. The beginning of Eccles Church, near Manchester, on the west, is referred by the archæologists, to about the year 1120, but probably it is one of the two mentioned in 'Domesday Book' in connexion with Manchester. The first distinct reference to it occurs in the 'Coucher Book' of Whalley Abbey, or about thirty years later than 1120. The Whalley monks held large estates both in Eccles and the neighbourhood, with granaries, &c.,—the modern 'Monton' is probably a contraction of 'Monks' town,' and the very name plainly indicates a church settlement. Ecclesiastical relics, of age quite or nearly as great, are found also near Preston, especially in the tower and chancel of the church of Walton-le-Dale, the former of no great elevation, but very strong, buttressed and embattled. Placed in a skilfully chosen position, on the crest of a little hill near the confluence of the Darwen with the Ribble, the aspect of the old place is distinctly picturesque ; the site at the same moment explaining the local appellation of ' Low Church,'—the Anglo-Saxon *low* or *law* denoting an isolated eminence, as in the case of Cheshire Werneth Low and Shuttlings Low. The date assigned to this ancient tower is 1162; to about thirty years after which time the oldest existing portions of Samlesbury, a few miles distant, appear to belong, the relics of the original here including the baptismal font. Didsbury Church, near Manchester, represents a chapel built about 1235, originally for the private use of the lord of the manor and a few families of local distinction, but a century afterwards made parochial.*

There are numerous indications also of ecclesiastical energy, if not of enthusiasm, temp. Edward III., to which period seem to belong the choir of Rochdale church, with its rich window tracery, the choir, probably, of Burnley church, and perhaps the older portions of Wigan church. As happens with many others, the history of the last-named is very broken. A church existed at Wigan in 1246, but the greater portion of the present pile belongs to two centuries later. That it cannot be the original is proved by the monument to the memory of Sir Wm. Bradshaigh and the unfortunate lady, his wife, the principal figure in the famous legend of Mab's, or Mabel's cross. The knight is cross-legged, in coat of mail, and in the act of unsheathing his sword ; the lady is veiled, with hands uplifted and conjoined as if in prayer. The deaths of these two occurred about the time of the Flemish weavers' settling in Lancashire, and of Philippa's intercession for the burghers of Calais.

Manchester 'old church,' since 1847 the 'Cathedral,' was founded, as before stated, in 1422, the last year of Henry V. and first of Henry VI.—that unhappy

sovereign whose fate reflects so dismally upon the history of Lancashire faithfulness. The site had previously been occupied by an edifice of timber, portions of which are thought to have been carried away, and employed in the building of certain of the old halls for which the neighbourhood was long famous, the arms of the respective families (who, doubtless, were contributors to the cost of the new structure) being displayed in different parts. But there does not appear to be any genuine ground for the belief ; and at a period when oak timber was so readily procurable as in the time of Henry VI., it is scarcely probable that men who could afford to build handsome halls for their abode would care to introduce secondhand material, unless in very small quantity, and then merely as commemorative of the occasion. Choice of a quarry by the builders of the new church was not in their power. They were constrained to use the red-brown friable sandstone of the immediate vicinity, still plainly visible here and there by the river-side. The exterior of the building has thus required no little care and cost to preserve, to say nothing of the injury done by the smoke of a great manufacturing town. There was a time when Thoresby's quotation from the Canticles in reference to St. Peter's at Leeds would have been quite as appropriate in regard to the Manchester 'Cathedral' —' I am black, but comely.' The style of the building, with its square and pinnacled tower, 139 feet high, is the florid Gothic of the time of the celebrated west front and south porch of Gloucester. The interior, in its loftiness and elaborate fretwork, its grand proportions, and ample windows, excites the liveliest admiration. The chancel-screen is one for an artist to revel in ; the tabernacle-work is, if possible, more beautiful yet.

The second best of the old Lancashire ecclesiastical interiors belongs to Sefton, near Liverpool, a building of the time of Henry VIII., upon the site of a pre-Conquest church. The screen, which contains sixteen stalls, is singularly beautiful in its carved work. There is also a fine carved canopy over the pulpit, though time with the latter has been pitiless. Very striking architectural details are also present, and, in addition, some remarkable monuments of Knights Templars, with triangular shields. Sefton church is further distinguished as one of the few in Lancashire more than a hundred years old which possesses a spire, the favourite style of tower in the bygones having been the square, solid, and rather stunted—never in any degree comparable with the superb ornaments of the Somerset churches, or with the circular towers that give so much character to those of Norfolk and Suffolk. A very handsome *octangular* tower exists at Hornby, on the banks of the Lune, built about the middle of the sixteenth century. Winwick church, an ancient and far-seen

---

* The existing church dates only from 1620, and in many of its details only from 1852 and 1855.

edifice near Warrington, and Standish church, near Wigan, built in 1584, supply other examples of the spire; and at Ormskirk we have the odd conjunction of spire and square tower side and side. Leland makes no mention of the circumstance—one which could hardly have escaped his notice. The local tale which proposes to explain it may be dismissed. The probability is that the intention was to provide a place for the bells from Burscough Priory, some of which, with a few of the old Stanley monuments, now sadly mutilated, were removed hither when the priory was dissolved. The existing spire is the third, dating only from 1832.

Many remains show that in Lancashire, in the time of Henry VIII., the spirit of church extension was again in full flow. Indications of it occur at Warrington, Burnley, Colne, and St. Michael-le-Wyre, near Garstang, also in the aisles of Middleton Church and in the towers of Rochdale, Haslingden, Padiham, and Warton, near Lancaster. Here, however, we must pause; the history of the old Lancashire churches treated in full would be a theme as broad and various as that of the lives and writings of its men of letters, and a simple catalogue of them would have no interest. There is one, nevertheless, which justly claims the special privilege of an added word, the very interesting little edifice called Langho Chapel, four miles from Blackburn, the materials of which it was built consisting of part of the wreck of Whalley Abbey. Sculptured stones, with heraldic shields and other devices, though much battered and disfigured, declare the source from which they were derived; and in the heads of some of the windows, which resemble the relics of others at the abbey, are fragments of coloured glass, in all likelihood of similar origin. The date of the building would seem to have been about 1557, though the first mention of it does not occur until 1575. How curious and suggestive are the reminders one meets with in our own country, comparing the small with the great, of the resort to the Coliseum by the masons of mediæval Rome!

The old Halls.—In old halls, mansions, and manor-houses, especially of sixteenth-century style, Lancashire abounds. A few are intact, held, like Widnes House, by a descendant of the original owner; or preserved through transfer to some wealthy merchant or manufacturer who takes an equal pride in maintaining the integrity of all he found—a circumstance to which we are indebted for some of the most beautiful archæological relics the county possesses. On the contrary, as would be expected, the half-ruined largely predominate, and these in many cases are now devoted to ignoble purposes. A considerable number, of stronger substance, have been modernised, often being converted into what are sometimes disrespectfully called 'farm-houses,' as if the home of the

agriculturist were not one of the most honourable in the land;—now and then they have been divided into cottages. Still, they are there; attractive very generally to the artist in their quaintness and often charming accessories, and always profoundly interesting to the antiquary and the historian, and to all who know the meaning of the fond care which clings to memorials of the past, whether personal or outside, as treasures which once lost can never be recovered. They tell of a class of worthy and industrious men who were neither barons nor vassals, who had good taste, and were fairly rich, and loved field-sports—for a kennel for harriers and otter hounds is not rare,—who were hospitable, and generous, and mindful of the poor.

The history of these old halls is, in truth, very often, the history of the aboriginal county families. As wealth increased, and abreast of it a longing for the refinements of a more elevated civilisation, the proprietors usually deserted them for a new abode; the primitive one became the 'old,' then followed the changes indicated, with departure, alas! only too often, of the ancient dignity.

In the far north a few remains occur which point to a still earlier period, or when the disposition to render the manorial home a fortress was very natural. Moats, or the depressions they once occupied, are common in all parts of the county, even where there was least danger of attack. In the neighbourhood of Morecambe Bay the building was often as strong as a castle, as in the case of the celebrated old home of the Harringtons at Gleaston, two miles east of Furness Abbey. These interesting ruins, which lie in a hollow in one of the valleys running seawards, are apparently of the fourteenth century, the windows in the lower storey being acutely pointed single lights, very narrow outside, but widely splayed within. Portions of three square towers and part of the curtain-wall connecting them attest, with the extent of the enclosure (288 feet by 170 where widest), that the ancient lords of Aldingham were alike powerful and sagacious. To-day Gleaston Castle is charmingly picturesque, being mantled with ivy, and well repays the artist's short railway trip from Grange. On the way thither, a little south of the village of Allithwaite, Wraysholme tells of similar times, though all that now remains is a massive, oblong, venerable-looking tower, the walls 3½ feet thick as they rise from the sod. The roof, reached by a spiral staircase in the wall at the south-west corner, once had a broad parapet, the corbels of which present some of the very few examples of the occurrence of hewn stones in this remarkable and very interesting old structure, near which, it will be remembered, according to tradition and the ballad, the last of the English wolves was killed. The fine old tower of Hornby Castle, the only remaining portion of a stronghold commenced soon after the Conquest, must be distinguished from these, being of very much later date, probably about 1520. That without being originally designed to withstand the attack of a violent enemy, more than one of these substantial old Lancashire private houses held its own against besiegers in the time of the civil wars is matter of well-known history. Lathom House (the original, long since demolished) has already been mentioned as the scene of the memorable discomfiture of Fairfax by Charlotte, Countess of Derby, the illustrious lady in whom loyalty and conjugal love were never parted.

The Elizabethan halls, so termed, though some of them belong to the time of James I., are of two distinct kinds,—the half-timbered, black and white, or 'magpie,' and the purely stone, the latter occurring in districts where wood was less plentiful or more costly. Nothing in South Lancashire, and in the adjacent parts of Cheshire, sooner catches the eye of the stranger than the beautiful old patterned front of one of the former;—bars vertical and horizontal, angles and curves, mingling curiously but always elegantly, Indian ink upon snow, many gables breaking the sky-line, while the entrance is usually by a porch or ornamental gateway, the windows on either side low, but wide, with many mullions, and usually casemented. The features in question rivet the mind so much the more delightfully because of the proof given in these charming old half-timbered houses of the enduring vitality of the idea of the Gothic Cathedral, and its new expression when cathedral-building ceased, in the subdued and modified form appropriate to English Homes—the things next best, when perfect, to the fanes themselves. The gables repeat the high-pitched roof; the cathedral window, as to the rectangular portion, or as far as the spring of the arch, omitting the trefoils, is rendered absolutely; the filagree in black and white, ogee curves appearing not infrequently, is a varied utterance of the sculpture; the pinnacles, and finials, the coloured glass, and the porch, complete the likeness. Anything that can be associated with a Gothic cathedral is thereby ennobled:—upon this one simple basis, the architecture we are speaking of becomes beautiful, while its lessons are pure and salutary.

Drawing near, at the side of the porch, are found seats, usually of stone. In front, closing the entrance to the house, there is a strong oaken door, studded with heads of great iron nails. Inside are chambers and corridors, many and varied, an easy and antique staircase leading to the single upper storey, the walls everywhere hidden by oaken panels, grooved and carved, and in the daintier parts divided by fluted

pilasters; while across the ceilings, usually low, run the ancient beams which support the floor above. So lavish is the employment of oak that when this place was built, surely, one thinks, a forest must have been felled. But those were the days of giant trees, the equals of which in this country will probably never be seen again, though in the landscape they are not missed. Inside, again, how cheery the capacious and friendly hearth, spanned by a vast arch; above it, not uncommonly, a pair of huge antlers, that talk of joy in the chase. Inside, again, upon the windows, one gets glimpses of heraldic imagery, commemorative of ancient family honours and alliances, rude perhaps in execution, but redeemed by that greatest of artists, the Sunshine, that, streaming through, shows the colours and casts the shadows. Halls such as these existed until quite lately, even in the immediate suburbs of Manchester, in the original streets of which town there were many black and white fronts, as to the present moment in Chester, Ludlow, and Shrewsbury. Some of the finest of those still remaining in the rural parts of Lancashire will be noticed in a future article. Our illustrations give, for the present, an idea of them. When gone to decay and draped with ivy, like Coniston Hall, the ancient home of the le Flemings, whatever may be the architecture, they become keynotes to poems that float over the mind like the sound of the sea. In any case there is the sense, when dismemberment and excessive modernising have not wrought their mischief, that while the structure is always peculiarly well fitted for its situation, the outlines are exquisitely artistic and essentially English. It may be added that in these old Lancashire halls and mansions the occurrence of a secret chamber is not rare. Lancashire was always a stronghold of Catholicism, and although the hiding-places doubtless often gave shelter to cavaliers and other objects of purely political enmity, the popular appellation of 'priest's room,' or 'priest's hole,' points plainly to their more usual service. They were usually embedded in the great chimney-stacks, communication with a private cabinet of the owner of the house being provided for by means of sliding shutters. Very curious and interesting refuges of this character exist to this day at Speke, Lydiate, Widnes, and Stonyhurst, and in an old house in Goosenargh, in the centre wall of which, four feet thick, there are two of the kind. In a similar 'hole' at Mains Hall, tradition says that Cardinal Allen was once concealed.

XI.

The Old Halls.—Continued.

ALTHOUGH the few perfect remaining examples of the old timbered Lancashire halls are preserved with the fondest reverence by their owners, the number of those which have been allowed to fall into a state of partial decay diminishes every year, and of

nation is entitled to insist upon their safe keeping and protection. Architectural remains, in particular, when charged with historical interest, and that discourse of the manners and customs of 'the lang syne,' are sacred. Let opulence and good taste construct

DARCY LEVER, NEAR BOLTON.

many, it is to be feared, not a trace will soon be left. Repairs and restorations are expensive ; to preserve them needs, moreover, a strong sense of duty, and a profounder devotedness to 'reliquism,' as some author terms it, than perhaps can ever be expected to be general. The duty to preserve is plain. The wilful neglect, not to say the reckless destruction of interesting old buildings that can be maintained, at no great cost, in fair condition, and as objects of picturesque beauty, is, to say the least of it, unpatriotic. The possessors of fine old memorials of the past are not more the possessors in their own right than trustees of property belonging to the nation, and the

as much more as they please on modern lines. Every addition to the architectural adornment of the country reflects honour upon the person introducing it, and the donor deserves, though he may not always receive, sincere gratitude. Let the builder go further, pull down, and, if he so fancies, reconstruct his work. But no man who calls himself master of a romantic or sweet old place has any right, by destroying, to steal it from the people of England ; he is bound not even to mutilate it. There are occasions, no doubt, when to preserve is no longer practicable, and when to alter may be legitimate ; we refer not to these, but to needless and wanton overthrow, such as unhappily has had examples only too many. There was no need to destroy that immemorial mansion, Reddish Old Hall, near the banks of the Tame, now known only through the medium of a faithful picture ;* nor was there excuse for the merciless pulling to pieces of Radcliffe Old Hall, on the banks of the Irwell, a building so massive in its under-structure that the utmost labour was required to beat it down. We need not talk of Alaric, the Goths and the Vandals, when Englishmen are not ashamed to behave as badly.

Of the venerated and unmolested, Speke Hall is, perhaps, the oldest in South Lancashire that remains as an example of the 'magpie,' or black-and-white half-timbered style. It stands upon the margin of the estuary of the Mersey, a few miles above Liverpool, with approach, at the rear, by an avenue of trees from the water's edge. As with all the rest of its class, the foundations are of solid masonry, the house itself consisting of a framework of immensely strong vertical timbers, connected by horizontal beams, with diagonal bracings, oak in every instance, the interstices filled with laths, upon which is laid a peculiar composition of lime and clay.

HALE HALL.

The complexion of the principal front is represented in our drawing, but no pencil can give a perfect idea of the exquisite repose, the tender hues, antique but not wasted, the far-reaching though silent spell with which it catches and holds both eye and fancy. Over the principal entrance, in quaint letters, ' This worke,' it is said, ' 25 yards long, was wolly built by Edw. N., Esq., Anno 1598.' The N. stands for Norreys, the surname of one of the primitive Lancashire families, still represented in the county, though not at Speke. A baronial mansion belonging to them existed here as early as 1350, but of this not a vestige remains. A broad moat once surrounded the newer hall, but, as in most other instances, the water has long since given way to green turf. Sometimes, in Lancashire, the ancient moats have been converted into orchards. Inside, Speke is distinguished by the beauty of the corridors and of the great hall, which

latter contains some very curious old carved wainscoting brought from Holyrood by the Sir Wm. Norreys who, serving his commander, Lord Stanley, well at Flodden, A.D. 1513, got leave to despoil the palace of the unfortunate monarch there defeated. The galleries look into a spacious and perfectly square central court, of the kind usually pertaining to these old halls, though now very seldom found with all four of the enclosing blocks of building. The court at Speke is remarkable for its pair of aged yew-trees, one of each sex, the female decked in autumn with its characteristic scarlet berries—a place for trees so curious that it probably has no counterpart. Everywhere and at all times the most imperturbable of trees, yews never fail to give an impression of long inheritance and of a history abreast of dynasties, and at Speke the association is sustained perfectly.

Near Bolton there are several such buildings, all in a state of more or less perfect preservation. In the time of the Stuarts and the Republicans they must have been numerous. Smithills, or Smethells, is one of these—a most beautiful structure, placed at the head of a little glen, and occupying the site of an ancient Saxon royal residence. After the Conquest, the estate and the original hall passed through various successive hands, those of the Ratcliffes included. At present it is possessed, fortunately, by one of the Ainsworth family above mentioned (p. 27), so that, although very extensive changes have been made from time to time, including the erection of a new east front in stone and the substitution of modern windows for the ancient casements, the permanency of all, as we have it to-day, is guaranteed. The interior is extremely rich in ancient wood-carving. Some of the panels are emblazoned in colours. Quaint but charmingly artistic decoration prevails in all the chief apartments ; everywhere, too, there is the sense of strength and comfort. In the quadrangle, open on one side, and now a rose-garden, amid the flower-borders, and in the neighbouring shrubberies, it is very interesting to observe how the botanical aspect of old England is slowly, but surely, undergoing transformation, through the liberal planting of decorative exotics.

Speke suggests the idea even more powerfully than Smithills. At each place the ancient Britons, the oak, the hawthorn, and the silver birch — trees that decked the soil in the days of Caractacus — wonder who are these new comers, the rhododendrons and the strange conifers from Japan and the antipodes. As at Clitheroe, the primæval and the novel shake hands curiously:—we are reminded at every step of the good householder 'which bringeth forth out of his treasure things both new and old.'

Hall i' th' Wood, not far off, so called because once hidden in the heart of a forest containing wild boars, stands on the brow of a precipitous cliff, at the base of which flows the little river Eagley, while from above there is a delightful prospect. Hall i' th' Wood, with its large bay window, may justly be pronounced one of the most admirable existing specimens of old English domestic architecture—that of the franklins, or aboriginal country gentlemen, not only of Lancashire, but of the soil in general, though some of the external ornaments are of later date than the house itself. The oldest part seems never to have suffered 'improvement' of any kind:—in any case, Hall i' th' Wood is to the historian one of the most interesting spots in England, since it was here, in the room with the remarkable twenty-four-light window, that Crompton devised and constructed his cotton-machine. The magnificent old trees have long since vanished. When the oaks were put to death, so large were they that no cross-cut saw long enough for the purpose could be procured, and the workmen were obliged to begin with making deep incisions in the trunks, and removing large masses of the iron-like timber. This was only a trifle more than a century ago.

Turton Tower, near Bolton, a fine old turreted and embattled building, partly stone, partly black-and-white, the latter portion gabled, originally belonged to the Orrells, afterwards to the Chethams, the most distinguished of whom, Humphrey Chetham, founder of the Chetham Free Library, died here in 1653. The upper storeys, there being four in all, successively project or overhang, after the manner of those of many of the primitive Manchester houses. The square form of the building gives it an aspect of great solidity; the ancient door is of massive oak, and passing this, we come, once again, upon abundance of fine wood-carving, with enriched ceilings, as at Speke. Turton has, in part, been restored, but with strict regard to the original style and fashion, both within and without.

The neighbourhood of Wigan is also celebrated for its noble old halls, pre-eminent among which is Ince, the ancient seat of the Gerards, and the subject of another of our sketches. Ince stands about a mile to the south-east of the comparatively modern building of the same name, and in its many gables,

surmounting the front, and long ranges of windows, is not more tasteful as a work of art than conspicuous to the traveller who is so fortunate as to pass near enough to enjoy the sight. Lostock Old Hall, black-and-white, and dated 1563, possesses a handsome stone gateway, and has most of the rooms wainscoted. Standish Hall, three and a half miles N.N.W., is also well worth a visit; and after these, time is well given to Pemberton Old Hall, half timbered, two miles W.S.W., Birchley Hall, Winstanley Hall, and Haigh Hall. Winstanley, built of stone, though partly modernized, retains the ancient transom windows, opposing a quiet and successful resistance to the ravages of time and fashion. Haigh Hall, for many ages the seat of the Bradshaigh family (from which, through females, Lord Lindsay, the distinguished Lancashire author and art-critic, descended), is a venerable and stately mansion of various periods— the chapel as old apparently as the reign of Edward II. Placed upon the brow of the hill above the town, it commands a prospect scarcely surpassed by the view from Billinge.

The old halls of Manchester and the immediate neighbourhood would a century ago have required a chapter to themselves. It has already been mentioned that a great portion of the original town was 'black-and-white,' and most of the halls belonging to the gentry, it would seem, were similar. Those which stood in the way of the fast-striding bricks and mortar of the eighteenth century, and the beginning of the nineteenth, if not gone entirely, have been utterly sacrificed. To-day there is scarcely a fragment left of Garratt Hall, in the fields close to which partridges were shot only seventy or eighty years ago. Hulme Hall, which stood upon a rise of the red sandstone rock close to the Irwell, overlooking the ancient ford to Ordsall—once the seat of the loyal and generous Prestwich family—is remembered by plenty of the living as the point aimed for in summer evenings by those who loved the sight of hedges covered with the white bells of Galatea's lovely convolvulus. Workshops now cover the ground; and though Ordsall Hall, its neighbour across the water, not long ago a mile from any public road, is still extant, it is hall only in name. Happily, it is in the possession of a firm of wealthy manufacturers, who have converted the available portions into a sort of institute for their work-people.* Crumpsall Old Hall; Hough Hall, near Moston; Ancoats Old Hall; Barton Old Hall, near Eccles; Urmston Old Hall, and several others, may be named as examples of ancient beauty and dignity now given over to the spirit of change. Leaving them as irrecoverable, it is pleasant to note one here and there among the

---

* Messrs. R. Haworth & Co., whose 'weaving-shed,' it may be added, is the largest and most astonishing in the world.

Hall in the Wood. By R. Kent Thomas

STONEYHURST.   *By R. Kent Thomas*

fields still unspoiled, as in the case of 'Hough End,' a building of modest proportions, but an excellent example of the style in brick which prevailed at the close of the reign of Elizabeth ; the windows square-headed, with substantial stone mullions, and transomed. This very interesting old mansion, now partly draped with ivy, was originally the home of the Mosleys, having been erected by Sir Nicholas Mosley, Lord Mayor of London in 1600, 'whom God,' says the old biographer, 'from a small and low estate, raysed up to riches and honour.' One of the prettiest of the always pretty 'magpie' style is Kersal Cell, so named because on the site of an ancient monkish retreat or hermitage founded temp.

quarterings — Stanley, Lathom, the Isle of Man, Harrington, Whalley Abbey, Hooton, and eleven others. The date of this is 1574.

The country immediately around Liverpool is deficient in old halls of the kind so abundant near Bolton and Manchester. This, perhaps, is in no degree surprising when we consider how thinly that part of Lancashire was inhabited when the manu-facturing south-east corner was already populous. Speke is the only perfect example thereabouts of its particular class, the black-and-white ; and of a first-class contemporaneous baronial mansion, the remains of the Hutte, near Hale, furnish an almost solitary memorial. The great stone transom of the

KNOWSLEY HALL.

Henry II. Another very interesting example of 'magpie' is found in Worsley Old Hall, though less known to the general public than the adjacent modern Worsley Hall, the seat of the Earl of Ellesmere, one of the most imposing edifices of its character in South Lancashire. With the exception of Worsley Hall, Manchester possesses no princely or really patrician residences. The Earl of Wilton's, Heaton Park, though well placed, claims to be nothing more than of the classical type so common to its class.

When relics only exist, they, in many cases, become specially interesting through containing some personal memorial. Barlow Hall, for instance, originally a grand old black-and-white, with quadrangle, now so changed by modernizing and additions that we have only a hint of the primitive aspect, is rich in the possession of an oriel with stained glass devoted to heraldry. One of the shields, parted per pale, apparently to provide a place for the Barlow arms, not inserted, shows on the dexter side those of Edward Stanley, third Earl of Derby, in seventeen

extant window, the upper smaller windows, the stack of kitchen chimneys, the antique mantel-piece, the moat, still perfect, with its drawbridge, combine to show how splendid this place must have been in the bygones, while the residence of the Irelands. It was quitted in 1674, when the comparatively new 'Hale Hall' was erected, a solid and commodious building of the indefinite style. Liverpool as a district is correspondingly deficient in palatial modern residences, though there are many of considerable magnitude. Knowsley, the seat of the Earl of Derby, is eminently miscellaneous, a mixture of Gothic and Classical, and of various periods, beginning with temp. Henry VI. The front was built in 1702, the back in 1805. Croxteth Hall, the Earl of Sefton's, is a large stone building of the negative character indicative of the time of Queen Anne and George I. Childwall Abbey, a mansion belonging to the Marquis of Salisbury, is Gothic of the kind which is recommended neither by taste nor by fidelity to exact principles. Lathom, on the other hand, is consistent, though opinions vary as to the amount of genius displayed in the detail—the very part in which genius is always declared. Would that there existed, were it ever so tiny, a fragment of the original Lathom House, that noble first home of the Stanleys which had no fewer than eighteen towers, without reckoning the lofty 'Eagle' in the centre—its outer walls protected by a fosse of eight yards in width, and its gateway one that in nobleness would satisfy kings. Henry VII. came here in 1495, the occasion when 'to the women that songe before the Kinge and the Quene,' as appears in the entertaining Privy Purse Expenses of the royal progress that pleasant summer, there was given 'in reward, 6s. 8d.' So thorough was the demolition of the old place that now there is no certain knowledge even of the site. The present mansion was built during the ten years succeeding 1724. It has a fine rustic basement, with double flight of steps, above which are rows of Ionic columns. The length of the northern or principal front, including the wings, is 320 feet; the south front overlooks the garden, and an abundantly wooded park. An Italian architect, Giacomo Leoni, was entrusted with the decoration of the interior, upon the whole very deservedly admired.

Ince Blundell is distinguished, not so much for its architecture, as for the very precious collection of works of art contained in the great entrance-hall, a model, one-third size, of the Pantheon. The sculptures, of various kinds, above 550 in number, are chiefly illustrative of the later period of Roman art, though including gems of ancient Greek conception; the paintings include works of high repute in all the principal Continental schools, as well as English, the former representing, among others, Paul Veronese, Andrea del Sarto, and Jan Van Eyck. This beautiful collection is certainly without equal in Lancashire, and is pronounced by connoisseurs one of the finest of its kind in the country.

The neighbourhood of Blackburn is rich in the possession of Hoghton Tower, five and a half miles to the W.S.W., a building surpassed only by Lancaster Castle and the abbeys in its various interest; in beauty of situation little inferior to Stirling Castle, and as a specimen of old baronial architecture well worthy of comparison with Haddon Hall. The estate was in the possession of the Hoghton family as early as temp. Henry II., when the original manorhouse, superseded by the Tower, stood at the foot of the hill, by the river-side. The existing edifice dates from the reign of Elizabeth, having been erected on its airy and commanding site by the Thomas Hoghton whose departure from 'merry England' is the theme of the pathetic old ballad, 'The Blessed Conscience.' He was one of the 'obstinate' people who, having been educated in the Catholic faith, refused to conform to the requirements of the new Protestant powers, and was obliged, in conse-

quence, to take refuge in a foreign country, dying an exile at Liege, June 3rd, 1580.

* * * * *

'Oh! Hoghton high, which is a bower
    Of sports and lordly pleasure,
I wept, and left that lordly tower
    Which was my chiefest treasure.
To save my soul, and lose the rest,
    It was my true pretence;
Like frighted bird, I left my nest,
    To keep my consciènce.

Fair England! now ten times adieu!
    And friends that therein dwell;
Farewell, my brother Richard true,
    Whom I did love so well—
Farewell, farewell, good people all,
    And learn experiènce;
Love not too much the golden ball,
    But keep your consciènce.'

The 'Tower,' so called, occupies the summit of a lofty ridge, on its eastern side bold and rugged, steep and difficult of access, though to the north and west sloping gently. Below the declivity flows the Darwen, in parts smooth and noiseless, but in the 'Orr,' so named from the sound, tumbling over huge heaps of rock, loosened from the opposite bank, where the wall of stone is almost vertical. In the time of its pride, the hill was almost entirely clothed with trees, but now it is chiefly turf, and the extent and grandeur of the prospect, which includes the pretty village of Walton le Dale, down in the valley of the Ribble, are enjoyed perfectly. The ground-plan of the building presents two ample courts, the wall with three square towers in front, the middle one protecting the gateway. The outer court is large enough for the easy movement of 600 men; the inner one is approached by a noble flight of steps. The portion designed for the abode of the family contains noble staircases, branching out into long galleries, which lead, in turn, to the many chambers. One of the rooms, called James the First's, is richly wainscoted. The stay of his Majesty at Hoghton for a few days in August, 1617, has already been referred to. It is this which has been so admirably commemorated in Cattermole's best picture, now in the possession of Mr. John Hargreaves, Rock Ferry. With a view to rendering this fine picture, containing some fifty figures, as historically correct as might be possible, the artist was assisted with all the records and portraits in existence, so that the imagination has little place in it beyond the marshalling. Regarded as a semi-ruin, Hoghton Tower is a national monument, a treasure which belongs not more to the distinguished baronet by whom it has lately been in some degree restored after the neglect of generations, than, as said above, to the people of England, who, in course of time, it is to be hoped, will rightly estimate the value of their heirlooms.

Stonyhurst, now the supreme English Jesuit College, was originally the home of the Sherburne family, one of whom attended Queen Philippa at Calais, while upon another, two centuries later, Elizabeth looked so graciously that, although a Catholic, she allowed him to retain his private chapel and domestic priest. It was under the latter that this splendid edifice took the place of one more ancient, though he did not live to complete his work. The completion, in truth, may be

in large measure, the singular interest of what it contains. In the philosophical apparatus room there is a fine *Descent from the Cross*, by Annibale Caracci. Elsewhere there are some carvings in ivory, and a *Crucifixion*, by Michelangelo, with ancient Missals of wonderful beauty, a copy of the Office of the Virgin which belonged to Mary, Queen of Scots, and antiques of miscellaneous character innumerable, those of the Christian ages supplemented most pleasingly by a Roman altar from Ribchester. A curious circumstance connected with Stonyhurst is, that the house and grounds occupy, as nearly as

HOGHTON TOWER.

said to be yet barely effected, so many additions, all in thorough keeping, are in progress. Not that they interfere with the stately original, its lofty and battlemented centre, and noble cupolas. The new is in perfect harmony with the old, and the general effect is no less fair and imposing to-day than we may be sure it was three hundred years ago. The interior corresponds ; the galleries and apartments leave nothing to be desired : they are richly stored, moreover, with works of art, and with archaeological and historical curiosities ; so richly that whatever the value of the museums in some of the Lancashire large towns, in the entire county there is no collection of the kind more inviting than exists at Stonyhurst. The house was converted to its present purpose in 1794, when the founders of the College, driven from Liege by the terrors of the French Revolution, obtained possession of it. They brought with them all they could that was specially valuable, and hence,

possible, the same area as that of the famous city which once adorned the banks of the Ribble.

A pilgrimage to that charming neighbourhood is rewarded by the sight of old-fashioned manor-houses scarcely inferior in manifold interest to those left behind in the south. Little Mitton Hall (so named in order to distinguish it from Great Mitton, on the Yorkshire side of the stream) is an admirable example of the architecture of the time of Henry VII. The basement is of stone, the upper storey of wood ; the presence-chamber, with its embayed window-screen and gallery above, and the roof ceiled with oak in wrought compartments, are singularly curious and interesting. Salesbury Hall, partly stone and partly wood, once possessed of a quadrangular court, now a farmhouse, was originally the seat of the Talbots, one of whom, in 1580, was Keeper of the Records in the Tower of London. Salmesbury, so splendidly monographed by Mr. James Croston, dates from the close of the fourteenth century,—a most fascinating old place, the inner doors all without either panel or lock, and opened, like those of cottages, with a latch and a string. Towneley Hall, near Burnley, with its glorious park, one of the most ancient seats in the county, is rich not more in pictorial than in personal history. The banks of the Lune in turn supply examples of the ancient mansion such as befit a valley picturesque in every winding, Hornby Castle and Borwick Hall counting as chief among them.

The halls above noticed may be the most interesting, but the list could be very considerably enlarged. Scarisbrick and Rufford, near Ormskirk; Yealand Redmayne, nine miles north of Lancaster; Swarthmoor, Extwistle, and many others, present features of singular though very various interest, and in the aggregate supply materials for one of the most delightful chapters still to be written for the history not only of Lancashire but of England.

SPEKE HALL. *By R. Kent Thomas*

XII.

The Natural History and the Fossils.

AN extended account of the flora of Lancashire, or of its fauna, or of the organic remains preserved in the rocks and the coal strata, is impossible in the space now at command: it is not demanded either by pages which profess to supply no more than general hints as to where to look for what is worthy or curious. A sketch of Lancashire, its contents and characteristics, would nevertheless be incomplete without some notice, however brief, of the indigenous trees and plants, the birds ordinarily met with, and the fossils. The zest with which natural history has been followed in Lancashire, for at least a century, has resulted in so accurate a discrimination of all the principal forms of life, that the numbers, and the degree of diffusion of the various species, can now be spoken of without fear of error. In those departments alone which require the use of the microscope is there much remaining to be done, and these, in truth, are practically inexhaustible.

Being so varied in its geology, and possessed of a hundred miles of coast, Lancashire presents a very good average flora, though wanting many of the pretty plants which deck the meadows and waysides of most of the southern counties. The wild clematis which at Clifton festoons every old thorn is sought in vain. In Lancashire no cornfield is ever flooded, as in Surrey, with scarlet poppies; the sweet-briar and the scented violet are scarcely known; even the mallow is a curiosity. Many flowers, on the other hand, occur in plenty, which, though not confined to Lancashire, are in the south seldom seen, and which in beauty compare with the best. Mr. Bentham, in his 'Handbook of the British Flora,' describes 1232 native flowering plants, and 53 of the cryptogamia—the ferns and their allies—or a total of 1285. Of these the present writer has personally observed in Lancashire more than 500. In the remoter corners another score or two, without doubt, await the finding. In any case, the proportion borne by the Lancashire flora to that of the entire island is, in reality, much higher than the figures seem to indicate, since quite a sixth part of the 1285 consists of plants confined to three or four localities, and thus not entitled to count with the general vegetation of the country. It is not, after all, the multitude or the variety of the species found in a given spot that render it enviable. The

excellent things of the world are not the rare and costly ones, but those which give joy to the largest number of intelligent human beings; and assuredly more delight has arisen to mankind from the primrose, the anemone, and the forget-me-not, than from all the botanist's prizes put together. Better, moreover, at any time, than the possession of mere quantity, the ceaseless pleasure that comes of watching manners and customs, or a life-history—such, for example, as that of the Parnassia. Not to mention all that precedes and follows, how beautiful the spectacle of the milk-white cups when newly open, the golden anthers kneeling round the lilac ovary; then, after a while, in succession rising up, bestowing a kiss, and retiring, so that at last they form a five-rayed star, the ovary now impurpled. In connexion with the dethronement of the natural beauty of the streams in the cotton manufacturing districts, it is interesting to note that, while the primroses, the anemones, and the forget-me-nots, that once grew in profusion, here and there, along the margins, have disappeared, the 'azured harebell' holds its own. Even when the white-thorn stands dismayed, the wood hyacinth still sheets many a slope and shelving bank with its deep-dyed blue.

On the great hills along the eastern side of the county, and especially in the moorland parts, the flora is meagre in the extreme. Acres innumerable produce little besides heather and whortle-berry. When the latter decreases, it is to make room for the empetrum, or the Vitis Idæa, 'the grape of mount Ida'—a name enough in itself to fling poetry over the solitude. Harsh and wiry grasses and obdurate rushes fill the interspaces, except where green with the hard-fern. Occasionally, as upon Fo'edge, the parsley-fern and the club-moss tell of the altitude, as upon Pendle the pinguicula and the cloud-berry. The hills behind Grange are in part densely covered with juniper, and the characteristic grass is the beautiful blue sesleria, the colour contrasting singularly with that of the hay-field grasses. The choicest of the English green-flowered plants, the truelove, *Paris quadrifolia*, is plentiful in the woods close by, and extends to those upon the banks of the Duddon. Everywhere north of Morecambe Bay, as these names go far to indicate, the flora is more diversified than to the south; here, too, particular kinds of flowers occur in far greater plenty. At Grange the meadows teem with cowslips, in many parts of Lancashire almost unknown. Crimson orchises—Ophelia's 'long-purples,' the twayblade, the fly-orchis, the lady's tresses, the butterfly-orchis, that smells only after twilight, add their charms to this beautiful neighbourhood, which, save for Birkdale, would seem the Lancashire orchids' patrimony. The total number of orchideous plants occurring wild in the county is fourteen; and of these Birkdale lays very special claim to two—the marsh epipactis and the *Orchis latifolia*. In the moist hollows among the sand-hills, called the 'slacks,' they grow in profusion, occurring also in similar habitats beyond the Ribble. The abundance is easily accounted for; the seeds of the orchids, of every kind, are innumerable as the motes that glisten i' the sunbeam, and when discharged, the wind scatters them in all directions. The orchids' Birkdale home is that also of the parnassia, which springs up less frequently alone than in clusters of from six or eight to twenty or thirty. Here, too, grows that peculiar form of the pyrola, hitherto unnoticed elsewhere, which counts as the Lancashire botanical specialty, looking when in bloom like the lily of the valley, though different in leaf, and emulating not only the fashion but the odour. It would much better deserve the epithet of 'Lancashire' than the asphodel so called, for the latter is found in bogs wherever they occur. Never mind; it is more than enough that there is whisper in it of the 'yellow meads,' and that in high summer it shows its bright gold, arriving just when the soft white cotton-grass is beginning to waft away, and the sundews are displaying their diamonds, albeit so treacherously, for in another week or two every leaf will be dotted with corpses. No little creature of tender wing ever touches a sundew except under penalty of death. Only two other English counties—York and Cornwall—lend their name to a wild-flower, so that Lancashire may still be proud of its classic asphodel.

No single kind of wild-flower occurs in Lancashire so abundantly as to give character to the county, nor is it marked by any particular kind of fern. The most general, perhaps, is the broad-leaved sylvan shield-fern (*Lastrea dilatata*), though in some parts superseded by the amber-spangled polypody. Neither is any one kind of tree more conspicuous than another, unless it be the sycamore. Fair dimensions are attained by the wych-elm, which in Lancashire holds the place given south of Birmingham to that princely exotic, the *campestris*—the 'ancestral elm' of the poet, and chief home of the sable rook—a tree of comparative rarity, and in Lancashire never majestic. The wild cherry is often remarkable also for its fine development, especially north of the sands. The abele, on the other hand, the maple, and the silver willow, are seldom seen; and of the beautiful group of hedgerow ligneous plants which includes the spindle-tree, the wayfaring-tree, and the dogwood, there is scarcely an example. They do not blend in Lancashire, as in the south, with the crimson pea and the tendrilled bryony. When a climber of the summer, after the bindweed, ascends the hedge, it is the Tamus, that charming plant which never seems so much to have risen out of the earth as to be a cataract of foliage from some hidden rill above. Wood-nuts are plentiful in the northern parts of the county; wild raspberries abound in the southern, as good in flavour and fragrance as the garden ones, wanting only in size. Bistort makes pink islands amid hay grass that waits the scythe. Foxgloves as tall as a man adorn all dry and shady groves. The golden-rod, the water septfoil, and the lady's mantle, require no searching for. At Blackpool the sea-rocket blooms again towards Christmas. On the extremest verge of the county, where a leap across the streamlet would plant the feet in Westmoreland, the banks are dotted for many miles with the bird's-eye primula.

THE BIRDS.[*]

WITH the Lancashire birds, as with the botany, it is not the exhaustive catalogue that possesses the prime interest. This lies in the habits, the odd and pretty ways, the instincts, the songs, the migrations, that lift birds, in their endless variety, so near to our own personal human nature.

Adding to the list of birds known to be permanent residents in Great Britain, the names of those which visit our islands periodically, either in summer or winter, the total approaches 250. Besides the regular immigrants, about a hundred others come occasionally; some, perchance, by force of accident, as when, after heavy weather at sea, the Stormy Petrel is blown ashore. In Lancashire there appear to be, of the first class, about seventy. The summer visitors average about thirty; and of winter visitors there have been noticed about a score, the aggregate being thus, as nearly as possible, one-half of the proper ornithology of the country. The parts of the county richest in species are naturally those which abound in woods and well-cultivated land, as near Windermere, and where there are orchards and plenty of market-gardens, as on the broad plain south-west of Manchester, which is inviting also in the pleasant character of the climate. Here, with the first dawn of spring, when the catkins hang on the hazels, the

---

[*] Condensed in part from the chapter on Lancashire Birds in *Manchester Walks and Wild-flowers*, 1858, long since out of print. I am indebted also to Mr. Charles E. Reade, of Stretford, for many interesting personal observations.

song-thrush begins to pipe. The missel-thrush in the same district is also very early, and is often, like the chief musician, remarkable for size, plumage, and power of song. Upon the sea-side sand-hills it is interesting to observe how ingeniously the throstle deals with the snails. Every here and there in the sand a large pebble is lodged, and against this the bird breaks the shells, so that at last the stone becomes the centre of a heap of fragments that recall the tales of the giants and their bone-strewed caverns. This, too, where the peacefulness is so profound, and where never a thought of slaughter and rapine, save for the deeds of the thrushes, would enter the mind. The snails are persecuted also by the blackbirds—in gardens more inveterately even than on the sand-hills —in the former to such a degree that none can refuse forgiveness of the havoc wrought among the strawberries and ripening cherries. Both thrush and blackbird have their own cruel enemy—the cunning and inexorable sparrow-hawk. When captured, the unfortunate minstrel is conveyed to an eminence, sometimes an old nest, if one be near, and there devoured. In almost all parts of Lancashire, where there are gardens, that cheerful and harmless little creature, the hedge-sparrow or dunnock, lifts up its voice. Birds commence their song at very various hours. The dunnock usually begins towards sunset, first mounting to the loftiest twig it can discover that will bear its weight. The sweet and simple note, if one would hear it to perfection, must be caught just at that moment. The song is one of those that seem to be a varied utterance of the words of men. Listen attentively, and the lay is as nearly as may be—'Home, home, sweet, sweet home; my work's done, so's yours; good night, all's well.' Heard in mild seasons, as early as January, the little dunnock sings as late as August. It rears a second brood while the summer is in progress, building a nest of moss, lining it with hair, and depositing five immaculate blue eggs. The robin, plentiful everywhere in the rural districts, and always equal to the production of a delightful song, never hesitates to visit the suburbs even of large and noisy towns, singing throughout the year, though not so much noticed in spring and summer, because of the chorus of other birds. The country lads still call it by the old Shaksperean name.

> *   *   *   *   'The ruddock would,
> With charitable bill (O bill, sore-shaming
> Those rich-left heirs that let their fathers lie
> Without a monument!) bring thee all this;
> Yea, and furr'd moss besides, when flowers are none,
> To winter-ground thy corse.'—*Cymbeline*, iv. 2.

The great titmouse is almost as generally distributed as the robin, and in gardens never a stranger, being busy most of its time looking for insects. Were coincidences in nature rare and phenomenal,

instead of, to the contemplative, matter of everyday delight, we should think more of its note as the token of the blooming of the daffodils. Making the oddest of noises, as if trying to imitate other birds, poor innocent, it only too often gets shot for its pains, the fowler wondering what queer thing can this be now? The blue titmouse, like the great, would seem to be very generally diffused. Exquisite in plumage, it attracts attention still more particularly while building, both the male and the female working so hard. The meadow pipit, or titling, loves the peat mosses, those decked with the asphodel, upon which the nests are often plentiful, a circumstance the cuckoos, when they arrive, are swift to take advantage of. No bird that builds on the ground has more work to do for the 'herald of summer.' From the end of April onwards—the cuckoo arriving in the third week—the titlings, whether they like it or not, get no respite. The young cuckoos are always hungry, and never in the least anxious to go away. How pretty the fondness of the cuckoo for its mate! Though apparently void of affection for its offspring, no bird, not even the turtle-dove, is more strongly attached to the one it has taken 'for better and worse.' Where either of the pair is seen, the other is sure never to be far away. Greenfinches and chaffinches are plentiful, the song of the former sweet, though monotonous, the latter rendered liberally, and always welcome. The chaffinch becomes interesting through choice of materials so very curious for its nest. One has been found—where but in Lancashire could it occur?—constructed entirely of raw cotton. The nest-building and the choice of abode constitute, in truth, a chapter in bird-life more charming even than the various outflow of the melody. The pied wagtail goes to the very localities that most other birds dislike—rough and stony places, near the water and under bridges; the tree-sparrow resorts to aged and hollow oaks, rarely building elsewhere; the long-tailed titmouse constructs a beautiful little nest, not unlike a bee-hive, using moss, lichens, and feathers; while the redpole prefers dead roots of herbaceous plants, tying the fibres together with the bark of last year's withered nettle-stalks, and lining the cavity with the glossy white pappus of the coltsfoot, just ripe to its hand, and softer than silk. The common wren—a frequent Lancashire bird—a lovely little creature, sometimes with wings entirely white, and not infrequently with a few scattered feathers of that colour, is one of the birds that prefigure character in man. When the time for building arrives the hen commences a nest on her own private account, goes on with it, and completes it. Her consort meantime begins two or three in succession, but tires, and never finishes anything. Among the Lancashire permanent residents, and birds only partially periodical, may also be named, as birds of singular attractiveness in their ways—

though not perhaps always tuneful, or graceful in form, or gay in plumage—the skylark, that 'at heaven's gate sings;' the common linnet, a bird of the heaths and hedgerows, captured, whenever possible, for the cage; the magpie, the common bunting, the yellow-hammer, the peewit, and the starling or shepster. The starlings travel in companies, and lively parties they always seem. The 'close order' flight of the peewit is well known; that of the starling is, if possible, even more wonderful. The sudden move to the right or left, of thousands perfectly close together upon the wing, the rise, at a given signal, like a cloud, from the pastures where they have been feeding, is a spectacle almost unique in its singularity. Near the sea the list is augmented by the marsh bunting, the curlew, and gulls of different kinds, including the kittiwake. In very tempestuous seasons gulls are often blown inland, as far as Manchester, falling when exhausted in the fields. They also come of their own accord, and may be seen feeding upon the mosses. Upon the sandhills a very curious, though frequent, sight is that of the hovering of the kestrel over its intended prey, which here consists very generally of young rabbits. The kestrel has little skill in building. Talents differ as much in birds as in mankind. Seldom its own architect, it selects and repairs an old and deserted crow's or magpie's nest, or any other it can find sufficiently capacious for its needs.

The history of the Lancashire summer visitants is crowded with interest of equal variety. The nightingale stays away. She has come now and then to the edge of Cheshire, but no further. Very often, however, she is thought to have ventured at last, the midnight note of the sedge-warbler being in some respects not unlike that of Philomel herself. The earliest to arrive, often preceding the swallows, appear to be the wheat-ear and the willow-wren. The sand-martin is also a very early comer. It cannot afford, in truth, to be dilatory, the nest being constructed in a gallery first made in some soft cliff, usually sandstone. While building it never alights upon the ground, collecting the green blades of grass used for the outer part, and the feathers for the lining, while still on the wing. The advent of the cuckoo has already been mentioned. In the middle of May comes the spotted fly-catcher, an unobtrusive and confiding little creature; and about the same time the various 'warblers' make their appearance. The males usually precede the females by a week or two; the black-cap going, like the hedge-sparrow, to the highest pinnacle it can find, and singing till joined by the hen; while the garden-warbler keeps to the bushes and gardens, and is silent till she arrives. The whinchat, the yellow wagtail, and the stone-chat, haunter of the open wastes where gorse grows freely, never forget. Neither do the

dotterel and the ring-ouzel, the latter in song so mellow, both moving on speedily into the hilly districts. To many the voice of the corncrake, though harsh and tuneless, is a summer pleasure, for she is heard best at those lovely hours when it is still too light for the stars, and the planets peer forth in their beautiful lustre.

The winter visitants comprehend chiefly the fieldfare and the redwing. In October and November these birds, breeding in Norway and Sweden, appear in immense flocks. Winging its way to the vicinity of farms and orchards, the one piercing cry of the redwing may be heard overhead any still night, no matter how dark. Siskins come at uncertain intervals; and in very severe seasons the snow-bunting is sometimes noticed.

Such are the ornithological facts which in Lancashire give new attraction to the quiet and rewarding study of wild nature. The few that have been mentioned—for they are not the hundredth part of what might be cited were the subject dealt with *in extenso*—do not pretend to be in the slightest degree novel. They may serve, nevertheless, to indicate that in Lancashire there is lifelong pastime for the lover of birds no less than for the botanist.

THE FOSSILS.*

ALTHOUGH the New Red Sandstone, so general in the southern parts, offers scarcely any attractions to the palæontologist, Lancashire is still a rich locality in regard to fossils. The coal-fields, and the mountain limestone, the latter so abundant near Clitheroe, make amends. The organic remains found in the mountain limestone almost invariably have their forms preserved perfectly, as regards clearness and sharpness of outline. The history of this rock begins in that of primæval sea; the quantity of remains which it entombs is beyond the power of fancy to conceive, large masses owing their existence to the myriads, once alive, of a single species of marine creature. A third characteristic is that, notwithstanding the general hardness, the surface wears away under the influence of the carbonic acid brought down by the rain, so that the fossils become liberated, and may often be gathered up as easily as shells from the wet wrinkles of the sands. Access to the mountain limestone is thus peculiarly favourable to the pursuits of the student who makes researches into the history of the life of the globe on which we dwell. How much can be done towards it was shown forty or fifty years ago, by the Preston apothecary, William Gilbertson, whose collection—transferred after his

---

* One or two paragraphs condensed from the seventh chapter of *Summer Rambles*, 1866. Long since out of print.

death to the British Museum—was pronounced by Professor Phillips, in the *Geology of Yorkshire*, at that moment 'unrivalled.' Gilbertson's specimens were chiefly collected in the small district of Bolland, upon Longridge, where also, at considerable heights, marine shells of the same species as those which lie upon our existing shores may be found, showing that the elevation of the land has taken place since their first appearance upon the face of the earth.

The quarries near Clitheroe and Chatburn supply specimens quite as abundantly as those of Longridge. Innumerable Terebratulæ, the beautiful broad-hinged and deeply-striated Spirifers, and the elegant discoid univalve well named Euomphalos, reward a very slight amount of labour. Here, too, are countless specimens of the petrified relics of the lovely creatures called, from their resemblance to an expanded lily-blossom and its long peduncle, the Crinoidea, a race now nearly extinct. A very curious circumstance connected with these, at Clitheroe, is that of some of the species, as of the *Platycrinus triacontadactylos*, or the 'thirty-rayed,' there are myriads of fossilized *heads*, but no bodies. The presumed explanation of this singular fact is, that at the time when the creatures were in the quiet enjoyment of their innocent lives, great floods swept the shores upon which they were seated, breaking off, washing away, and piling up the tender and flower-like upper portions, just as at the present day the petals of the pear-tree exposed to the tempest are torn down and heaped like a snow-drift by the wayside, the pillar-like stems remaining fast to the ground. There is no need to conjecture where the *bodies* of the creatures may be. At Castleton, in Derbyshire, where the encrinital limestone is also well exhibited, there are innumerable specimens of these, and few or no examples of heads. The bodies of other species are plentiful at Clitheroe, where the Actinocrinus is also extremely abundant, and may be detected, like the generality of these beautiful fossils, in nearly every one of the great flat stones set up edgeways, in place of stiles, between the fields that lie adjacent to the quarries.

The organic remains found in the coal strata rival those of the mountain limestone both in abundance and exquisite lineaments. In some parts there are incalculable quantities of relics of fossil fishes, scales of fishes, and shells resembling mussels. The glory of these wonderful subterranean museums consists, however, in the infinite numbers and the inexpressible beauty of the impressions of fern-leaves, and of the stems of the great plants well known under the names of Calamites, Sigillaria, and Lepidodendra, which in the pre-Adamite times composed the woods and

groves. In some of the mines—the Robin Hood, for instance, at Clifton, five miles from Manchester—the roof declares, in its flattened sculptures, the ancient existence hereabouts of a vast and splendid forest of these plants. At Dixon-fold, close by, when the railway was in course of construction, there were found the lower portions of the fossilized trunks of half-a-dozen noble trees, one of the stone pillars eleven feet high, with a circumference at the base of over fifteen feet, and at the top, where the trunk was snapped when the tree was destroyed, of more than seven feet. These marvellous relics of the past have been carefully preserved by roofing over, and are shown to any one passing that way who cares to inquire for them. Beneath the coal which lies in the plane of the roots, enclosed in nodules of clay, there are countless lepidostrobi, the fossilized fruits, it is supposed, of one or other of the coal-strata trees. Two miles beyond, at Halliwell, they occur in equal profusion; and here, too, unflattened trunks occur, by the miners aptly designated ' fossil reeds.' Leaves of palms are also met with. The locality which in wealth of this class of fossils excels all others in South Lancashire, would appear to be ' Peel Delph.' In it are found calamites varying from the thickness of a straw to a diameter of two or three feet, and as round as when swayed by the wind of untold ages ago. The markings upon the lepidodendra are as clear as the impress of an engraver's seal. In another part there is a stratum of some four feet in depth, consisting apparently of nothing besides the fossil fruits called trigonocarpa, and the sandy material in which they are lodged. With these curious and beautiful triangular nuts, no stems, or leaves, or plant-remains of any description have as yet been found associated. All that can be said of them is that they resemble the fruits of that singular Japanese tree the Salisburia.

At Peel Delph, again, a stratum of argillaceous shale, five or six feet in thickness, contains innumerable impressions of the primæval ferns, the dark tint thrown forward most elegantly by the yellow of the surface upon which they repose. The neighbourhood of Bolton in general is rich in fossil ferns, though Ashton-under-Lyne claims, perhaps, an equal place, and in diversity of species is possibly superior.

Thus, whether considered in regard to its magnificent modern developments in art, science, literature, and useful industries; its scenery and natural productions; or its wealth in the marvellous relics which talk of an immemorial past, Lancashire appeals to every sentiment of curiosity and admiration.